P9-BYJ-701

OUTSMARTING GOOGLE®

EVAN BAILYN
with
BRADLEY BAILYN

800 East 96th Street,
Indianapolis, Indiana 46240 USA

Outsmarting Google®: SEO Secrets to Winning New Business

Copyright © 2011 by Que Publishing

All rights reserved. No part of this book shall be reproduced, stored in a retrieval system, or transmitted by any means, electronic, mechanical, photocopying, recording, or otherwise, without written permission from the publisher. No patent liability is assumed with respect to the use of the information contained herein. Although every precaution has been taken in the preparation of this book, the publisher and author assume no responsibility for errors or omissions. Nor is any liability assumed for damages resulting from the use of the information contained herein.

ISBN-13: 978-0-7897-4103-5
ISBN-10: 0-7897-4103-2

Library of Congress Cataloging-in-Publication data is on file.

Printed in the United States of America

Fourth Printing: January 2013

Trademarks

All terms mentioned in this book that are known to be trademarks or service marks have been appropriately capitalized. Que Publishing cannot attest to the accuracy of this information. Use of a term in this book should not be regarded as affecting the validity of any trademark or service mark.

Warning and Disclaimer

Every effort has been made to make this book as complete and as accurate as possible, but no warranty or fitness is implied. The information provided is on an "as is" basis. The authors and the publisher shall have neither liability nor responsibility to any person or entity with respect to any loss or damages arising from the information contained in this book.

Bulk Sales

Que Publishing offers excellent discounts on this book when ordered in quantity for bulk purchases or special sales. For more information, please contact

> U.S. Corporate and Government Sales
> 1-800-382-3419
> corpsales@pearsontechgroup.com

For sales outside the United States, please contact

> International Sales
> international@pearson.com

Editor in Chief
Greg Wiegand

Acquisitions Editor
Rick Kughen

Development Editor
Rick Kughen

Managing Editor
Sandra Schroeder

Senior Project Editor
Tonya Simpson

Copy Editor
Keith Cline

Indexer
Cheryl Lenser

Proofreader
Language Logistics,
Christal White

Technical Editor
Steve Baldwin

Reviewers
Peter Shankman
Simon Salt

Publishing Coordinator
Cindy Teeters

Book Designer
Anne Jones

Compositor
Mark Shirar

CONTENTS AT A GLANCE

TABLE OF CONTENTS

About the Authors

Evan Bailyn is an Internet entrepreneur, speaker, and child advocate. He is best known for being an expert at search engine optimization, having used his ability to rank at the top of Google to build and sell five businesses, including one of the largest children's websites online. His Facebook page, which provides daily inspirational thoughts, has more than 100,000 "likes," making it one of the most popular non-celebrity pages on Facebook.

He has been interviewed on ABC and Fox News and featured in *The New York Times*, *The Wall Street Journal*, *The New York Post*, *The International Business Times*, and *Crain's New York Business Daily*. He is a frequent speaker and television guest.

In 2010, Evan established The Evan Bailyn Foundation, which awards grants to groups that promote emotional awareness in children.

Bradley Bailyn is an Internet marketing expert and co-founder of First Page Sage. He tracks Google's algorithm on a daily basis, ensuring that clients' websites remain optimized for maximum exposure on Google. He also helps clients tune their websites to convert as many visitors as possible into buyers—a science known as conversion optimization.

Bradley graduated from New York University's Stern School of Business, where he studied accounting, and then went on to Brooklyn Law School, where he did legal work for various government and international agencies, including the United Nations and United States Agency for International Development. He briefly ran his own law practice, and then left to join forces with Evan and pursue a shared dream of building a business that made a real difference in people's lives. He has been profiled in *The New York Times*, *Crain's New York Business Daily*, and *The Daily News*.

Dedication

This book is dedicated to two very special people: my brother Brad, who is my partner in all things business, and my soon-to-be wife, Sasha, who is my partner in life.

Acknowledgments

I would like to acknowledge the people whose gracious help contributed to the creation of this book.

Peter Shankman, you are awesome.

Rick Kughen, thanks for making this book happen.

Bella, you have been there for Brad as his wife and life companion.

Uncle Dave, your generosity and support means more than you know.

Lulu, we are very grateful for your guidance.

Russell, thank you for being a great brother and best friend. You are the first author in our family.

Ma, your love and support means everything to me.

Bear, you taught me to believe in myself—no amount of thanks can equal that.

We Want to Hear from You!

As the reader of this book, *you* are our most important critic and commentator. We value your opinion and want to know what we're doing right, what we could do better, what areas you'd like to see us publish in, and any other words of wisdom you're willing to pass our way.

As an editor in chief for Que Publishing, I welcome your comments. You can email or write me directly to let me know what you did or didn't like about this book—as well as what we can do to make our books better.

Please note that I cannot help you with technical problems related to the topic of this book. We do have a User Services group, however, where I will forward specific technical questions related to the book.

When you write, please be sure to include this book's title and author as well as your name, email address, and phone number. I will carefully review your comments and share them with the author and editors who worked on the book.

Email: feedback@quepublishing.com

Mail: Greg Wiegand
Editor in Chief
Que Publishing
800 East 96th Street
Indianapolis, IN 46240 USA

Reader Services

Visit our website and register this book at quepublishing.com/register for convenient access to any updates, downloads, or errata that might be available for this book.

Introduction

If you own any other books on search engine optimization, throw them out. They belong to the mass of misinformation that has been swimming around for years, keeping people from making their websites truly appealing to search engines. And no surprise, Google loves it.

What I am about to share with you are the real, gritty, tried-and-true tactics that have made my websites consistently show up at the top of Google for seven years and have made me a millionaire. My relationship with Google is love/hate. On the one hand, I am astounded by the brilliance of a company that makes my life easier every day and continues to come out with innovative products that push the level of communication and organization in our society to new heights. On the other hand, they have done everything they can to stymie my efforts to publicize websites that are so content-rich, so original, and by any stretch of the imagination so *deserving* of good placement in the search results.

One thing I should make clear from the beginning: I don't do any black-hat stuff. For those who aren't familiar with search engine jargon, that means I don't partake in unethical schemes or employ any tactics that do nothing more than fool Google into thinking my websites are more valuable than they actually are. No, what I have done is become intimately familiar with Google's rule book—the one they would do anything to hide from the public—and play by those rules *very closely*.

You see, outsmarting Google is not a matter of being a mathematical genius like many of the people they hire. It's a matter of looking at Google's intentions as a search engine, studying the accepted rules of SEO (search engine optimization), and then patiently trying every method that comports with and breaks each of those rules until you've brewed the perfect concoction. That can take years, of course, but reading this book should take only a week.

I first got started with search engines in 2004 after dropping out of law school to start my own company, a college counseling service. Soon enough, I learned that I had no idea how to acquire customers. Search engines were already pretty mainstream, and it was a fair guess that people were going to use them to find pretty much everything in the future—including college counselors. So I decided to focus on them head-on. Short on money, I spent eight months sitting in front of the computer reading about SEO on an online forum called webworkshop.net. In researching for this book, I see that the forum still exists, but it doesn't have the energy it used to. Back in 2005 when I was on it every night from 11 p.m. to 4 a.m., it was a hive of eager amateurs mixed with some so-called experts all trying to figure out how certain sites showed up at the top of the search results, and others weren't even in the first 1,000 results. The amount of ignorant nonsense that was spewed in that forum could fill the Library of Congress. But a few valuable tricks slipped in.

Instead of racking my brain trying to figure out which information was credible and which wasn't, I spent a lot of my time researching the people on the forum. I would Google their usernames and connect them to their business websites and then see whether those websites ranked for the keywords that they were obviously targeting. Most people's websites, including the moderators of the forum, were either nowhere to be found or hanging around in the top 50 search results. But a couple actually had top 10 rankings. I was on those guys like white on rice. I would go back and read every post they had ever written, trying to figure out what they knew. I looked for commonalities among them. Soon enough, I found a couple: phrases like "anchor text links" and "meta title tags." And I wrote myself a little playbook filled with my best guesses of what made Google happy.

Around that time, I had about $6,000 in the bank, at the bottom of which was a ticket to go back to Long Island, live at home, and start looking for 9–5 jobs. Running out of money was my greatest fear. I had spent $650 buying and developing a website for my college counseling business. I had spent another $500 buying a few other websites to play around with and teach myself about the way sites relate to each other. Having studied the Google founders' original position papers, which established the idea of Google, I knew that they believed that the relationships between websites were the best way to determine the value of each individual online property. That is, if websites were people, who would be the most well liked? Is it the guy who simply knows the most people? Or the guy who has the most powerful friends? It certainly isn't the guy who just moved to town and doesn't know anybody. Soon it became clear that Larry Page and Sergey Brin, who went on to found one of the most successful companies of the last decade, thought of the Web as a big popularity contest.

My $500 bought me three crappy websites, but more than anything, it bought me an education. Apparently, gone were the days when all you had to do to get a top ranking in the search engines was write your keywords a thousand times on your home page. Search engines, especially Google, had gotten much smarter, and now all that mattered was how many times other websites linked to you and how they linked to you, and when, and why. I hadn't the foggiest idea how to make my website show up at #1 in Google yet, but I did know one thing: It had everything to do with links.

That brought on a painful six months of trying every way of linking from my three test websites to my college counseling website. By day, I handed out flyers at Penn Station trying to make up the cost of my office rent, and by night, I linked. In that stretch of life, I linked in big letters, small letters, bold letters, italic letters, invisible letters, and no letters at all. I linked from the top of the page, bottom of the page, side of the page, and not on the page at all. I linked at 9 a.m. each day and every other Tuesday. I linked in plain text, images, and Flash; on every page of the website and on only one; on the home page and in the site map; and from each website to every other website. Damn, was it boring! The worst, and most devilishly clever part of it all was, Google updates its rankings only once per week, so every little permutation of linking I tried required a week of saint-worthy patience. And yet, none of it was working. My website had never—and it seemed, would never—show up in the top 100 results. Every day felt like walking through complete darkness, swinging my arms around in the hopes that I would hit something. I was very near giving up by the time that momentous Monday morning rolled around.

That Monday, just the same as every other day, I typed "college admission essay" (my keyword of choice, given that editing essays was one aspect of what I was attempting to do for a living) into the search box of Google. Thousands of times I had done this, and thousands of times Google had come up with the same search results, a tired collection of established companies and institutions of higher learning. But that day, to my shock and delight, the #1 result was *my* website.

"Oh my god! Oh my god! I did it! I cracked Google!" My neighbors in the tiny office suite poked their heads in to see what the racket was. Annoyed that it was nothing more than an overzealous 24-year-old screaming at his computer, they went about their business as I hugged my brother and business partner, Brad.

From that point on, my college consulting business got a steady stream of customers. And in the following two years, armed with the power to rank at the top of the search results for any keyword, I started lots of different companies. Now, five sold businesses and lots of experience later, I still work side by side with my brother, but we apply what I discovered back then (which I've honed greatly over the past six years) to other people's businesses to make them money. My reputation as a search engine guru has spread, making its way to the ear of an editor at Pearson Education. And that is how this book came to life.

Now that you know a little of my history, sit back and get ready to learn what Google is dreading you'll find out.

What's In This Book

This book contains everything you need to know—no more and no less—to get your website to rank on the first page of Google's search results. The 13 chapters of *Outsmarting Google: SEO Secrets to Winning New Business* are organized as follows:

- Chapters 1 and 2 explain the system underlying Google's algorithm, TrustRank, and the five ingredients of successful Google optimization. By themselves, these two chapters could bring a novice up to proficiency in this area.

- Chapters 3, 4, and 5 are filled with specific strategies to get your website to rank at the top of the results, discussing links, aging, and the ultimate ranking strategy—the Nuclear Football.

- Chapters 6 and 7 are the technical chapters. They are intended to provide support as you become a more advanced search engine optimizer, covering Google AdWords and Google's search operators.

- Chapters 8 and 9 are all about clarity and contain interesting information about optimizing for Google that will help clear away common myths and misunderstandings.

- Chapter 10 tells you what you need to know to rank on Yahoo! and Bing.

- Chapter 11 is a particularly important complement to search engine optimization, detailing the best ways to convert your search engine traffic into revenue for your business.

- Chapters 12 and 13 cover the role of social media in Google—both now and in the future—and the ways in which social media and search engines will meld together to form a new basis for discovering information, products, and services.

Who Can Use This Book?

Outsmarting Google: SEO Secrets to Winning New Business was written for all knowledge levels—from the casual Internet user to the professional search engine optimizer. More than anything, it was written for people who are seeking simple and direct information about how to get their websites to rank at the top of Google's results. I have assumed a blank slate and built a picture of the search engine's algorithm from the ground up, using simple language and analogies. I also have tried to keep the book moving along quickly, never getting too philosophical or bogged down with dense material. This book was meant to be like celery—crisp, easy to eat, and nutritious—and yet, even those who have years of experience in the field of search engine optimization should find a fresh perspective in these pages. I hope you enjoy the read.

1

Trust: The Currency of Google

If we could peer into the secret room where Google keeps the computers that rank every website on the Internet, this is what I think we would see (see Figure 1.1).

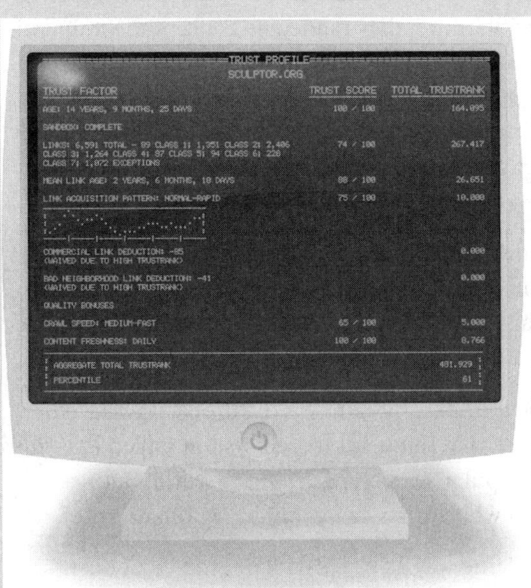

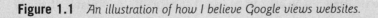

Figure 1.1 *An illustration of how I believe Google views websites.*

Google analyzes unimaginable amounts of data from millions of websites and whittles it down to the ten most relevant results for your search. As you will soon see, only a few factors ultimately determine the order of search results. But the big G likes to have all sorts of data available so that it can return relevant web pages for highly specific searches such as *why does my dog like watching baseball*? After all, most searches *are* specific. General searches such as *dog* make up a relatively tiny slice of the search pie.

As a website owner or marketer, you don't need to worry about the more arcane data points that Google analyzes. Your focus should be on the three most important factors for ranking on Google:

- Links
- Page title
- URL

Understanding how to optimize these factors allows you to rank for popular search terms, which causes you to get the most visitors to your website in the shortest time. But before I show you how to do that, you need to understand how Google looks at the Web.

PageRank

When Larry Page and Sergey Brin set out to organize all the Web's information as eager, bushy-tailed grad students at Stanford, they made one concept the foundation of their entire algorithm: links. Links, they hypothesized, were the currency of a new, democratic World Wide Web, just as votes are the currency of an election. After all, a voter only casts his ballot for the candidate he believes in, and similarly, a website owner only links to another website if he finds it genuinely valuable... right?

Nope. Not in a free-market economy. The moment people figured out that Google ranked websites based on links, a new cottage industry was born. People started buying, selling, and trading links like it was their job. And for some, it was. Today, the link industry is worth more than one billion dollars.

Even after the purity of the Google founders' system was disturbed, it was tremendously innovative for its time. In fact, that same link-based system, called *PageRank*, is still the foundation of the most popular search engine in the world. But nowadays, dozens of restrictions apply to which links can count as legitimate votes.

PageRank works in very much the same way as popularity in grade school. Generally speaking, the more friends you have (and the cooler they are), the better. So if you have six friends who are sort of cool, you're pretty comfortable. If you have only three friends, but they happen to be the coolest kids in the school, you're even higher in the pecking order. But of course, the most enviable situation of all is to be the most well-liked kid in the whole school. Then you have more *aggregate coolness* than anyone.

Now let's turn to the way Google looks at PageRank. Technically, PageRank is a predictor of how relevant a web page will be for any given search. It is similar to popularity, which could be said to be a predictor of how much a person will be liked by any other given person. Every web page on the Internet is assigned a PageRank, which is a number from 0 to 10. The higher the PageRank, the more relevant Google considers the page to be, and the better its chance of showing up at the top of the search results. It is exponentially more difficult to achieve higher PageRanks in each successive bracket, and most websites never get past a 4 or 5. PageRanks of 6 are hard to come by, and 7s are downright rare. 8s and higher are reserved for the Apple.coms and Microsoft.coms of the world, and there are fewer than a dozen PageRank 10 websites on the entire Internet, including Facebook, the World Wide Web Consortium, and Google itself. You can see a site's PageRank by downloading the Google toolbar and enabling the PageRank bar (see Figure 1.2).

Figure 1.2   *This is what PageRank looks like on the Google toolbar. This particular PageRank is a 5 out of 10.*

As in the grade school analogy, PageRank is based on how many other sites like you—that is, *link* to you. More important, if the sites that link to you are very popular—that is, well-*linked*—themselves, you get an even higher PageRank. So even if only one website links to your page, if it's a super-high PageRank site like, say, Huffingtonpost.com, your page will get a much higher PageRank than one that has 20 links but all from lesser-known sites. And of course, the best situation of all is to be that universally liked kid in school and have many websites of varying PageRanks linking to you. That gives you the highest *aggregate PageRank* of all. A shining example of a site that everyone seems to like is Wikipedia, which is why it has a PageRank of 9.

The analogy goes even further when you consider the special rules that Google has imposed on PageRank (see Figure 1.3). You know how it stinks to be the new kid in school—how it takes a few months to make friends and establish a reputation? Well, it's exactly the same with new websites. Even though Google assigns a PageRank to a new site pretty quickly, they won't allow it to enjoy the value of that PageRank—that is, rank well in the search results—until the site has been around for a couple of months.

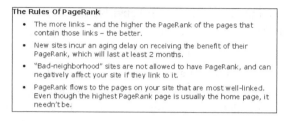

The Rules Of PageRank
- The more links – and the higher the PageRank of the pages that contain those links – the better.
- New sites incur an aging delay on receiving the benefit of their PageRank, which will last at least 2 months.
- "Bad-neighborhood" sites are not allowed to have PageRank, and can negatively affect your site if they link to it.
- PageRank flows to the pages on your site that are most well-linked. Even though the highest PageRank page is usually the home page, it needn't be.

Figure 1.3   *The rules of PageRank.*

A second important rule of PageRank is this: You are who you hang out with. If you hang out with the druggies and the dropouts, you are considered one, too. Similarly, if your website has anything to do with porn, pills, or gambling, consider yourself an outcast that will never gain PageRank. Simply put, if you run any sort of adult site, search engine optimization is not for you.

On the other side of the coin, if you keep company with the valedictorian and the salutatorian, you can expect a sterling reputation in the community; and in the same way, if your site is linked to by educational, governmental, or high-profile nonprofit websites, you can expect a generous helping of PageRank.

The third and final special rule of PageRank is that it flows unevenly throughout the pages on your site. Instead of being assigned to your website as a whole, PageRank is spread among all of your website's pages based on the number and quality of links each page has. Even though your home page is usually the page with the highest PageRank—as it is the one other websites typically link to—it is possible for another page on your site to have a higher PageRank. The most common example of an *inner page* that might have a higher PageRank than the home page is a blog. If your blog is the main attraction on your site but is housed within a larger website, say http://www.yourname.com, then http://www.yourname.com/blog will probably have a higher PageRank.

I might be going out on a limb here to extend this analogy, but I liken this rule of unevenly spread PageRank to the kid who is popular only because of his baseball card collection, or his swimming pool, or his hot older sister. He may still be considered popular overall, but those specific aspects of his life are more popular than he himself. If you have an inner page on your website that gains a higher PageRank than your home page, you should place an ad for your product or service on that page because it is more likely to rank highly in the search results.

TrustRank

Now, I hope you don't kill me for saying this, but...PageRank doesn't matter that much anymore. Back in 2004, it was basically synonymous with high rankings. Today, it is more of an indicator, a correlation rather than a conclusion. Above all,

PageRank is a pretty mirage to keep you from thinking about the real measure of a site's popularity, better known as TrustRank. TrustRank is the degree to which Google *trusts* that your website will be valuable to visitors if presented as a search result.

So why did I explain PageRank in the first place? Simply because it's a must-know term, probably the most commonly used of any vocabulary word associated with Google optimization. Also, it happens to be the only publicly available measure of a site's value. TrustRank is a far more closely guarded concept, one that Google has never officially recognized. Back in 2007, when it became clear that a high PageRank didn't necessarily guarantee a good ranking, we in the search engine optimization (SEO) industry needed a word to describe what we all thought we were talking about when we said PageRank—that is, *the actual importance of a web page in Google's eyes.*

So let it be known from here on out: When I talk about PageRank, I am talking about the press piñata, the public evaluation that Google gives to every page on the Internet but which has only a loose correlation with a page's actual value in Google's eyes. When I talk about TrustRank, I am referring to the bottom line for every optimizer—Google's willingness to place your website highly in the search results and therefore deliver new business. TrustRank is earned in the same way that PageRank is: by receiving links from other sites. The age of a site also increases its TrustRank.

If every web page had a public TrustRank value the way it has a public PageRank value on the Google toolbar, the link industry would be revolutionized. There would be a gold-rush-like frenzy to buy links on web pages that Google truly trusts. But Google would never make a search engine optimizer's life that easy. If they did, getting your website to the top of the search results would be as easy as having a good relationship with a commercial link broker.

Note

A word about link buying: At a certain point in most people's SEO education, they realize that there are webmasters out there who sell links. The link buying process can be as simple as "Pay me X dollars, and tell me what site to link to and how you would like the link to look." If you didn't know anything about SEO, you'd think it was a pitiful form of advertising—a tiny link on the side of a site being sold for the same price as your cable bill every month. These links aren't even designed to be seen or clicked on. Their entire value is in being recognized by Google so that they can pass TrustRank from the site that is hosting them to the site that bought the link.

For years—and even today—the standard way for people to determine the value of a link in the open market was by looking at its PageRank. A web page with a PageRank of 2 usually gets around $25 per month for each link it sells, and PageRank 7 links sell for up to $2,000 per month. This system is remarkably flawed, and literally millions of dollars have been wasted on it. Why? High-PageRank links will not necessarily increase your Google ranking! To begin with, the PageRank found on the Google toolbar, on which the entire commercial link industry relies, is updated only every two to three months, so the PageRank you see today could be very different from the page's actual PageRank, which is tabulated daily by Google.

Most important, Google has publicly stated that they penalize websites that sell links by crippling their ability to transfer TrustRank. And they have been equally public about the fact that they do not inform penalized websites that they have lost the ability to pass TrustRank to other sites. This change has made the commercial link industry into a shell of what it once was. I estimate that 60% of the links that are sold today are from penalized pages and have absolutely no value to their buyers. Determining which sites haven't been crippled, and thus truly pass TrustRank, has become the most important skill for a professional search engine optimizer to possess nowadays. SEO today is just as much about how to avoid acquiring penalized links as it is about acquiring as many high-quality links as possible.

Clearly, the question on the lips of everyone in the SEO community right now is this: *How do I know whether my web page has high TrustRank?* Very few people are able to answer that question. I am one who can.

In late 2008, I developed a tool for measuring the TrustRank of a web page, which is now the engine behind my SEO company. I would tell you how it works, but that would be very boring, and I fear that I might find more than a few Google ninjas at my door if I gave away all their secrets. Not to fear, though; I won't leave you in the lurch.

The best way to determine a site's TrustRank, and the foundation of my proprietary tool, basically comes down to taking an educated guess. Here is the logic:

1. Google gives the most TrustRank to sites that have links from well-linked web pages. (Or, in grade school language: Google gives the most popularity to kids who have lots of popular friends.)

2. Google does not allow sites that sell links to pass trust but shows no indication of the sites that have been disallowed to pass trust. (Nature punishes the corrupt popular kids who have allowed their friendship to be bought, making them unable to confer popularity on other kids. Even though these punished kids remain popular, they cannot make anyone else popular.)

3. Therefore, a site has a high TrustRank if its links are from websites that, to the best of your knowledge, have never sold links. (If you only

become friends with the kids in your grade who have never sold their friendship for money, you can be sure that you are truly popular.)

Guessing which sites are penalized versus unpenalized is easier than you would think. If a site looks professional, has been around a while, and doesn't have anything spammy written on it, it is likely to be in good standing with Google and will transfer TrustRank properly. You should approach as many of these sites as possible and ask them if they'd be willing to sell or trade for a link on their site.

Figure 1.4 shows an example of a web page that has the ability to pass TrustRank—the home page of my foundation. If I had never seen this page before, I would believe it was unpenalized because it looks like a legitimate, "un-spammy" page and doesn't appear to be selling any links.

Figure 1.4 *A site that appears to be unpenalized, free and clear to pass TrustRank.*

In contrast, Figure 1.5 shows a page that I believe is penalized, and I wouldn't request a link from in a million years.

Notice the difference between the two pages. Figure 1.4 shows a home page from a nonprofit website, appears to be professional, and cares about the user's experience. The layout is clean, the message is coherent, and there are links to other respected nonprofit websites at the bottom. Figure 1.5 shows a site that is disorganized and covered in links, including many that are clearly paid links. I would bet money that a link on the first site would pass TrustRank and boost your site's Google rankings, and a link on the second site would do absolutely nothing for your website's rankings. The six or seven companies that purchased links on the second site do not realize this fact or they wouldn't be wasting their money. And just in case my earlier statement about PageRank being irrelevant wasn't clear enough, note that both of these sites show a PageRank of 4 on the Google toolbar.

Figure 1.5   *A site that appears to be penalized, unable to pass TrustRank.*

You know a site is penalized when it *seems* to be actively selling links. When the title of the page is My Travel Diary, and it inexplicably links to websites that sell insurance, poker chips, and software programs...it's penalized. If you can plainly see the links on the site have an unnatural quality to them, then Google probably can too. Through their legions of Stanford- and MIT-trained engineers, in addition to turning webmasters on each other by asking them to report sites that sell links, they have gotten very good at spotting link sellers and penalizing them. It is because of this new skill for identifying link sellers that Google is getting ever closer to their original ideal of a perfect Internet, where links are given based on merit, not money. But they will never truly reach their goal because the SEO community is one step ahead of them all the time.

Google's Circus

To Google, TrustRank is a closely guarded secret. It is the very essence of its algorithm—the last remaining relic of Larry and Sergey's original vision of how the Web should be organized. That is why they want professional optimizers nowhere near it. And to make sure that search engine optimizers never gain insight into TrustRank, they have created the ultimate distraction by continuing to include a

PageRank meter on the Google toolbar. That little green bar—an essential tool to most search engine optimizers—is nothing more than a mirage to keep intelligent people expending their brainpower on *anything but* TrustRank. Sound like a stretch to you? Consider this: If displaying a page's PageRank really helped search engine optimizers do their job better, why would Google continue to do it? After all, the feature is used only by SEOs. Nobody *but* a search engine optimizer would even take the time to enable the PageRank meter through the toolbar's settings menu.

In keeping with their strategy of distraction, Google appointed a spokesperson by the name of Matt Cutts in 2007. His job is to interface directly with the SEO community, encouraging webmasters to use the Internet in the same way they did before Google came along—mostly by linking to only relevant, interesting content. Matt provides his fair share of drama by describing in great detail Google's latest algorithm updates and giving them fancy names such as "Big Daddy" and "Caffeine." Not surprisingly, his presence prevents a lot of innovation in the SEO industry from occurring. A person very much like me, who has the ambition to truly learn how to cause his or her site to rank higher on Google, could easily spend months digesting the carefully worded corporate messaging that Matt imparts and never spend a moment doing real, productive work. That is not to say he doesn't offer good business advice; it just isn't good for people trying to rank high on Google. You could sum up his entire message in one sentence: Create a website that people truly get value from, and it will naturally rank well on Google over time. Again: completely true statement, just not helpful to most businesses.

The first time I visited Matt Cutts's blog, I was struck by the fact that he is not a member of the search relevance department; instead, he is the lead spam engineer. This was the moment I realized that Google considers search engine optimizers to be spammers, and I knew not to trust anything they put forth specifically for search engine optimizers.

What Google has done with releasing the PageRank meter is similar to Coca-Cola releasing one of the most irrelevant ingredients of its secret formula. Although it seems obvious that Coke could reap no benefits from doing so, nobody seems to notice. Instead, they fixate on it as if it were accidentally leaked information and try to discover what makes Coke taste the way it does. Meanwhile, the company continues to avoid telling people that the ingredient plays no real role in the soda's taste despite existing in small traces. Rival soda companies take the bait and spend years analyzing this ingredient. Coke then goes a step further and appoints their head of anticompetition to be their official liaison from the company. He is a nice guy, and his message usually goes something like this: Develop a delicious soft drink, and people will buy it. Yet none of the rivals see anything wrong with this picture, instead choosing to believe that Coke is really going to help them re-create its formula.

When we understand that Google's strategy for protecting its algorithm is to create a circus to divert people's attention from the real measure of a site's value—TrustRank—we can get back to the job at hand, which is to figure out how to make our website rank higher on Google.

How to Mine TrustRank

So now that we know not to believe what Google tells us about SEO, how do we clear the fog and figure out which sites have real TrustRank and therefore would be good targets for us to approach about selling or trading links? I've already covered the "is it spammy looking?" intuitive test. But there is an even simpler way to determine a site's TrustRank. In fact, it's so simple that it might have already crossed your mind—just look at where a site ranks in the search results. For instance, if you sell apple peelers, type *apple peeler* into Google. The top 40 results definitely have TrustRank. The top 10 results definitely have *a lot* of TrustRank.

When using this method to determine a site's TrustRank, remember to only search for competitive terms. If you enter an uncommon search term (if you own an apple peeler site, an uncommon term would be something like *top rated metal apple peelers*), even your first five results might not have a lot of TrustRank, as Google will probably be scraping the bottom of the barrel to find you results that are relevant to your search.

To solidify your understanding of this method of mining TrustRank, let's go through two examples. In fact, let's make them a little bit more fun than the apple peeler company. Let's say you just opened an online surfing supply store. Naturally, you will want to receive as many high-TrustRank links as possible to beef up your own TrustRank. You should start by typing *surfing* into Google (as shown in Figure 1.6).

> ✉ *Note*
>
> You will see in Chapter 8, "Google Optimization Myths," that I am one of the few people who doesn't think the links you acquire need to be especially relevant to your website; however, relevant sites are often a convenient place to start looking for links.

As you scan the top 10 results, you should be looking for organizations, resources, conference pages, and any other established site that might be likely to link to your website merely because you are a member of the industry. Those kinds of pages are the low-hanging fruit for which you would typically be looking. Apart from industry sites, you should be seeking out any site from which you have a reason to request a link. Let's dive in and see what we find.

Figure 1.6 *A Google search for the term* surfing *is a good place to start.*

Because *surfing* is a high-volume search and these are the top 10 results for it, we can immediately feel certain that each of the 10 results has a good amount of TrustRank. Therefore, any of them would be good targets to approach about acquiring a link on their sites. Because two of them—Surfer Magazine and Wikipedia—are editorial in nature, you can immediately assume that there is no way they will link to your business on their sites (although, if they did, your site would get a big shot of TrustRank). So that leaves the others. Examining them, I see that a few are informational sites about surfing, which are perfect places to put your link, providing you can convince them that your website is worthy of inclusion. (I address the many ways to secure links in Chapter 3, "How to Reel In Links.") If you could get a link on even four of the sites on this first page, you'd be well on your way to the top of the results for most surfing-related keywords.

Next, let's try a slightly less-common search (see Figure 1.7): *surfing supply*.

Here we find 10 results that we can still feel pretty good about, TrustRank-wise. *Surfing supply* is a common enough phrase, and looking above the results I see that companies are buying ads alongside the search results. When you see a lot of ads come up around a search, it usually means that the search seemed worthy enough to other businesses that they were willing to invest money in it. That's a sign that the search is competitive and the top 10 results probably had to earn their spots on the first page with a healthy amount of TrustRank.

So once again, I'd feel good about getting a link from any of these sites, but notice that the two editorial sites, Wikipedia's "Surfing" page and Surfer Magazine, aren't on this page. I also don't see any other surfing names I've heard of (I have a bit of familiarity with surfing), so I would definitely say that this group of sites is a notch below the *surfing* search in terms of TrustRank levels.

Finally, Figure 1.8 shows a search for a much less-competitive phrase: *premium surfing supply.*

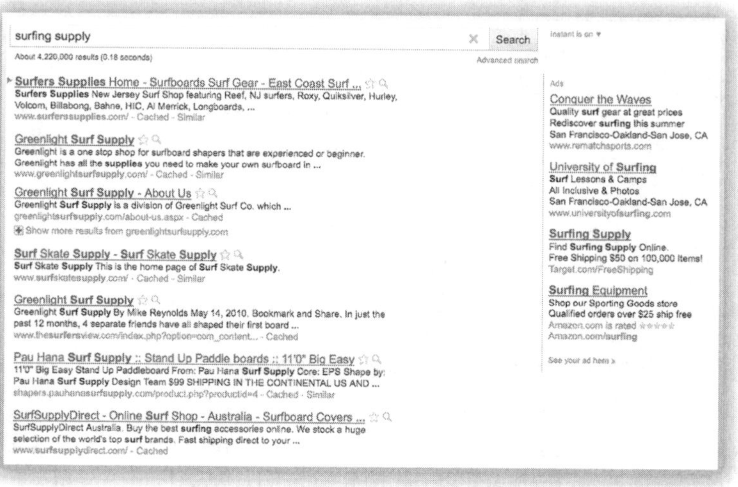

Figure 1.7   *A Google search on the term* surfing supply.

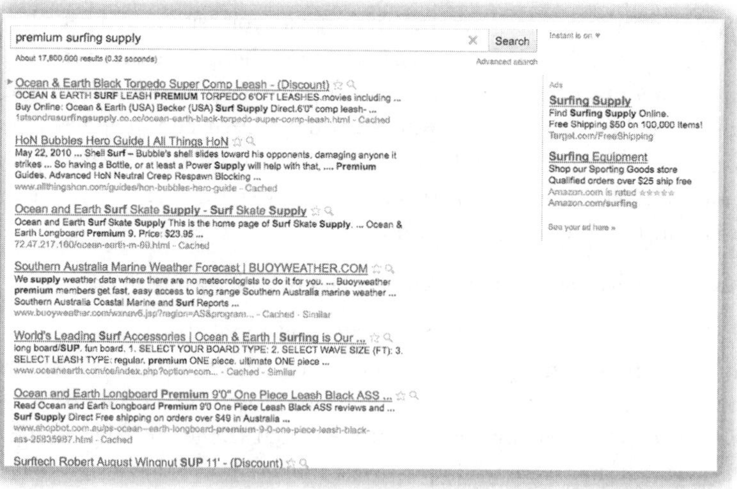

Figure 1.8   *A Google search on a much less competitive phrase,* premium surfing supply.

Before even seeing the results, we can infer that because the search is obviously not an especially common one, we are not going to be able to feel confident that any of these sites have enough TrustRank to spend our energy approaching them about links.

When we actually inspect these results, we observe that a number of them are not actually surfing supply stores, but rather individual product pages about random items like surfboard leashes. This indicates that the Big G was straining to find relevant sites and so had to dig deeper into its repository. If this were a clear product-oriented search like *buy surf boards* I would expect plenty of product pages, but because *premium surfing supply* is more of a store search, it's clear Google was unable to return good results. Now is the time when the intuitive test I described earlier would kick in. Clicking the sites on this page, I see that almost all of them are pages from e-commerce sites. There is very little chance that an e-commerce site would link to another website because it would distract buyers from making purchases. Some of these websites, however, are worth considering based on the fact that they have links right on the landing pages, such as buoyweather.com. This site appears to be a legitimate weather website and has a row of links in its right column. If I were in the surfing supply business, I would probably reach out to that website asking for a link.

Now that you have an easy way to see which web pages are most trusted, you can quickly compile a list of websites that you should be approaching to ask whether they would be willing to link to your site. If your site were to receive a link from every website that shows up in the top 40 or 50 results for your most competitive search terms, I guarantee it would soon become the #1 spot on Google, and you would be flooded with business. In reality though, you would never get all those webmasters—many of which are competitors—to agree to give your site a link, so we need to come up with some more creative ways of gaining high-TrustRank links for your business.

A Final Word on TrustRank

In the game of search engine optimization, you should now be at the point where you understand what the playing field looks like from a high level. If you haven't been paying attention, it basically comes down to this:

- Try to get a lot of websites to link to your website that
  - Have many inbound links
  - Have never sold links
- This will give your site TrustRank and cause Google to send it traffic.

The next few chapters explain how TrustRank interacts with other factors to determine your website's Google rankings and how to use SEO to get the most targeted visitors to your site.

2

The Five Ingredients of Google Optimization

By now, I've shed some light on how Google ranks the millions of sites on the Web. As a business owner or marketer, you are on a constant quest to gain Google's trust. And on your quest, you will need to keep exactly five factors in mind. I call them the five ingredients of successful SEO. You already know the most important one: links (the very currency of trust in Google's eyes). The others are keyword selection, meta page title, URL structure, and time. Even if those terms sound like jabberwocky to you right now, I promise they'll be second nature by the time you finish this chapter.

Before we get started, I want to make sure you understand a few basic vocabulary terms that will make your reading of this chapter much easier:

- **Keywords**—Keywords, or search terms (*these expressions are interchangeable*), are the words that are typed into search engines such as Google.

- **Inbound links**—As Google is analyzing its vast database of websites, trying to determine which ones to select as the 10 final, first-page contestants, it puts a high price tag on what's known in the industry as inbound links. Inbound links are links from other websites that point to your website, which hopefully result in your site gaining Google's trust.

- **TrustRank**—We know from the preceding chapter that the more links your site receives from other trusted websites, the higher its TrustRank will be, and therefore the higher its likelihood of showing up at the top of the search results. TrustRank is one of the two main factors Google uses to determine which results to show on the first page for a search.

- **Meta page title**—A meta page title, the other main factor used by Google to determine which results to show on the first page for a search, basically is a short description of what your site is about, which people who program websites put into a special area of the website code. It is like the headline of a newspaper. There is a different meta page title for every page on your site, and Google pays special attention to it.

- **URL**—A uniform resource locator (URL) is the same thing as a domain name, or a web address. It's the http://www.example.com that you type in when you want to visit a website.

Ingredient One: Keyword Selection

Now that you understand some of the basic terminology and concepts behind ranking, let's get down to the nitty-gritty of keyword selection. Selecting your search terms (or keywords) is not difficult. All you do is think about what you would like people to type into Google to make your website pop up. For example, I would like it if my personal website, http://www.evanbailyn.com, were the first result when someone typed in *Who is the handsomest man on earth?* This would cause people to believe that I am considered the handsomest man on earth. Why? Because Google says so! People put a lot of trust in Google's rankings.

If I managed the website for a personal injury law firm in New York, I would want that website to show up when someone types in *personal injury lawyer new york*. How did I choose that search phrase? I just thought about it for two seconds and decided that people would probably type it in if they were looking for a personal injury lawyer in New York.

Those phrases, *who is the handsomest man on earth?* and *personal injury lawyer new york*, are *keyword phrases*. I chose them because they seemed like the best searches to bring new visitors to the two websites in question for their respective purposes.

Of course, there are more scientific methods for choosing keywords in addition to the "think about it for two seconds" method. Here they are.

Take an Informal Survey

Ask your friends what they would type into Google if they were looking for the product or service your company sells. If you own a website that sells shampoo for people with dry hair, ask people around you: What would you type into Google if you want to find a new moisturizing shampoo? Their answers might be as general as *buy shampoo*, or they might specifically search for *dry hair shampoo*, or they might start with some research and type, *what are the best shampoos for dry hair?* These are three very different keyword phrases, and it is invaluable to know which of them most people would type so that you can set your strategy.

Use the Google AdWords Keyword Tool

This free tool is the de facto standard for keyword selection in the SEO world (see Figure 2.1). It shows global and local statistics of how many people are searching for the keywords you enter, along with a list of related terms and their search volumes. You can access the tool directly using this link: https://adwords.google.com/select/KeywordToolExternal. Without a doubt, bookmark this tool for future use.

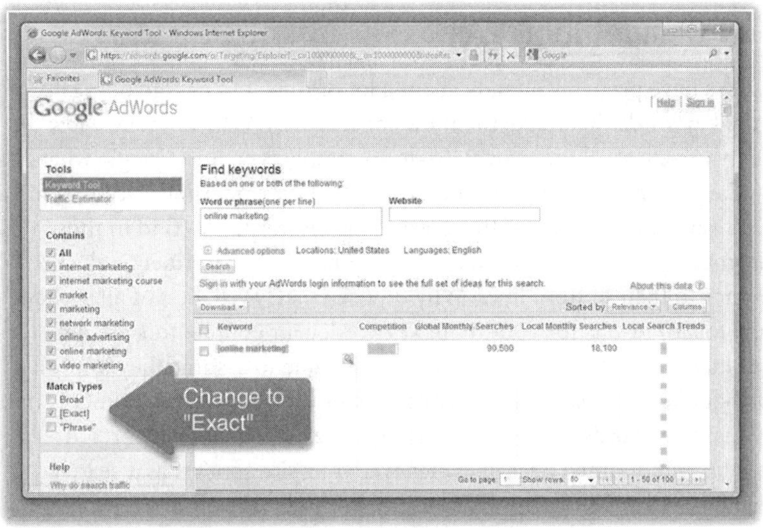

Figure 2.1   *The Google AdWords Keyword Tool. Always change the default Broad match type to Exact.*

BE CAREFUL WITH ADWORDS' SEARCH VOLUME NUMBERS

A crucial note about this tool is that its search volume numbers are inflated. I can't tell you how many clients I've gotten on the phone with who tell me breathlessly that if I can just get their sites to #1, they will get 10 million visitors per month! In reality, the keyword they are referring to will deliver a tiny fraction of that number of visitors. I have learned this lesson firsthand, having optimized my kids' website to the top five results of Google for the term "games" a few years ago. According to the Google Keyword Tool, "games" receives more than 400 million global searches per month. Getting even 1% of that number would make my site one of the most popular game sites online. So how many did I receive the month that I was on the first page of Google? Around 56,000.

To get a more accurate picture of the type of search traffic you can expect from the Keyword Tool, filter your results using the Exact match setting rather than the default Broad match setting. Then look in the Local Monthly Searches column. Take that number and divide it by three. The final number you get is somewhere close to the number of visitors your site would get if it ranked #1 for the search term in question.

Capitalize on Competitors' Work

Your competitors have probably already spent a lot of time and energy doing research on the keywords that make them the most money. Why not take a few seconds and avail yourself of all that work? To do so, simply type into Google what you believe to be your main keyword, and look at the blue underlined heading of each of the 10 results that subsequently appear. The keywords you find in those headings are probably the ones that your competitors have determined make the biggest difference to their bottom lines. Why do I say that? Well, first of all, to have gotten into the top 10 results for your main keyword, your competitors are definitely doing something right, SEO-wise, so it's reasonable to assume they know a thing or two about keyword selection. Second, one of the oldest rules in SEO is that you put your main keywords into your meta page title, which Google ports directly into your site's blue underlined heading whenever your site appears as a search result.

So let's say I sell gift baskets. Is the right keyword for me *gift baskets?* Perhaps it's *gift basket* as a singular. Or perhaps it's *order gift baskets online.* I'm not sure, but I'm going to see what my competitors think by typing *gift baskets* into Google (see Figure 2.2).

Figure 2.2 *Don't overlook what you can learn about the keywords your competitors deem important.*

After a quick glance at the headings of these results, I can immediately see that my competitors believe the keyword *gourmet gift baskets* is a lucrative one. Two out of the top four websites have the keyword *gourmet* in their headings or descriptions. So I will now add it to the list of keywords I want to optimize for my gift baskets company. It also seems that my competitors like *birthday gift baskets, food gift baskets,* and *wine gift baskets.* All three of these keyword phrases will be considered because I know from looking at these websites that they have put a lot of work into their companies, so they probably have a good sense of which keywords deliver the most new sales.

Another somewhat sneakier and more awesome way of capitalizing on your competitors' hard work is using free traffic measurement services to spy on the keywords for which your competitors are already ranking. I used to think that this kind of tool couldn't possibly exist because only I have access to my internal traffic logs and therefore know which search keywords bring my site the most traffic, but then I tried running the tool against my own site and found that it was about 90% accurate.

The best free keyword-spying tool is Alexa. Go to http://www.alexa.com, type in a competitor's website, click the Get Details button, and then click the Search Analytics tab. On the right side, you will see Top Queries From Search Traffic (see Figure 2.3).

Top Keywords from Search Traffic

The top keywords driving traffic to imdb.com from search engines. Updated monthly.

Keyword	Percent of Search Traffic
1 imdb	1.96%
2 megan fox	0.22%
3 avatar	0.19%
4 surrogates	0.14%
5 paranormal activity	0.14%
6 inglorious bastards	0.13%
7 500 days of summer	0.12%
8 imdb.com	0.12%
9 morena baccarin	0.11%
10 district 9	0.11%

Figure 2.3   *Alexa.com's Search Analytics report for imdb.com, showing the top keywords delivering traffic to IMDB.*

Using Alexa or other free keyword-spying tools is one surefire way to know which keywords are actually delivering traffic to your competitors. The keywords from which they receive traffic might be the best keywords for you; however, keep in mind that just because a keyword delivers traffic to a site doesn't mean it delivers *new sales* to a site. If there were a New Sales Spying Tool out there, it would be quite popular. However, the next best thing to a New Sales Spying Tool is a pay-per-click campaign.

Spend a Few Bucks on a Pay-Per-Click Campaign

There is no better way to understand the effect of your website showing up on the first page for a particular keyword than instantly getting it to the first page and seeing how many sales you make from it. This is essentially what you can do with a Google AdWords campaign (http://www.google.com/ads/adwords/). For a few hundred dollars, you can get your website to show up above the regular (organic) search results, in the shaded Sponsored Results area. While the sponsored results are less trusted by the average searcher than the organic results, there are definite advantages to spearheading an SEO effort with a brief Google AdWords campaign.

The most significant benefit of running a paid campaign on Google is that you can quickly learn which keywords produce the most sales for you. In the keyword selection process, this knowledge is invaluable. Not only can you try out the couple of keywords you think would bring the most benefit to your business, you can try out hundreds of keywords at once and not pay unless someone clicks your ad. In doing so, you might stumble upon the fact that the plural of your main keyword performs much better than the singular; one of your three most obvious keywords outperforms the other two by a wide margin; or some random keyword you never would have thought of is a sleeper, producing numerous sales.

When you gain a better understanding of your best-performing keywords, you can gradually wean yourself off the expensive Google AdWords system and focus on SEO (although there is nothing wrong with keeping a pay-per-click campaign running at the same time as doing SEO, as long as you are carefully watching the campaign to make sure you are making more money than you are spending). Google AdWords can work very well for targeting the lesser-searched keywords in your industry because of the rule that you pay only when someone clicks. I have some clients that use paid search only for those lesser-searched keywords and focus their entire SEO efforts on the three or four big keywords that bring in the most sales; this approach generally works well. I give a full tutorial on how to start a Google AdWords campaign to complement your SEO campaign in Chapter 6, "Google Adwords as a Complement to SEO."

Ingredient Two: The Meta Page Title

Do not skip this section, even if it sounds boring. I promise I won't hammer you with techie-talk. The meta page title is the second most important factor in all of SEO.

When your website was first created, whoever was programming it had to fill in a section of the coding called the *meta page title*. If your web designer knows a thing or two about SEO, he or she will have paid special attention to this seemingly random bit of code that is a part of every website.

The reason this primitive bit of information matters so much is because search engines have, for a while now, considered the meta page title to be the one true description of a website. The meta page title is like the headline of a newspaper story or the front cover of a book. It encapsulates a web page in about 15 words or fewer.

Google's decision to make it such a huge factor in ranking websites is pretty arbitrary. They could have made the meta description title, the meta keywords, or any other section of the website code the defining attributes of a website. But because they decided that this area matters so much, we are compelled to pay attention to it, too.

First off, let's get this out of the way. Figure 2.4 shows what the meta page title actually looks like inside your website's Hypertext Markup Language (HTML) code. I use the code from my website as an example.

Figure 2.4 *An example of how the meta page title appears in a web page's HTML code.*

Feel free to forget that image if it seems complicated. What that code turns into on your website is the words at the very top of your Internet browser, above the address bar (see Figure 2.5).

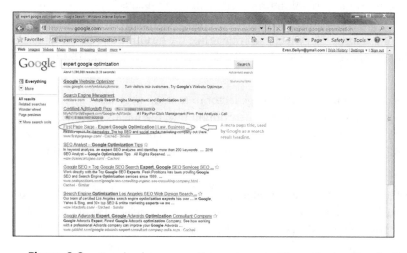

Figure 2.5 *The meta page text is what appears at the very top of the user's web browser.*

The only other place you will encounter meta page titles as a normal Internet user is when you are looking at search engine results. Those blue underlined headings on the first line of every Google result are simply a direct copy of each site's meta page title, as shown in Figure 2.6.

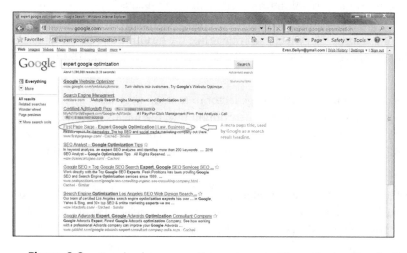

Figure 2.6 *Google also uses a site's meta page title as the heading for its search results.*

It is your job to decide what your page title should be before asking your web designer or tech person to put it into your site's code. But not to fear—when creating a meta page title, you need to know only the following three things:

1. It needs to summarize what your site is about in a simple way for the sake of visitors but also contain keywords so that Google knows which terms your website should rank for.

2. Keep it to a maximum of 100 characters, although Google will show only 65 or so.

3. After you've finished formulating it, send it to your web designer (or anyone who does your web work) and say, "Please make this sentence the meta page title of my site's home page."

Now that you see this meta page title thing is quite doable, let's go into how you can maximize its impact.

Maximizing the Effectiveness of Your Meta Page Titles

The key to a really effective meta page title is including all your most valuable keywords in a human-friendly *and* Google-friendly way. To demonstrate this idea, I will give an example of a long-time client of mine, a criminal lawyer in Los Angeles. He wants his website to show up at the top of Google whenever someone is looking for a criminal lawyer in Los Angeles. After doing his research, he realized that all his keyword phrases contain the words *lawyer, attorney, los angeles, criminal,* and *defense.* In other words, if you combine these words in different ways, you will end up with the various keywords that people type in when they are looking for a criminal lawyer in Los Angeles (for example, *criminal defense lawyer los angeles*). He also wants his website to rank high for searches related to criminal law representation in three areas outside of Los Angeles: Glendale, Pasadena, and Burbank. Add those three city names to the list of words that a potential client might enter into Google to find him, and he's looking at more than 20 different keywords. That's a lot of keywords to stuff into a 100-character title. How will he do it? Well, back in 2004 or 2005, it would have been common for webmasters to simply list their keywords, in order of importance, in the meta page title tag like this:

Los angeles criminal lawyer, los angeles criminal attorney, los angeles criminal defense attorney, los angeles criminal defense lawyer, los angeles criminal defense, los angeles lawyer, lawyer in burbank, glendale, pasadena

That type of meta page title is not only unfriendly to visitors, but would probably get your site labeled as spam and dropped to the bottom of the results. The main thing that this meta page title lacks—other than adherence to the character limit— is the fact that Google can read words in any order as long as they are written one time. So if your three keywords are *red delicious apples, delicious apples,* and *apples,* you could simply make your page title "Red Delicious Apples For Sale."

That would cover all three keywords just fine. With that rule in mind, here is a perfect meta page title for my client, the Los Angeles criminal lawyer:

Los Angeles Criminal Lawyer | Defense Attorney in Burbank, Glendale, and Pasadena

This meta page title incorporates all the words that my client wishes to rank for, and because Google doesn't care about word order, my client is getting credit for every permutation of those words. This means that if someone types into Google *pasadena defense lawyer,* Google will consider my client's website an ideal match. Same with *criminal defense attorney los angeles* or any other permutation of the words in his site's meta page title. We've covered them all in a short, human-friendly way.

So far I've been focusing on just your home page meta page title. But nowadays, especially with Google's newest algorithm updates, it is important to get many pages of your site, not just your home page, to rank. This means you should be specifically concerned with the meta page titles on all the pages of your website, not just your home page. My client, for instance, did not need to construct a meta page title for his home page that covers every important keyword. He could have a specific page that focuses just on criminal defense in Burbank, and the meta page title of that page could be "Burbank Criminal Defense Lawyer | Attorney in Burbank, California." Creating separate pages, all with unique meta page titles for every keyword, is a good idea because it gives visitors a page that specifically suits their search, whatever it may be. It also gives Google lots of opportunities to rank your website's pages for niche keywords. Ultimately, it is the sites that have hundreds, or even thousands, of pages on niche topics that receive the most overall traffic from Google. I discuss this strategy further in Chapter 5, "The Nuclear Football."

If you totally understand how to craft the perfect meta page title now, skip ahead to the "Ingredient Three: Links" section of this chapter. For those who really want this idea hammered home, I have included two case studies.

Case Study One: The Baby Store

A client of mine has an online store that sells clothing for babies and toddlers. Using the Google AdWords Keyword Tool, she found that her potential customers type in the obvious—*baby clothing*—but also use the word *clothes* in place of *clothing* and add the descriptors *girls* and *boys* in their searches. So already she was looking at the following list of keywords:

baby clothing
baby clothes
girls baby clothing
girls baby clothes
boys baby clothing
boys baby clothes

On top of that, potential customers with older kids were also typing in *toddler clothing* and *kids clothing*. So there were at least a dozen more permutations of keywords she wanted her site to rank for. After much thought, here is the page title we came up with:

The Baby Store | Baby and Toddler Clothing | Kids Clothes for Girls and Boys

As you can see, all the words that make up the keywords she wanted to rank for are represented in this innocent-looking page title. It just took a few minutes to arrange the words in a way that seemed natural but was also rich with keywords. As you can see, I'm a fan of the "spoke," the long vertical line that is above the Enter key on most keywords, because it separates bits of the page title neatly.

Case Study Two: Games

A client of mine who owns a games website wanted to rank for the keywords: *free online games, fun games,* and *best games.* Let's say his site name was Floofy.com. (I just made that up because it's fun to say.) A good page title for him would be this:

Floofy.com | The best fun, free online games

As with the other two examples I've given, this page title incorporates all the words that make up his three keywords, and therefore would be called forth by Google when someone types in *fun games, free online games,* or *best games.* Because this is a relatively short page title, he could include some other keywords as well. Or he might want to keep it that way because people do make the decision of which site to click on in the search results based on that blue underlined heading, which, once again, is a direct copy of the meta page title.

Ingredient Three: Links

You should now understand the meta page title, but how does it fit within Google's algorithm? Well, if I were an oversimplifying kind of person, I would tell you the following:

When someone does a search on Google, the first thing Google does is locate every site whose meta page title contains the words in that search. It then looks at how many trustworthy links each web page in that result set has and puts the ones with the most trustworthy links on the first page and the ones with the least trustworthy links at the very end.

So once you've got the right page title, it's all about links.

It amazes me how much I still hear that SEO is about the things that are on your website. In fact, the main service most so-called SEO companies sell is one where they work on your website to cause it to attract search engine traffic. This boggles my mind because, other than the meta page title, what's on your website barely even matters to Google! *It's all about links.*

Links are to Google what grades and SAT scores are to a college admission officer. Does the admission officer care what you look like on your interview? Sure. But he wouldn't have invited you for the interview in the first place if you didn't have high enough grades and SAT scores. Similarly, does Google care about how user-friendly your website is, what's written on it, and how fast it loads? Absolutely. But they won't even look at it if you don't have the right quality and quantity of links.

That being said, if you have great links but maintain a poorly coded, slow website with nonsense copy written on it, you won't have much luck ranking on Google. Just as you wouldn't have much luck getting into college if you have perfect grades and SATs but show up late to your interview wearing sloppy clothes and making wisecracks at your admission officer.

The point I'm trying to make is this: Links matter far more than any other factor. And if you get the link component and the meta page title component right, you've got 85% of the job done right there.

In Chapter 1, "Trust: The Currency Of Google," I went over how to determine a high TrustRank link versus a low TrustRank link. And in the next chapter, I go over how to acquire links. So for now, let me just explain a bit more clearly what a link is and what makes it valuable so that you know exactly what you're hunting for.

For the purposes of this book, a *link* is anything on a website that, when clicked, brings you to another web page. The granddaddy of links, the one that was there in 1994 when the Internet was still something only nerds cared about, is the *text link* (or, as I like to call it, the "blue underlined link"). Figure 2.7 shows a snippet from my bio on evanbailyn.com that contains two text links.

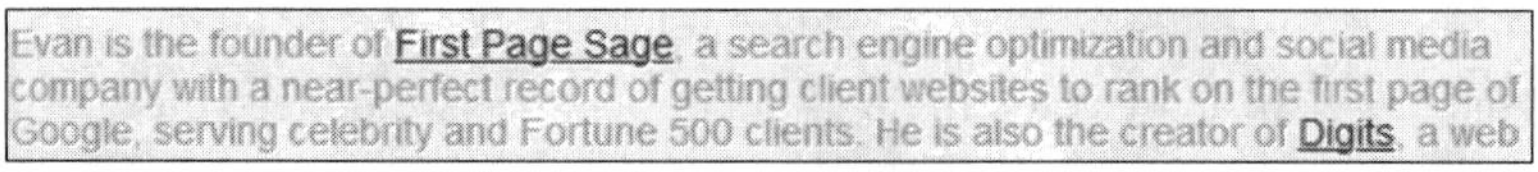

Evan is the founder of **First Page Sage**, a search engine optimization and social media company with a near-perfect record of getting client websites to rank on the first page of Google, serving celebrity and Fortune 500 clients. He is also the creator of **Digits**, a web

Figure 2.7 *An example of the way links are used inside text: they guide visitors to other web pages to supplement the information on the current page.*

I had my web designer add these two text links into my bio so that people could see my web properties with a simple click. That is generally the purpose of links—to allow people to discover new web pages with a quick mouse click.

Text links are usually blue and underlined, but there are exceptions. Sometimes you'll catch webmasters being creative with their text links. Also the color of a text link usually changes when you click it; this is to remind you that you've already visited the site that the link references. A clicked-on link will typically be purple, but again, that is up to the web designer. No matter what color it is or what it looks like, if it takes you to another page, it's a link.

The other type of link is the *image link*. As the name implies, this kind of link is in the form of an image but functions exactly like any other link in that it brings you to another web page when you click it. We've all seen plenty of image links; every advertisement on every website is an image link.

You know by now that Google gives your website credit every time another website links to your website. However, certain types of links are more valuable than others. Text links are the most valuable types of links because Google can easily read the words in and around the text link to get a sense of what the link is referring to. An image link has the same magnitude of value as a text link, but without all the description. In other words, an image link is like an overall vote for a political candidate, one that says "I like this candidate." A text link is like a detailed vote for a political candidate, the equivalent of "I like this candidate because of his stance on health care and education." Text links are valuable because they tell Google what a site is about. This information allows Google to decide which specific keywords to rank that website for.

As I explained in Chapter 1, the reason links are so important is because they pass TrustRank. Text links pass highly detailed TrustRank. Image links pass general TrustRank. When asking other websites for links, you should request a text link, but if you absolutely can't get one (for instance, if text links don't fit into the site's aesthetic), you can settle for an image link. Ultimately, your site will rank higher with a mix of both, because Google's engineers have determined that most sites would attract both types of links in a world without SEO.

When requesting a text link from another site, you should usually ask for one that has your keywords inside the linked text. For instance, if I print business cards for a living, I want my link to appear in underlined text reading "business cards." These links could stand on their own or appear in the context of a sentence or paragraph. You do not want a link that simply has your website's address in the linked text. So to be clear...

The three ways you *want* your link to appear on another website:

➡ <u>business cards</u>

➡ Print your <u>business cards</u> quickly and inexpensively.

➡ Nowadays there are many ways to send people your contact details. A simple email signature can suffice. You could share your Twitter username. And of course, we must not underestimate the old-fashioned convenience of <u>business cards</u>.

The two ways you *do not* want your link to appear on another website:

<u>www.yoursite.com</u>

Business Cards

I would be finished writing this section if it were 2008 right now. For the vast majority of Google's existence, simple text links with keywords inside of them have been
the greatest weapon in any search engine optimizer's arsenal. But alas, in mid-2009
Google slammed the SEO world with an algorithm update that punished sites that
have too many same-keyword text links pointing to them. In other words, if I had
been telling webmasters for years to only link to me like this—<u>business cards</u>—my
site would have dropped way down in the rankings. I wondered why it had taken the
arsenal of highly paid Stanford and MIT graduates at Google so long to realize that
keyword-rich text links were overused by optimizers and were unnatural looking.

At the time the keyword-rich text link party was ending and hundreds of search
engine optimizers were in their home offices crying, I remained relatively calm. I
had outsmarted them before and was determined to do it again. How should I react
to Google's rebellion against unnatural-looking link patterns? By adopting natural-
looking link patterns, of course. I started linking to my clients in a smattering of
different ways. Some links had the keyword a few words away in a paragraph, some
had the keyword as only part of the text link, some had the keyword not mentioned
at all, and some had the keyword inside the text link exactly the way I did before.
Following is my recipe for the perfect "natural" linking pattern for your site. In
other words, this is the formula for how other websites should link to your website
under ideal circumstances. I have used "business cards" as the example keyword
that I am aiming to optimize for.

- 20% links in text *around* your keyword but not *on* your keyword (for
  example, "When I need business cards, I contact <u>this company</u>.")

- 30% links that include your keyword but also include other words in a
  sentence (for example, "I ran out of my <u>brand new business cards</u> today.")

- 30% links that include only your keyword (for example, "I love my
  <u>business cards</u>.")

- 20% image links

In other words, I am saying that, if your site had 10 total inbound links, each link
from a page on a different website, it would be ideal if

- Two of those pages contained your keyword but linked to your website
  from text near that keyword, not from the keyword itself.

- Three of those pages contained your keyword and linked to your website from your keyword in addition to the word or two that is next to it.

- Three of those pages contained your keyword and linked to your website directly from it.

- Two of those pages contained images and linked to your website from those images.

For the professional search engine optimizers among you, this recipe might seem like the cream of this entire book. Why not wait until nobody's looking, rip it out of the book, and stick it in your wallet, right? I must warn you that although this recipe works very well at the time of this printing, remember that Google is always shifting their algorithm. Your best shot to always fall ahead of the curve is to obtain as many natural-looking links as possible in a variety of formats.

Dummy Links

Before moving on to the next ingredient, I must warn you about a certain type of link that passes no TrustRank at all and must be avoided at all costs. I call these types of links *dummy links* because they look just like real links but contain none of the substance that helps your website to rank. You should keep dummy links in mind because there is nothing worse than finding out that some of the links you have worked hard to earn are not actually passing any TrustRank. Here are the two types of dummy links:

- **Redirect links**—If a webmaster is trying to prevent TrustRank from being passed via the links on his site, he can have them coded in such a way that when someone clicks a link to an outside site, that person is first sent to a page on his own site before arriving at his final destination website. This is called a redirect. In other words, there is an intermediate page that the visitors hit before they get to the page they intended to visit. Usually the visitor is on the intermediate page just for a split second so that they never even notice they visited an intermediate page. This is a sneaky way of withholding the site's vote—that is, their TrustRank—from ever being cast. Google gives all the TrustRank they would have given to the outside site to the intermediate page, which is just some random page on the originating site. You can identify this kind of dummy link by hovering your mouse over any link on another site that seems to be going to your site and then looking at the bottom left corner of your screen where the URL that the link is pointing to is displayed. As long as it reads http://www.yoursite.com, you're

good. If it reads something like http://www.othersite.com/
redirect.php?url=www.yoursite.com, it is a dummy link.

- **No-follow links**—The most sinister type of dummy link is the no-follow link, simply because you can't tell that it isn't passing TrustRank
  without looking at the HTML code of the web page. No-follow links are
  normal links that have been intentionally crippled via a short bit of
  code to prevent TrustRank from leaving a web page. They are an invention of Google, created to give webmasters a way to link to advertisers
  without "voting" for advertisers. For a couple of years, the no-follow
  link has been a subject of debate in the SEO world. Google holds that
  they are merely trying to figure out which links are editorial mentions
  and which are paid mentions. (Google only wants to give ranking credibility to the former.) Many webmasters think that they should not have
  to change the way they link to advertisers just to please an outside company, even one as important as Google. Naturally, advertisers don't like
  being labeled with a no-follow tag because that TrustRank is one of the
  chief things that they are paying for.

When another site links to your site as part of an arrangement you
made, ask your webmaster to check to see whether it has a "no-follow
tag" on it. If you catch a site linking to you with a no-follow tag, you
have license to be very upset with them. The only good use of a no-follow tag, in my opinion, is in the comments of a blog because there are
so many spammers who leave comments with links in them just to steal
TrustRank from your site. Many sites, includes the *New York Times*
website, place a no-follow tag on all comments. If you'd like to check a
link yourself for a no-follow tag, find the View Source button on your
web browser's menu (often you can access the code by right-clicking
the page as well) and do a search for your site's URL. If you see
rel=nofollow next to your link, you know that the webmaster is withholding TrustRank from being passed to your site.

Ingredient Four: URL Structure

Sometimes Google is so easy to read that people miss what it's trying to tell them.
The role of the URL in SEO is one of those times. Simply put, your main keyword
should be in your URL. Preferably, it should be the entire URL. For example, if you
own a video-sharing site and your keyword is *funny videos,* the best domain name
you could ever get is http://www.funnyvideos.com. If you have many keywords, as
most webmasters do, you'll want to make sure that every keyword has its own landing page with the keyword somewhere in the URL. The most standard way to format keyword-specific URLs is as follows:

http://www.yoursite.com/keyword1.html
http://www.yoursite.com/keyword2.html
http://www.yoursite.com/keyword3.html

When I speak about this topic, I always get lots of questions about the best way to include your keywords in your URL. So let me break it down for you. We'll start with the most fundamental part of your URL: your domain name. I'm sure Google has some dusty tablets lying around that define the top-level domains (or TLDs, such as .com, .net, .org) they trust the most, but the most I can do is give you my educated guess.

When choosing a domain name, you should first try to get your keyword in a .com form (for example, http://www.funnyvideos.com). If you can't get that— which you probably can't without paying the spammer who probably owns the domain lots of money—try for the .net or the .org version of that domain. If you can't get either of those, you will definitely be able to find a domain name that has your keyword in it with another word before it, as in http://www.yourfunnyvideos. com. While far less valuable than http://www.funnyvideos.com, a domain name with an extra word in it will give you some extra ranking credibility with Google for that keyword. If you can't manage to find a domain with your main keyword in it, you can either try a hyphenated domain (such as http://www.best-funnyvideos. com) at the risk of looking a bit low quality, or simply use a URL without a keyword in it and optimize a page that is named after your main keyword, as in http://www.yoursite.com/funnyvideos.

If you have multiple very important keywords and have time and money, buying multiple URLs, one for each keyword you care about, is a strategy I've seen work quite well for clients. But keep in mind that each URL will need its own website with unique content. If you try to throw the same website on multiple URLs, Google may penalize all but one of them for having duplicate content.

There are probably many people reading this book who do not have the option of deciding how to integrate their keywords into their domain names because they already have a website or need to use the names of their companies as their domain names. If that's your situation, you should focus on having an excellent URL structure for all the pages on your site. And in this case, excellent means simple.

Determine your keywords in advance and have a separate web page for every keyword that has the keyword as the full name of the page, as follows:

http://www.yoursite.com/funnyvideos
http://www.yoursite.com/sillyvideos
http://www.yoursite.com/crazyvideos

Remember what we went over in the "Ingredient Two: The Meta Page Title" section of this chapter: Your meta page title should contain the keyword that your page is about, as well. A content management system (CMS) like WordPress will automatically create these kinds of URLs for you. They call them SEO-friendly URLs, and they work quite well. Some CMSs, on the other hand, create dynamic URLs that look sort of like this:

http://www.example.com/article/bin/answer.foo?language=en&answer=3&sid=98 971298178906&query=URL

These types of pages, although readable by Google, are not as helpful to your site's Google rankings as simple, static URLs such as the ones I listed previously. When executed correctly, a page on your website designed to attract searches for a particular keyword should look like the site in Figure 2.8.

Figure 2.8 *A website with a recommended URL structure and meta page title when the keyword being targeted is* pregnancy.

This page is targeting the keyword *pregnancy,* and so its URL is correctly formatted oh-so-simply as http://www.fornewmoms.com/pregnancy. Note that the meta page title also includes the word *pregnancy.*

After you have your keywords together, links to your website, proper meta page titles, and the correct URL structure, you've done an excellent job impressing Google. Like a well-prepared prom date, you have shown up to meet your date's parents looking your best, armed with compliments, polite manners, and diplomatic answers. And you've succeeded: The parents like you! But you haven't earned their trust quite yet.

Ingredient Five: Time

Like the prom-goer who has impressed his date's parents on the first meeting, you will be in great initial shape to rank high on Google if you've implemented the first four ingredients correctly. Now it's up to you to continue this good behavior. Bring her home at 4 a.m. on prom night, and you are *out*, buddy. Bring her home before midnight and keep exhibiting good manners in the coming weeks and months, and you're building real trust. Google is just as unforgiving as a pair of protective parents; they can handle imperfections and a few awkward missteps, but cross a line that violates their trust, and you will not be welcome inside Google's house again for a long time.

In a website's first month, it cannot rank for any competitive keyword. I've heard about websites that were just released and immediately hit the top of Google, but I've never seen one; and the times I *have* seen sites that claim this meteoric rise, they were ranking for wholly uncompetitive keyword phrases such as *turkish cotton substitute*.

Google intentionally imposes a ranking delay on new websites. This tradition originates back in the days when Google was still combating spam sites, which were threatening to take over their index. These spam sites, most of them automatically generated blogs made up of paragraphs of senseless content to fool Google into thinking they were legitimate websites, had found a way to rank on Google for hundreds of thousands of keywords. The situation had gotten so bad that it was threatening the relevance of Google's results. I remember this period well; although the search experience on Google was not awful, for most searches you typed in you had about a 10% chance of clicking a site that seemed to be written by a lunatic. The new ranking delay (which used to be more severe—preventing most sites from ranking for up to one year) stopped the spammers cold in their tracks. No longer could they throw a website up, get it to rank in a week, make a few bucks from ads or identity-theft schemes, and then disappear. Now they had to stick around and prove their worth for a while, a task very few of them seemed eager to take.

Nowadays, a website gets its first real opportunity to rank for a competitive keyword around the two-month mark—just as long as it has lots of high-TrustRank, natural-looking links. And yet Google still keeps an invisible rubber band around its waist, holding it back from reaching its full potential. A website *can* rank after two months but will be playing with a handicap for about four years in progressively smaller degrees. If I had to guess the amount of "holdback"—that is, inability to rank—a website suffers from its inception to its fourth birthday, the chart would look like what's shown in Table 2.1.

Another way of expressing this chart is that, in month one, the TrustRank of your site's links will have no impact on its Google rankings because your site is completely held back. In month six, however, every link gets about half credit for the

TrustRank it should be conferring on your website. By the 3-year mark, your links receive almost the entire value of their TrustRank, and therefore your website can rank quickly for any term for which it has enough links. That slow-release system is the reason why it is extremely advantageous to buy an old website that already ranks for some of your keywords rather than starting a brand new site. For example, if I sold fortune cookies, instead of simply registering http://www.evansfortunecookies.com, I would type *fortune cookies* into Google and try to find a site that ranks on the first five pages or so that the owner is willing to sell. Although it is difficult to find sellers willing to let their sites go for a reasonable price, if I were to buy an old website that already ranks for my main term, I'd be skipping the entire holdback period and saving myself a ton of time and money.

Table 2.1   Estimated "Holdback" Placed on Sites by Google

Month	Holdback
1	100%
2	75%
6	50%
12	25%
24	10%
36	5%
48	0%

Time is not just a friend of your website; it is a friend of your website's *links*, as well. Confusing as it may sound, a high Google ranking is not just dependent on site age, but also on link age. That is to say, if you have a very old website, and thus experience none of the holdback period whatsoever, you still wouldn't rank high for the keywords referenced by your links if those links were only a few days or weeks old. Google likes to make sure that your links are there for the long haul, not just rented for the month to see whether they will boost your site's rankings (a common situation among buyers of commercial links).

In summary, time will be kindest to websites that have waited long enough and whose links have been there from the very start.

Congratulations on having made it through this chapter. It is, by itself, a record of everything that causes a website to rank on the first page of Google. If you feel like you understood most of the information discussed, you officially know more about Google optimization than the vast majority of Internet business owners. Now it's time to deepen that knowledge.

3

How to Reel
In Links

At this point, I am confident that you understand how important links are to your website's rankings. Now it's time to show you how to actually acquire them. The easiest way to get a link on another website is to ask a webmaster—by email, phone, smoke signal, or whatever—to place a link on their website that points to your website. They will probably know how to do it, but if not, they can always ask whoever handles their web development. It should take about two minutes for someone to decide whether there is room to place a link on their website and then publish it there.

Now, when I say that the easiest way to get a link is to ask a webmaster for one, I am being a little bit oversimplistic; most webmasters are protective about links on their sites, thinking of them as Google does—as editorial votes that only merit passing out to highly worthy web pages. So for the most part, when you are trying to attain links, especially high TrustRank ones, you have to be quite clever.

Good and Bad Neighborhoods

Before I get into the many exciting ways to acquire links, I want to make sure you understand which links are worth having. As I mentioned in Chapter 1, "Trust: The Currency of Google," you do not want links from any website that promotes spam or adult content. Although Google has implied that links from outside sites cannot affect your website's rankings because they are beyond your control, it is in fact the case that too many bad neighborhood links can get your website penalized. I believe that Google has an algorithmic way of determining whether a website appears to have an intentional association with low-quality sites. If Google determines that your site has such an association, you might as well kiss your online presence goodbye. I doubt many readers of this book are involved in spam or adult content (if you are, oops—this book is about "white hat" SEO only). I emphasize this point only because, in the process of attracting links, you will undoubtedly come across emails from various spammers promising you "expert link building" or something of the sort, which usually means placement on hundreds of already-penalized spam websites. Although joining up with spam networks such as this is often an innocent decision, it's about as innocent as joining a devil-worshipping cult under the pretense that you were just trying to make some new friends. Your "new friends" will surely ruin your reputation.

A much more common mistake when link building is to trade with, or buy links from, sites that actively buy, sell, and trade links as part of an aggressive link-building strategy. In general, you want to receive links from websites that are a lot less aggressive than you are as far as link building goes. In late 2010, Google put the whammy on sites that buy and sell links even casually. Unlike the case with spam and adult sites, these links will not get your website penalized; they will just fail to pass TrustRank to your website, and therefore acquiring them will be a waste of your time and money.

It is worth reemphasizing here that, when seeking out links, you should look to sites that already rank high on Google. Sites that don't rank high for the keywords that define their site probably have very low TrustRank and will not confer much ranking value on your website.

Link Building 101

I think by now you have an understanding of which sites you definitely should *not* seek links on and which sites you definitely *should* seek links on. Now here is a list of the kinds of links you should look for first, the low-hanging fruit:

- **Family and friends' websites**—Because any link on a "good neighborhood" site is a good link, why not start in the obvious place: your network of family and friends? Does your Uncle Dave have a blog? Does your cousin Suzie have a website for her start-up? Maybe your bro from college knows a guy who has a *Jersey Shore* fan site and would totally link to your business website if you asked him nicely. Work all those avenues!

- **Other websites in your industry or niche**—No matter what business you're in, other people do the same thing, or at least something similar.

These are the members of your industry, or in some cases, your niche within an industry. Often, you can ask these folks for links on their websites, and they'll be responsive to it. Competitors are a tossup: Either they will totally not get why they should do anything to help you, or they will feel a kinship with you and be happy to help. Sometimes you can get the latter result with a simple explanation: "I know we vie for the same customers, but helping each other out is a lot more productive than pretending the other one doesn't exist. If we help each other to succeed, we can both take more of the pie as a result, and who knows, maybe even make the pie larger for all of us."

Tip

An even easier road to take is to approach complementary sites in your industry. Got a cookie site? Approach a milk site. Got a fishing site? Approach a bait site. Got an airplane site? Approach a yacht site. You get the picture.

- **Every social media site on Earth**—Social media sites are uniquely valuable to SEO because they are free to join and their pages often have high TrustRank. It takes all of 10 minutes to join a social media site and set up a page that contains a link to your business website. This means 10 minutes per new link for you! The greatest part is that there are hundreds of random social media sites. Start with Facebook (the most popular), and then go to YouTube, Twitter, Tumblr, Foursquare, Digg, Reddit, Friendster, Orkut, and yes, even MySpace. Type *list of social media sites* into Google to find a huge number not mentioned here. Then you can go to blogging sites, online journals, business directories, and any other site that publicly lists profiles. (We don't want privacy here; if your profile page doesn't show up publicly on Google, it is of no value to your link-building efforts.) When creating all of these pages, just make sure to set up a separate email address so that your main email doesn't get overrun with all of the confirmation and welcome emails these sites will send you.

Obtaining links on the social media sites should be pretty straightforward. The other two types—family and friends links and industry links—take a bit more effort. Depending on your personality type, it can be either quite easy or quite difficult to gain dozens of links on other people's websites. Doing so is a straight sales job. If you're charismatic and a good closer, you will pile on the links and gain top rankings quickly. If you are more of a behind-the-scenes kind of person, you might find the process frustrating. Every link deal involves a personal exchange with another webmaster or marketer, and those who get along best with others and can think of creative business solutions will come out ahead. In a few pages, I reveal every way I can imagine to acquire links. But because we're still talking Link Building 101, just consider one method: writing a simple email asking whether the webmaster would mind linking to your website, either as a favor (in the case of family and friends) or as a resource (in the case of industry sites).

In the course of your courtship of these low-hanging-fruit website owners, at some point you will probably receive a reply that reads something like "I suppose I can add your link, but I don't know where I'd put it. I don't really link out to other websites that much."

You should say, "I'm glad you asked. There are plenty of places you could place my link on your website that are out of the way and won't cause visitors to be distracted from what you're trying to accomplish or leave the site. After all, I'm not necessarily looking to get new visitors to my website from this link. I just want Google to spot it and give me credit for having it there."

From there, you can suggest one of the following locations:

- **The home page**—You always want to try to get a link on a website's home page if you can because Google gives more TrustRank to links from home pages. Although having *only* home page links would ultimately cause Google to distrust you, you will naturally receive so many links from inside pages (that is, pages other than the home page) that you might as well try to get the most valuable links when you can. If there is not already a place for links on the home page (such as a blog roll—a listing of favorite websites on the side of a blog), you can suggest placing your link on the edge or bottom of the page. Figure 3.1 shows an example.

Figure 3.1 *A home page link on the side of my blog, under a category I call "Friends." This list of links does not interfere with my site's aesthetic or draw much traffic, but each link passes TrustRank to the website it points to.*

- A **"Resources" page**—There's no harm in creating an extra page on your site just to link to other websites (see Figure 3.2). Usually, this is called a Resources page. If your request for a link is turned down by a webmaster who says there is no room for your link, remind him how useful Resources pages can be and show him an example of one.

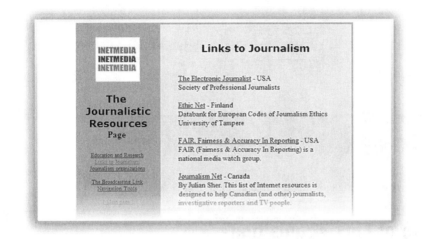

Figure 3.2 *A Resources page: a great place to host links when there is no other convenient spot on a website.*

- **The bottom of a page**—If a webmaster refuses to place your link anywhere even remotely visible, as a last resort you can ask him to just throw your link way at the bottom of one of the pages (see Figure 3.3). Keep in mind that you don't want to have your link at the bottom if there are many other sites down there (especially if they're unrelated to each other), because this is a common linking tactic for which Google might discount the TrustRank value of the link. A recommended way to get your link placed at the bottom of a website is when you have done work, such as web design, programming, or consulting for that site.

With this basic tutorial, you should now have a way to get started on your link-building journey. Just utilizing these tactics alone, you could build 50+ links and reach the first page of Google for a medium-competitive to competitive keyword, assuming you have the proper meta page title and URL structure on whichever page you're trying to get to pop up in the results. But this first push will not be enough to rank on the first page for highly competitive keywords. Are you ready for the big guns?

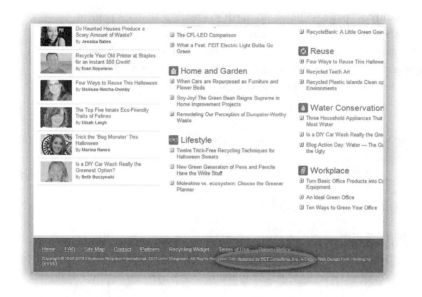

Figure 3.3   *A web designer's link at the bottom of a site's home page.*

The Bible of Link Acquisition

In the coming sections, I include every tactic for gaining links that I can think of. Most of them fall into one of two broad categories:

- Systematic link building involves doing a lot of repetitive work to gain links, and I recommend getting an intern to do these tasks after you've mastered them yourself.

- Link bait, or creating something so interesting or useful that people really want to link to it, is a highly creative—and sometimes quite ambitious—endeavor.

> ✉ *Note*
>
> Many of these techniques result in general links to your site's home page, which do not have the proper link text and therefore do not cause your website to move up higher for a specific keyword. However, both techniques improve your site's overall link popularity and, over time, increase your website's ranking for all keywords. All links that pass TrustRank to your website are valuable.

Systematic Emailing

The surest way to get a large volume of links is through good, old-fashioned cold emailing. Find a list of webmasters in a specific niche, put their names, websites, and email addresses into a table, and then go down the list, writing a personalized form letter requesting a link to each person. This method has garnered me many links. Here is an example of a simple, customizable form letter you might send to a website from which you are seeking a link.

Hey [Name],

I hope all is well. I've been a fan of your site for a while now. [Something personal like "You really do have the best quotes from 90s sitcoms—they crack me up!"]

I actually just created a site of my own, [yoursite.com]. It's basically a site about [topic]. I am quite passionate about this topic, having wanted to create this website for many years. Finally, I realized my dream just recently.

I was wondering if you'd be interested in linking to my website. I see you have a [blogroll/ resource section/ friends box]. If you'd be kind enough to add my site, I would be more than happy to return the favor in some form. I have numerous contacts and am pretty resourceful, so whatever you need, please ask, and I will see if I can help.

If you do decide to link to my site, please create the link in the following way if you could:

[keyword]

Thanks and I hope to have the opportunity to build a relationship.

Sincerely,

[Your Name]

[Your contact info]

With a letter like this one, which contains a line or two of personalization but is otherwise fairly general, I'd say your response rate will be about 1 in 15. The more you personalize your email, the higher your response rate will be.

Press Releases

Ah, the press release: the age-old art of attempting to interest people in what you're doing by writing it in the form of an objective article. No matter how self-conscious this method might make you feel (you usually have to quote yourself), it still works quite well. The services that blast out press releases to hundreds of online outlets create lots of links for you. Just make sure your links are formatted correctly in your press release and that you are comfortable with the content you've written because these suckers will stay around for a long while, popping up whenever someone uses Google to search for your company's name. Try prnewswire.com, prweb.com, or any of the dozens of others that show up when you search for *online press release* on Google. Some of these services charge a fee. The most basic press package is often worth purchasing, but none of the more expensive ones are worth the money. If you plan to use press releases to build links, keep in mind that some press release services such as businesswire.com change all links to "smart links," more commonly known as redirected links, which prevent the link from passing TrustRank (see Figure 3.4). These links are of no SEO value to you.

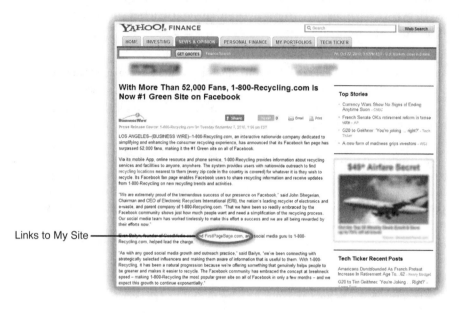

Links to My Site ——————

Figure 3.4 *A press release containing what appears to be a normal link to my website. However, this site uses redirected links, which send visitors to another web page for a micro-second before sending them to the link's intended destination, thus eliminating the passing of TrustRank. As a result, this link has no search engine value.*

Create Funny or Ridiculous Content

Got a penchant for humor? An eye for the outlandish? Even if your site is completely serious, there is always room for an offbeat-yet-tasteful section, and it doesn't even need to be linked from a place where your everyday visitors will see it (that is, your home page). Many sites will link to your website if people find a piece of content genuinely entertaining, and those links will count toward your site's overall link popularity.

So what kind of crazy stuff could you create? Well, it depends on your industry. I have had the fortune of running an online paper doll site for girls, which gave me the opportunity to create online paper dolls of characters that weren't just for kids. For instance, during the 2008 primaries, I created dress-up dolls of then-candidates Barack Obama, Rudy Giuliani, and Hillary Clinton. I made sure to look up all I could about their personal lives first so that I could add all kinds of gimmicks—

from campaigning props to college sweatshirts—that political junkies would get a kick out of. My goal was to attract at least 10 links from political sites, hopefully even the online versions of newspapers because I knew those sites carried a lot of TrustRank. With that goal in mind, I emailed about 50 political writers whose names and email addresses I got from a site that rounds up articles by various pundits. I told them merely that I had created these dress-up dolls, that they could find them at a particular URL on my website, and that I hoped they would have some fun with them. Figure 3.5 shows one of the dress-up dolls I sent them.

Figure 3.5 *A dress-up doll of Barack Obama I created in 2008 to "bait" political websites to link to my kids' paper doll site.*

The dress-up dolls were a hit. They attracted links from 34 different websites, most of them blogs. The writers apparently found the dolls wacky enough that they just *had* to share them. And the jewel of the whole effort was the fact that the *New York Times* blog picked it up, as well, delivering my site a gloriously high TrustRank link.

When trying to procure funny material, it helps a great deal to use people or subjects that already matter a lot to people. Politics is an especially fertile ground for humor because people take it so seriously. And if you satirize a political figure, you stand to benefit from the many people who dislike that figure, or at least find him or her too stuck up or self-righteous for his own good.

During the time of the Eliot Spitzer scandal, for instance, we had a moment when a man whom many people disliked was publicly embarrassed. I guarantee that if you had taken action the moment the news broke, writing a mock public apology from the desk of Eliot Spitzer or a song that made fun of his perceived hypocrisies, people would have loved it. Whatever site you hosted this content on would have gotten links aplenty. The same with Tiger Woods. If you do a Google search for *tiger woods humor* or *tiger woods funny,* you will see dozens of joke pieces that people created to capitalize on his 2009 cheating scandal. And so, while I'm not necessarily telling you to use people's tragedies for your own benefit, I am telling you to use topics of mass public interest to attract links because many people already find them fascinating.

But be careful not to be too general. There are lots of things that are universally funny, such as tripping and falling, but the Internet is built around niche interest groups. So if your site can attract the attention of political junkies, or car lovers, or lawyers, or equestrians, it will quickly spread around to the many websites in that contingent's circle and garner you a payload of links.

To give you another example of a successful piece of link bait catering to a niche group, a few years ago I created a humorous website on a domain I own, www.irony. com. Because I wasn't doing anything with this great domain name, I figured I would try to create a highly linkable website and see what happened. I hired an artist to draw cartoons that satirized different issues of importance to many people. I targeted a number of interest groups, one being Internet geeks. Figure 3.6 shows one cartoon I came up with, called *If the World Wide Web Were a City*.

Figure 3.6 *A cartoon called* If the World Wide Web Were a City, *which I created to attract links to my website from Internet tech websites.*

This cartoon drew the attention of about 15 blogs and computer interest sites after it was featured on the home page of a particularly popular blog.

Just be careful because people can be sensitive. Use your judgment to make wise decisions based on the comfort level of your intended audience.

Create Interesting Content

Although humor is a particularly popular content category, it falls within a larger category that matters much more—things that are interesting. If you can make something that someone will look at and say "Hmm!" to themselves, you've just created an excellent piece of link bait.

Of course, many things could be considered interesting, but the Internet makes it much easier for us to know what people like. If you want to know which videos people find the most interesting, for instance, look on YouTube's Most Popular or Most Viewed pages. If you want to know which Internet news stories people find the most interesting, look at the front page of Digg.com. If you want to know which topics people are talking about the most, look at Google Trends or the Trending Topics area of Twitter. These are all excellent ways to draw inspiration for your very own piece of interesting content.

Probably the most popular above-board area of interest in the United States is celebrities. That is what gave me the idea to add a new section to my SEO and social media website that is essentially a ranking list of celebrities in order of their popularity. I know that celebrities sound like they have nothing whatsoever to do with an SEO company, but because attracting links to my website is so important to me, I found a connection. I reasoned that one way to measure the popularity of a celebrity is to look at how many mentions, followers, and fans they have online. And because one of the main things my company does is increase the mentions, followers, and fans people and businesses have online, I knew I could couple this list with a tool to find out just how popular you or your business is on the Internet; and once you saw where you ranked compared to the celebrities and invariably felt that you would like to be *more* popular, I'd serve you an advertisement for First Page Sage's promotional services.

"The List," as I call it, includes the top 200 celebrities in eight different categories, and is shown in Figure 3.7.

Because a function of this page is that it actively reports changes in the popularity of celebrities, I have fresh news—which I've manufactured—every day. "Ashton Kutcher fell 5 slots in popularity," or "Britney Spears is at it again and climbed 15 spots in the rankings," or "Lady Gaga has held onto her top spot for the 27th straight week!" I then send all these pieces of "news" to various celebrity sites. Usually, they find the concept of a straight-up ranking chart for celebrities to be pretty interesting. People tend to love charts, tables, and graphs, especially when they oversimplify information. And when people love my rankings, they give my site links that it would normally never receive.

You don't have to create an entire tool the way I did to make a successful piece of link bait. You can simply give your outlook on a breaking piece of news in an original way or find some cool pictures and put them in a context in which they aren't normally presented. For example, one article I created for a client website was on 12 rarely seen animal emotions (see Figure 3.8). It was just a collection of funny pictures of animals that seemed to indicate a particular emotion (a dog looking sad, a donkey looking mad, a llama looking suspicious), but presenting them in the way I did, as a concise and easily consumable exposé on animal emotions, got the site more than 100 links!

Figure 3.7   *A section on my SEO and social media business website that ranks celebrities in order of their popularity.*

Figure 3.8   *An article on animal emotions I created for a client to attract links to her blog.*

Top 10 Lists

I could have discussed top 10 lists in the preceding section, but they're so important that they require their own heading. People love lists. David Letterman has proved this over many years of reading a top 10 list every night. There's just something appealing about knowing that an official list has been made and only 10 items have "made" it, and only *one* item is at the very top of that list. I might even go as far as to say that top 10 lists are the quickest, easiest form of link bait.

Another great thing about top 10 lists is that they can be written for almost any kind of website. If you're in an industry where you can unbutton your top shirt button at least some of the time, you can write a top 10 list for your website. To prove my point, here are some examples spanning vastly different fields, beginning with the starchiest:

- **Accounting**—Top 10 Most Annoying Things About QuickBooks
- **Real Estate**—Top 10 Most Expensive Homes Sold in This Decade
- **Law**—Top 10 Most Impactful Decisions in the Modern Era
- **Jewelry**—Top 10 Gaudiest Engagement Rings
- **Dog Training**—Top 10 Must-Knows for the Advanced Show Dog
- **Extermination**—Top 10 Scariest Insects Ever to Invade a Home
- **Music**—Top 10 Greatest Rockers of the 20th Century

Top 10 lists give us license to be superlative. What is the best, the greatest, the most essential of your field? That kind of information interests people—and will earn you links.

Compendiums

If this chapter were online, it would probably get a lot of links. Why? Because it's a compendium: a definitive, organized set of information. I intentionally named this section something cool sounding, "The Link Acquisition Bible," so that it would get psychological credit for being a comprehensive resource. Even if I have missed a link acquisition technique in this chapter, its name is confident enough to cause people to link to it. You can do the same in your industry, no matter what it is. And as with top 10 lists, your creativity is key. I'll brainstorm through a number of examples, and hopefully my doing so will spark an idea for you.

My first example has nothing to do with any website I can picture a reader of this book having, but I think a list and description of every candy ever made would be awesome. I guarantee that if you created *The Ultimate Candy Encyclopedia*, it would get a ton of links because so many people would like to get the official background on their favorite childhood candies. If that has anything to do with your business, please do it. Next time I'm in the mood for something sweet (probably in about an hour), I'll thank you for it.

Here are compendium ideas across a few different industries:

- **Sports**—A glossary of sports terms (strike, let, balk, nutmeg, shuttle-cock—there's plenty of great material there).

- **Environmental**—A "Green People" directory. It might not be the first compendium that comes to mind for the environmental industry, but there are already so many green dictionaries. I would think it would be cool to compile a list of the people who are most influential in the green world. I haven't seen that done before, and I believe if you wrote up bios of even the green industry folks who don't have Wikipedia pages, it would attract links for being an original and interesting compendium.

- **Horticulture**—A list of endangered rare plants. Compendiums of natural wonders are particularly fascinating to people of all ages. Add a sense of limitedness (hence the "endangered," "rare" adjectives), and you have a very link-worthy list.

- **Fashion**—A timeline of fashion throughout the last century. Although this sort of idea has been done before, I believe it would be interesting to many people, especially if categorized by social class so as to capture the full spectrum of fashion in each decade.

- **City culture**—A guide to bathrooms in the city. Bathrooms are a part of every restaurant and nightclub, and everyone has a personal experience with them, but few people publicly comment on them. So I think it would make an engaging list. Even if you start with just one tiny area of the city and try to evaluate every bathroom, I can guarantee you that anyone who sees your list will be intrigued by it. That means links.

When you're thinking about making a compendium—be it a dictionary, glossary, encyclopedia, or plain old list—here are a few things to keep in mind:

- Try to limit your time expenditure on this project to a certain number of hours, days, or weeks. After all, a compendium is meant to be link bait and not a direct route to sales. So although it justifies a real time commitment, it should not distract you from focusing on your core business responsibilities.

- It doesn't have to be exhaustive; it just has to have enough information that it can *pass* as exhaustive.

- You can get almost all the information from the Internet. That means it won't be hard to collect. Just try to get your info from credible sources. People appreciate that.

- You need to tell people about it or else your awesome compendium might never be seen. If it's cool enough, sending a personalized email to 25 blogs that are somewhat related to your compendium should do the trick; after all, it takes just one or two good mentions to make a piece of content go viral.

Contests

Self-servingly, contests usually give something away to attract attention. Attention can easily equal links, especially if your contest is interesting or offers a good prize. Take a treasure hunt, for instance. I hadn't thought about clue-driven quests since I was a teenager until I saw a link for a modern-day treasure hunt on a blog. While checking the links for the website that was holding this treasure hunt (see Chapter 7, "Tracking Your Progress with Search Operators," for an explanation of link checking commands), I saw that dozens of other sites also found this concept cool enough to link to, including the online versions of some local newspapers. With the same money and creative resources, this treasure hunt site could have built a compendium or interesting online tool. But instead, they buried some gold coins probably worth about $3,000, wrote 10 clues, and emailed some blogs to tell them about it. The cool nature of their contest took care of the rest.

A tried-and-true method to draw links to your contest is to involve the users of your site or some extension of them. Classic case study 1 is a Cutest Pet contest. People love their animals and take any opportunity to get them featured as the cutest or the best at anything. If your site has any lifestyle component to it and already has at least a few thousand visitors per month, try holding a Cutest Pet contest. After you have a few hundred entries, put a picture of each pet on its own unique page, and then tell everyone that the one with the most online votes will win a year's supply of pet food and supreme recognition on your website. People's reactions will be to immediately send out emails and post all over their social media sites "Vote for my dog on this website!" Each of these posts are potential links for your site (depending on whether they're on public or private pages), as are any "Please vote!" blog posts you elicit from readers who maintain a blog.

This concept can be applied to many things that people become passionate about. Cutest Baby, Best Nature Photograph, and Coolest Car are three photo-related contests that jump to mind. Videos are great, too, because most computers and many phones have simple video-creation functionality. I think that Best Singer, Best

Dancer, Most Talented Pet, and Funniest Baby are good subjects for video contests. If you want to keep it simple, you can hold a Community Member of the Month contest or Most Inspiring Teacher contest asking for a few sentences about why a person in one of your readers' community should be recognized on your site. Even if you just get 10 good entries, the benefit for you will be in all the links to your contest page that your submitters will create in an effort to get people to vote for their entry.

Press

Press is exposure, and in today's Internet-driven society, that equals links. Investing in a good publicist was one of the best decisions I ever made. Having worked with two different publicists in the past five years, I have found that if you can find someone affordable, publicity can be a real boon for your business. It can provide credibility, new business connections, better customer conversion on your website, and links all at once.

There are generally two types of press hits:

- **National**—The most obvious type is big national hits, the kind you dream about when you hire your first publicist: "I'm calling to tell you that I have just secured a feature on your company in the *New York Times*." Even a less-substantial outlet like a mid-sized city's largest newspaper or a local TV station can get your business's phone ringing. This is the best type of press hit in terms of overall value.

- **Blogs and Internet publications**—The less-obvious press hit, the one you don't think about much when you bring on a publicist, are the blogs and Internet publications that get only a few thousand visitors a month. Often, the proprietors of these outlets can ask for a lot of your time, and in the end, not a single phone call or even website visitor may come from the opportunity. But these are the hits that matter in terms of getting links. Make sure to ask the reporter in advance if he or she would be kind enough to link to your company's website in the article when it's posted. Obviously, tact is required when making a request such as that because some reporters don't like having to link to every source they use for an article. But if you get enough of these smaller blog articles and they all contain links, they will amount to lots of link love for your website. Notably, the kinds of blogs that consider themselves news sites typically have a lot of TrustRank. Figure 3.9 shows a press hit from a small blog.

A Link to My Website

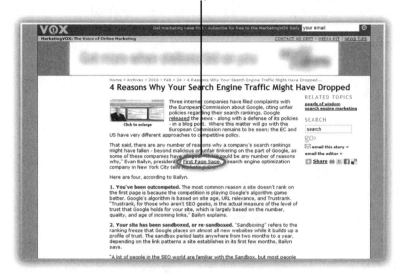

Figure 3.9 *A typical press hit from a small blog containing a link to my website.*

Widgets

A widget is a small online application that helps people do something simple, such as editing a photo, creating an icon, or looking up the meaning of a name. You can easily place a widget on any web page, and almost all widgets contain a link to the site that created it. A widget is an excellent way to attract links to your website.

The key to making this strategy work is to create a widget that is so interesting or useful that lots of webmasters want to place it on their sites. Facebook, for example, has done an excellent job making a widget that people genuinely want to put on their sites. Facebook's widget displays your latest status updates and your number of friends or "likes" and can be placed on any web page or blog (see Figure 3.10). Because people often want to show off their Facebook page on their personal website, this widget is widely used and amounts to tens of thousands of links back to Facebook.

Another exceptionally popular widget—and, in fact, one of the best examples of link bait I have ever seen—is the statcounter.com widget. It is a tiny box that goes at the bottom of your website that simply displays how many times your website has been visited in the past 30 days (see Figure 3.11). If you click it, it brings you to that site's web statistics page on statcounter.com. Because thousands of people like the idea of publicly displaying their visitor count, statcounter.com has become a Goliath of link popularity and ranks exceptionally high on Google. It even has a

PageRank of 8. Offering this widget for free was a brilliant move by statcounter.com and has been the key to the wide exposure the company has received.

Figure 3.10   *One version of the Facebook fan page widget from my personal website.*

Figure 3.11   *One of statcounter.com's simple, free widgets that measure website hits. You can place this at the bottom of your website if you want to show visitors your site traffic.*

A widget I also like a great deal was conceived by a client of mine, 1800Recycling.com. They offer a free little search box that tells you the location of your nearest recycling center (see Figure 3.12). A simple idea, this widget appears on many high-TrustRank websites, conferring tremendous SEO value on 1800Recycling.com.

This should give you an idea about what widgets are and how their simplicity makes them so appealing. Creating one, on the other hand, is not always easy. It requires an experienced programmer who has made widgets before. Depending on the complexity of programming behind the widget, it can become costly to produce. To give you a relative scale, a widget that converts text typed into a box into a shareable online sticker would probably be on the lower end of the price scale, about as much as a new computer. A widget that reports the rock density of a given land mass by latitudinal and longitudinal points, on the other hand, could have expensive technology behind it and cost as much as a car.

Figure 3.12   *The Recycling Location Finder widget created by 1800Recycling.com.*

Social Media

Creating a page on a social media site and listing your website on it is a great way to get a superbly valuable website to link to you. Facebook, Twitter, YouTube, and LinkedIn may be the most popular names in social media, but they are by no means the only ones. There are hundreds of social media sites that offer you the opportunity to create a free profile, on which you can place your link.

> ✉ *Note*
>
> Want to see a thorough listing of all (or least most) of the social media sites out there? Check out http://traffikd.com/social-media-websites/.

Awards

If you think your site has any prominence within your industry (oh hell, even if it doesn't!), come up with an award to give out to certain websites. These sites can be within your industry or in a related industry. The key to this form of link bait is that your "award" is a graphic that the winning sites place on their home or about page, which links back to your website.

When inventing an award, focus on quality. Have an excellent graphic designer make the award graphic so that sites will want to feature it. Think carefully about the recipients of the award: Do they truly deserve an award, and would other people feel the same way? Even more important, does this award recognize a characteristic that they value highly and would be good for them to display on their websites? For instance, because of the value of recruiting good employees, many companies would be thrilled to receive a Best Places to Work award. This would attract job applicants. Another example: Best Web Design. Any site that has clearly done something original with its design would love to receive recognition for it. But be sure not to give the Best Web Design Award to a company that doesn't take pride in their design; it will just be wasted. Your recipient should feel they worked hard for, and highly deserve, your award.

When informing proprietors of sites that they have won an award, be sure to word your messaging carefully. If there is any inkling that the award is a gimmick to gain a link on their websites, your plan will be foiled. The voice of your email should be lighthearted, yet take itself seriously. Something like this...

Subject: Excellence in Customer Service Award

Dear Recipient.com:

I am writing to say congratulations on behalf of ABCstaffing.com. We've chosen your site as a winner of this year's Excellence In Customer Service Award. As a staffing agency that has been in the business of placing qualified candidates in jobs for over a decade, we know good customer service when we see it. Recipient.com is a leader in this category, and we are proud to have selected it from among 500 candidates to receive this award. To see the other four winners, please visit our awards page.

The attached graphic may be added to your site's home page or about page simply by copying the attached code into the HTML of the page. If you have any questions, please feel free to contact Bob Smith at 212-XXX-XXXX.

Keep up the great work!

Sally Anne Jones, CEO

ABCstaffing.com

www.yoursite.com

212-XXX-XXXX

Take special note of the mention of "the attached code" in this email. Any web designer can provide you with code that adds a graphic to a website. The purpose of giving the award recipients a code is ostensibly so that it will be easier for them to place it on their websites, but it is also to ensure that the graphic links back to yours. And if they choose to add the graphic without the link (which some savvy companies might do), make sure the name of your company is at the bottom of the award. It won't help your site's TrustRank, but might send over some visitors.

Here are some other nice touches for your award:

- Mail a physical copy of the email to the recipients on your company stationary to give it that old-fashioned, take-me-seriously feel.

- Establish a yearly tradition of giving out the award so that you can refer to the award's history each successive year when you give out the award ("Our Third Annual Best Marketing Award").

- Do some press—or at least some press releases—around the award so that when recipients Google it there is something for them to look at.

I will leave you with one final note: As with other forms of link bait, if you take pride in your gesture, thoughtfully picking out the winning sites and genuinely believing they deserve an award, your effort will be more successful.

"Advertising"

The reason the title of this technique is in quotes is because I am not actually recommending advertising as a method of acquiring links. I am recommending buying a text link from a site that would normally not sell one and *calling* it advertising. As you learned in Chapter 2, "The Five Ingredients of Google Optimization," buying links used to be the best way to get a high ranking on Google, but because nearly all sites that openly sell links are crippled—unable to pass TrustRank—nowadays, you need to appeal to webmasters who are against selling links. How do you do that? By calling it advertising.

Your targets when looking for sites to publish your links are small, high-quality blogs owned by hardworking people who are trying to make a living from blogging. These are exactly the kinds of people who will appreciate an advertising request the most. In fact, an advertising inquiry is one of the best types of email they can receive. It validates their creativity and long hours, attaching a monetary reward.

When requesting a link on one of these kinds of sites, your approach is key. First, consider the psychological difference between "I'd like to pay you to put a link on your site so my search engine rankings will go up" and "I'd like to be one of your site's first advertisers." The former approach sounds foreign to most people and a little off-color. The latter approach sounds supportive and is backed up by decades of messaging that advertising is a highly legitimate practice. (Perhaps one day SEO will feel 100% legitimate to the average person, but we're not there yet.)

After you receive a response from the webmaster, you have three obstacles to get over, which, after some practice, will be fairly straightforward. You either get over them quickly or move on to the next website:

- **Obstacle 1: Price**—The kinds of people you will be talking to will no doubt have a great deal of pride in the work they've created, and might believe that an "advertisement" on their website is worth more than the market dictates. This depends on what other people have told them that ads go for. Make sure to tell them that you are not looking for a big display ad, just something small, because you don't have a big budget.

- **Obstacle 2: Getting a text link instead of an image link**—The form of advertising you are looking for is a simple bit of text on their site that is linked to your website. Why? Well, you can be completely honest with them and say it partially has to do with search engine rankings, or you can just explain that you think that this kind of advertising is less intrusive and more effective. (After all, Google does it!) You'll also need to mention that the text should be somewhere near the top of the page rather than way at the bottom.

- **Obstacle 3: Permanence**—Negotiating with individual webmasters can build up excellent links for your site, but it does take a while. So the last thing you want is for your "advertisement" to come down after a month, or even three months. You want your link to be on the site for one year at the very least. The way to go about getting a long-term link is another matter of psychology. Instead of saying, "I'll pay you $X per month," where $X is a pretty low amount (about the price of lunch), multiply $X by 9 or 10 and then offer that amount for a year of advertising. The sound of the lump sum is much more appealing to the webmaster. It also usually gets you a discount. If you have the chips and believe the site will continue to grow in prominence, you might even pay for 16 months up-front and ask for the link to last indefinitely.

The advantage to this form of advertising is that it yields an excellent quality of link. It is essentially going back to the kind of manual labor that commercial link brokerages used to handle for you, which was great before they got onto Google's blacklist. These links will never arouse Google's ire because they are one-time links on substantial sites that do not routinely sell text links.

If you plan to use this method for most of your linking, be warned once again that Google does not like it when too high a percentage of your links are text links. You need a good mix of image links, URL-only links, and text links. But having a few text links from great sites is absolutely essential to first page rankings.

Guest Posts

Most blogs, including the prominent ones, are always looking for material. A guest post is a welcome suggestion to the owners of these blogs, providing that the post is well written, on topic, interesting, and not too self-serving. Reaching out to blogs to secure a guest post is the kind of job that a publicist usually handles for you, but you can easily do it yourself. The goal of a guest post (in addition to the visibility it may get you) is the link to your website that is typically included in your accompanying bio.

To score a guest post on a popular blog, you need to be good at "pitching," but in all truth, this is not so hard for anyone with good people skills and writing ability. Just compose an earnest, mildly flattering email suggesting that you contribute a blog post and include some reasons why you are qualified to write such a post. Puff up that bio of yours as best you can; work those accomplishments! This is the time when they need to shine.

If you are not confident in your ability to sell your guest post to the owner or editor of the blog, hire a writer to do the pitch and—if successful—the blog post for you. A tip on hiring writers: There are many great ones out there who are just getting started and don't charge much. You do not need anyone beyond a bright recent college grad, and you do not need to pay a lot of money for this task.

To guide you in the right direction, here is an email I sent to the owner of a popular Facebook blog requesting a guest post.

> Hey Guys,
>
> I am a daily reader of Facebookblog.com. It has replaced TechCrunch as my #1 read. I would love to do a guest post explaining how to get tens of thousands of fans for your personal brand. I have 57,000 fans all gained within the last eight months. There are very few noncelebrities besides me with that level of fans.
>
> If this idea is interesting for you, I can write up a draft for you today.
>
> Thanks for taking the time to read my email.
>
> Best,
>
> Evan Bailyn

If you are concerned that you don't have a standout accomplishment to mention in your letter such as my high number of Facebook fans, don't sweat it. First of all, pick a topic to write about based on the best accomplishment you can think of. Even if it's a science award in high school, you can mention it, but maybe just call yourself "award-winning" instead of getting into how your science teacher made the award on his home computer and made a copy for each of the 20 students who received one. The other route is to state that you have done extensive research on the topic and would like to report your findings. Ah, and what better transition into our next link acquisition strategy?

Research Results

One of the awesome things about the Internet is that anyone can become a journalist or researcher. If I take a survey of 500 people of varying demographic characteristics and then write up a well thought-out analysis of my findings and it gets published on a high traffic blog, it will probably reach more people than research conducted at significant expense and published in a trade journal. Granted, it might be trusted less, but that's not the point here; the point is that research is a respected form of content that *you* can create—and it can be an easy way to get a link from another website.

The trick here, as in many other link acquisition techniques, is to make the research results interesting and relevant to the site you are pitching it to, and to write the email in a genuine but excitement-inducing way. Let me bring you through an example. Let's say I want to get a link on a big social media blog. I begin by identifying what the blog cares about. A social media blog exists for the purpose of observing the phenomenon of people being social on the Internet. In a larger sense, this kind of blog probably sees itself as a beacon of the progress of the Internet in our society. This is just my hunch. So I would think that a survey whose results are that people spend more time on the Internet than they do watching TV would be very interesting to them; it would signal a major societal change.

Now obviously I am not going to submit this information unless it's true and I have a reasonable way of taking the survey. So I am going to test it. The only cost-efficient way for me to do this is by polling the members of my website. After I get at least a few hundred, hopefully even a thousand responses, I will make my conclusion. It is essential, however, that I do not rely on the results of my poll alone. I must analyze these results and publish my analysis on a page of my website that is well designed and includes cool charts and graphs. After the information has been neatly packaged, it is ready to be pitched. If you make the subject of your email a few-word summary of the results, your email is likely to be read.

There is a site I love to read called rjmetrics.com. It is one of the better procurers of research that I've ever seen. Granted, it is a research company, not a business that is looking to publish some interesting research results to get a link. But its authors write analytical blog entries so well, coming up with original findings on topics that range from Twitter to sports feats. In one blog entry, they researched the likelihood that a minor league baseball player would break the league's all-time hitting streak (see Figure 3.13).

A website that covers minor league baseball would very likely be intrigued by this study and link to rjmetrics.com's blog. The presentation of information in this blog post is well executed. There is a simple-looking graph of the probability of this player breaking the record, followed by a chart of probabilities of him achieving certain hitting milestones. Any similarly well-executed explanation of a study—no matter how carefully the study was conducted—would attract links from blogs.

Link Reverse Engineering

With a bit of simple know-how, anyone can see the links pointing to a given website. I will give you that simple know-how: http://siteexplorer.search.yahoo.com/. This is the URL of Yahoo! Site Explorer, the only reliable tool for showing all the links a website has accumulated. (Google's link tool is not helpful because it shows only a sample of the links it knows about.)

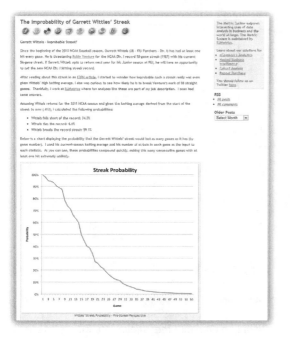

Figure 3.13 *A blog that presents homegrown research very neatly, tempting other websites to link to it.*

By looking through the links earned by competitors or sites in related industries, you can get a sense of some of the techniques they have been using to get new links. And even though anyone could theoretically look up your site's links as well, most business owners don't know about Yahoo's Site Explorer, shown in Figure 3.14.

To see all the links pointing to a given website, just go to Yahoo.com and in the search box type in the following (where *http://www.example.com* is the site you're researching):

  linkdomain: *http://www.example.com*

That will bring you to the Site Explorer. Make sure the Inlinks box is selected. You should also click the drop-down menu to the right of Show Inlinks and choose Except from This Domain. That option spares you from having to wade through tons of internal links.

To help you understand how to use this tool, here is an example of an internal dialogue I might have if I were the owner of a website that competes with dog.com and I were browsing that site's links on Yahoo! Site Explorer.

  Hmm, they have a link from garden.com. What the heck is that? Wonder if these people own a bunch of one-word .com domains and they interlink from all their sites. Not a bad idea, actually. Maybe I should start a couple more sites just to link to my main website from.

Make sure the Inlinks box is selected.

Choose Except from This Domain.

Figure 3.14   *Yahoo! Site Explorer, the only online tool that shows you all the links pointing to any given website. This specific page came from going to Yahoo.com and typing in linkdomain: http://www.dog.com.*

Ah, a link from American Kennel Club. Let me check out what kind of page the link is on and see whether this is just a listing of dog sites or if they're paying to advertise on this site. If the AKC is just listing them as a resource, I should reach out to them right away so my site can get a link from them, too.

Lots of blog links. Looks like they are getting some links just for having such a good domain name and because people are typing it in. I can't do much about that.

Actually, upon further inspection, it looks like their images are getting linked a lot. I can't believe I didn't think of that sooner. If we create a bank of images of all different kinds of dogs, we would probably pick up lots of natural links over time just like they did. And better yet, if I can get some pictures of lesser-known, rare dog breeds the links would probably start coming in even quicker.

A link from horse.com? Okay, these people definitely own a ton of one-word .com domains. Linking from all the sites in their network must help their search engine rankings a lot.

As you can see, a huge amount can be learned in just a few minutes about any other site's linking strategy purely by using Yahoo's Site Explorer.

"Link-Only" Photos

Not a photographer? Wait, don't skip this section yet! One of the newest, cleverest ways I've seen people attract links to their sites is by having a page of their own interesting photos on their websites. Every webmaster knows the difficulty of obtaining photos for his or her site. Most companies pay a stock photo site for their website's images; however, the same stock images are typically found on multiple websites, shattering the illusion that those professional-looking folks actually work at your office. The other option—getting professional photos—is expensive. There is a third option that is becoming more and more popular, and that is taking photos that are licensed under the "attribution" condition of Creative Commons. What this basically means is that you can use them on your website as long as you link back to the original site that posted the photos. For the site doing the posting, this can create a gold mine of links, providing the images are interesting enough. Here is the link to the Creative Commons search engine so that you can browse the tens of thousands of images licensed in this way:

   http://search.creativecommons.org/

So whether you've ever seriously taken pictures or not, this might be an interesting link acquisition strategy. Either try your hand at taking useful or striking photos or hire an amateur photographer to take them for you. Amateur photographers, like writers, are often not going to charge a lot for their work.

Wikipedia

One of the most elusive links out there is the highly coveted Wikipedia link. The two main ways that Wikipedia links naturally occur is when your site is listed as a source in a Wikipedia article or when your site provides more information about the subject of a Wikipedia article. In other words, if you act as a news or information site about something important enough to be included in Wikipedia, you might get a natural link.

These conditions apply to very few businesses except the very biggest. So, you ask, is there any other way?

There is, but it's highly difficult to pull off. You have to write an article on a highly specific subject and make it as scholarly as possible, complete with sources. Then edit a Wikipedia article that relates to that subject, adding information that is backed up by the article on your site, and then list your article either as a source or in the External Links section at the end of the entry. The likelihood that your link will be taken down is 95%, and if you do this enough times, your IP address will be banned, and you won't be able to edit Wikipedia again. When attempting this method, it is best to create an article of true value that adds something to the body of research being cited. Real, highly discerning editors will be viewing your article, so genuine effort counts.

Some of these techniques will be better for your business than others. It's all about getting the creativity flowing. There are many ways to go about the essential task of link building, and there will also be new, innovative approaches invented all the time; that is the lifeblood of search engine optimization.

4

Using Time to Gain Trust

No matter how many links and pages your new website has, it will not be able to rank on the first page for any competitive keyword for a couple of months. This core principle of Google optimization nearly put me out of business at one time. It just didn't make sense. I had great content and lots of links; why wasn't my website even in the top 100 results? The answer: because in the world of Google, you just have to wait. I picture an old farmer sitting on the back of a truck, chewing on a piece of grass, saying, "Life ain't fair, kid." It's just one of those rules.

The Sandbox

A mandatory ranking delay for new sites is the kind of SEO principle that doesn't make sense for most websites but benefits the entire ecosystem. Google instituted the sandbox, or the waiting period that all new websites must incur before they can rank properly, to keep fly-by-night spammers out of the index. As I mentioned in Chapter 2, "The Five Ingredients of Google Optimization," if you were doing a lot of Googling in the early 2000s, you might have noticed that there were many spammy sites in the search results. These sites were set up for the purpose of making money quickly and unethically, and then shuttering their online doors after just a few weeks. Using link farms, or vast, interconnected networks of low-quality links, these sites were able to rise to the first page quickly due to Google's then-weaker algorithm. Many of them took a lot of money from people before Google discovered and banned them.

Because of this group of scammers, we all have to suffer. As I was saying, the sandbox nearly broke me when I was first learning about SEO. It took a full year and a half for my college consulting website to finally see the light of page one. If another three months had gone by without reward for my work, I would have run out of money. Thankfully for all of us, nowadays the sandbox period is shorter than it used to be.

To make sure that you are adequately informed of what to expect when you have a new website, allow me to take you through the phases of aging a site on Google.

- **0–2 months: The Period of Nothingness**—Until your website is about two months old, even the most awesome, link-juiced-up site will be snubbed by Google like a smelly kid at the school dance. But this does not mean you should be inactive. This is exactly the time when you need to get busy building links. Google is watching every link built in this period, seeing whether your site deserves to jump out of the sandbox, into power, within the next few months. If you do not build links in the first two months, your site will continue to be sandboxed until you *do* build links.

- **2–4 months: Behold, a Brave New World**—After your site has been around for a couple of months, it might peek into the top 100 results, but only if it has a couple of high TrustRank links. Typically, you are not going to see first page rankings for difficult keywords in this phase. Google basically has your site on probation.

- **4–6 months: The Winds of Trust**—If you were building links in a casual, nonaggressive way for the past few months, your site will now be able to rank for moderately competitive keywords. It *could* even rank for a competitive keyword. However, if your site has the same number and quality of links as another website that is two years older, it will rank below that other website.

- **6–12 months: Dropping Anchor**—Your site will now be able to rank for any keyword except the top 2% most coveted keywords out there. So, no *mesothelioma, structured settlement,* or *airline tickets* for you...but yes to *jewelry store Hollywood, customized silverware,* and the like.

- **1–2 years: Welcome to the Land of Trust**—The door is now 90% open to you, and your site can rank for any keyword, providing you have spent the past year building high TrustRank links. Google will now view you the way society views a young, roguishly handsome doctor or lawyer—as impressive and capable of great feats but not as well respected as you will be later on in your career.

- **2–4 years: A Seasoned Citizen**—By now your site should have a number of old, trusted links and be a shining member of the community. Not only are you ranking well for long tail keywords and competitive keywords alike, but your site is a highly sought-after influencer—a site from which any other site would feel privileged to gain a link.

- **4 years +: The Golden Years of Trust**—These are the good times. Google now considers you a fully indoctrinated member of its kingdom. With a history of building links in a natural way and continuing to attract links on a regular basis, your site may rise in search results as you please. Your site joins the ranks of those "unbeatable" websites that are always on the first page for the most competitive keywords.

The sandbox has been the subject of much pontification and misinformation. Simply put, if you focus on building links in a slow, natural way—say, getting three to five links per month—your site will come out of the sandbox and rank normally in sync with the preceding timeline. On the other hand, if you spend too much time reading articles about the sandbox and getting yourself worked up about why Google isn't giving your site a fair shake, you will make less progress. In my opinion, the sandbox is a great time to work hard on your web design, create interesting pages for your site, attract links to those pages, and get your site ready to be seen by lots of people once it emerges. Think of it like a beauty pageant. Do your primping and preening and choosing your best outfits before you are called to walk out on stage. If you've prepared well enough, you will be a winner come time for the looks and talent competitions.

The Power of Aged Websites

The age of a website should matter to you in three contexts.

- The first, which we just discussed, is the age of your website as it applies to being able to rank for competitive keywords.

- The second is the age of other websites when analyzing the strength of the links going back to your site.

- The third is knowing the age of websites that you are considering purchasing to augment your SEO efforts. Because I haven't previously addressed the idea of making strategic website purchases, I cover the third context later in this chapter.

How to Measure the Value of a Link Based on Aging Factors

After discussing in depth the methods of gaining links in the last chapter, it might be helpful to explore using aging factors to help determine the value of a web page's links. Because age plays a role in the amount of trust Google gives a website, we know that the age of a website relates to the value a link from that site gives.

You should always use the Internic whois lookup to check the age of each website you are considering approaching about a link.

> ✉ *Note*
>
> In this book, I emphasize the idea of proactively approaching other web-sites for links instead of waiting for other websites to offer you a link. Most websites that go around offering links are new themselves and hence do not have enough TrustRank to merit your consideration.

Although it might seem that the most valuable sites are the oldest ones according to the whois database, keep in mind that it is not the age of the domain that confers TrustRank, but the age of the website that sits on top of the domain. So if you see that a domain was registered in 1997, don't drop everything to gain a link on that site because it is possible that the domain was parked for 10 years before a website was built. Even if a website was built right from the start, if the website was later taken down and the domain was parked for any substantial period of time, Google will have perceived that the domain was transferred to a new owner and reset what-ever TrustRank it earned in the past. So before giving a site credit for being well aged, you should ask, "Has a website been continuously running on this domain since it was registered?" And note that if a website *has* in fact been running, unin-terrupted, for many years, it retains its TrustRank no matter how many redesigns of the site occurred; Google expects that. Google resets the TrustRank of a website only if the domain has been parked.

Now let's go a step further. Let's suppose a site has been online continuously for a few years. Does this make it instantly link-worthy? Almost. As explained in the sec-tion "The Sandbox," at the beginning of this chapter, a site with links is eons more trusted than a site without links, no matter how old it is. So for a site to be truly valuable as a linker to your site, it must also have a bunch of links that have been pointing to it for a long time.

If you really want to be thorough, you can attempt to determine the age of a web-site's links before requesting a link to your site. Doing so is similar to determining the age of an antique. Most of the time you will not know for certain, but there are various clues you can search for that will each increase the chances that the link is from a certain date.

1. First, you need to identify pages containing links you want to investigate. Second, look for clues on those pages as to the age of the relevant links.

2. The following are the two best ways to find links to the page you are investigating:

   • **Googling its URL**—Googling the URL of the web page enables you to see what other pages reference it. Assume you are interested in the age of the links to http://www.sculptor.org/Children/. Googling this URL brings up the page http://42explore.com/sculpture.htm. This page (as of the time this book went to press) features sculptor.org and contains a link to www.sculptor.org/Children/. At the bottom it states, "Updated, 04/01." So we can assume this link is 10 years old. Are we certain this link was not added later? Of course not. But based on the statement at the bottom of the page and the lack of any evidence to the contrary, it would be a reasonable guess. If other pages that reference http://www.sculptor.org/Children/ display similar circumstances, we could guess that at least some of those links really are quite old.

   • **Using Yahoo's linkdomain operator**—You can use the linkdomain operator to locate other pages that link to the page in which you are interested. Assume we are interested in investigating the home page of www.mjartstudios.com. Typing linkdomain:www.mjartstudios.com into Yahoo's search bar shows many pages that link to www.mjartstudios.com. One of those pages is www.sculptor.org/Jobs/CommercialSculptorsWanted.htm. This page contains paragraphs that each begin with a date. The paragraph discussing www.mjartstudios.com is clearly labeled March 15, 2002. Therefore, it can reasonably be assumed that this link is at least nine years old. As with Googling a URL, there is no guarantee that this date was not inserted later, but taken along with other similar pages, it is good evidence that this site has well-aged links.

3. Look for clues on a linking page as to the age of its links. There is no single silver bullet here. The better a detective you are, the more evidence you will discover about the age of the links on a page. Here are some of the most common "smoking guns":

   • Is the link contained within the text of an article that has a date somewhere on the page (for example, http://www.10weablog.com/?m=200801)?

- Is the link contained on a blog page that is categorized by date, either on the page or in the URL of the page itself (for example, http://www.10weablog.com/?m=200801)?

- Is the link contained on a page that allows comments with dates on them (for example, http://www.servicesnitch.com/site/article/ wedding_planners_bridal_consultants_wedded_to_your_wallet/ #comments)?

- Does the page have a PageRank of 3 or higher? (It takes three to six months for a web page to get a PageRank of 3 or higher.)

- Is there a date in the URL of the page itself (www.example.com/ 2009/06/article.html)?

- Are there any dates on the page at all that could lead to useful assumptions (for example, a contest that requires a reply by January 5, 2006)?

- Is there any reference on the page to any current events that can be traced back to a certain point in time? (For example, a reference to a certain politician indicating he might run against Bill Clinton would indirectly indicate the age of the link.)

4. If none of those methods work for you, it is also possible, although tedious, to use archive.org to determine when a site added the link in question. There you can look through archives of a webpage to pinpoint exactly when the new link appeared.

If you're just looking for the quickest way to determine whether a site has a good number of old links but you don't want to spend a lot of time on it, use Google's "link" command. Just go to Google.com and type *link:example.com* into the search box. If you see web pages from at least, say, 10 different domains listed (ignore all the internal results from the site you are looking up), the site has a substantial link history. If you are a big-timer buying a multi-thousand-dollar site, you'll want to see approximately 40 or more distinct domains linking to the site. Remember that I am giving you rough numbers here; 3 links from exceptionally high-TrustRank websites would be enough to make a website a very valuable linker, and 15 links from brand-new websites would make a website a pretty mediocre linker.

Link Aging and Link Churning

Whether you've built a website from scratch, diligently attracting links yourself, or bought a website that already has a high level of TrustRank, it is important to make sure that your links do not disappear. That is why it is a smart idea when purchasing an aged website to include a clause in your contract with a website seller that they do not do anything that could cause links to be removed. It is also why earlier I recommended that you make long-term link relationships. The longer a link to your site stays in place, the more Google trusts it.

My experience has taught me that some small amount of TrustRank is granted to a website when a link points to it for at least a month. However, if that same link were to remain for six months, a much larger percentage of the TrustRank that link is capable of passing will in fact be passed. Many people think that if they get a bunch of links to their sites, and then those links are removed later on, that they are left back where they started—with no added TrustRank. This is not so. I used to believe this theory, too, which is why, when a particular client did not pay his bill for 30 days, I removed the links I had built for his site, thinking his rankings would drop and he would get the message to pay his bill on time. In fact, his rankings stayed the same for six months! That client had been paying for link-building efforts for more than six months, which is probably why Google did not remove the TrustRank corresponding to those links. If his links were only three weeks old, for instance, I believe that none of their TrustRank would have remained with his site after the links were removed.

Does this mean that you should try to get tons of links and keep them around for six months, and then systematically drop them? Certainly not. Google does credit sites for links earned in the past, but it also penalizes sites for link churning: bulk removal of links in a short period of time, often followed by adding new links. I don't know the exact math, but I'd estimate that if you drop more than 20% of your site's links at one time, Google will put your site in the penalty box.

Because I have never specifically defined a penalty, I address that concept here. Google has several levels of distrust that it can apply to websites: sandboxing, penalty, deindexing, and blacklisting (see Figure 4.1). Except for sandboxing, you can avoid Google's distrust by being discerning about the sites from which you receive links and the manner in which you acquire them. In the hierarchy of Google distrust, penalty status is less severe than deindexing and *much* less severe than blacklisting.

✉ *Note*

As you'll recall from earlier in this chapter, sandboxing is a different concept because it doesn't have to do with bad behavior (although its effect is similar to a penalty). Google uses the sandbox, or the waiting period that all new websites must incur before they can rank properly, to keep fly-by-night spammers out of the index.

Figure 4.1 *A typical parked domain. When looking for websites to purchase, skip these spam pages.*

Levels of Distrust

Table 4.1 is a handy-dandy guide to the levels in which Google may distrust your website.

Table 4.1 The Guide to Google Distrust

Act Of Google Distrust	Cause	Effect	Road To Recovery
Sandboxing	A site is new or has never built links before.	Google will not allow a site to rank in its top 100 results for any competitive keyword until the site has built some links and at least two months have passed from the start of the link building.	Build links. Wait.

Table 4.1   The Guide to Google Distrust

Act Of Google Distrust	Cause	Effect	Road To Recovery
Penalty	Building too many unnatural-looking links at once (for example, 40 links that all say "converter cables") or dropping a substantial percentage of your links at one time.	Google moves your website off the first page for one or more of your main keywords, often frustratingly to the top of the second page, but potentially to the third or fourth page or even out of the top 100.	Remove the offending situation if there is one, and wait. Google will intentionally not inform you that your site is being penalized because, suspecting you of engaging in rogue SEO tactics, they want you to get confused and just give up. If you make your linking pattern more natural, it will take two to six months for your rankings to return.
De-indexing	Your site contains links to "bad neighborhoods" such as gambling, pills, or adult websites; or your site engages in offensive SEO tricks such as link farming or keyword stuffing.	Your site does not appear in the search results for any searches. It does not even show up when you type your domain name into Google (for example, www.firstpagesage.com). You might be notified by Google on your Google Webmaster Tools control panel.	Access your Google Webmaster Tools control panel at www.google.com/webmasters/tools. Fill out the form that allows you to submit your site for reconsideration. Giving a good reason, such as your site having been hacked or your being the hapless victim of a web marketing firm, will result in reinstatement.
Blacklisting	Your site has engaged in black hat SEO tactics such as writing code that shows search engines different content than your site's visitors see; or your site is considered spammy or scammy.	Your site does not appear in the search results for any searches. You might be notified by Google on your Google Webmaster Tools control panel.	You can try submitting your site for reconsideration in the Google Webmaster Tools control panel, but Google probably will not allow your site back in the index. It is best to buy a new domain name and disassociate with the offending practices if you care about receiving traffic from Google.

Link churning is equal only to overoptimization in its capability to cause Google to prevent a website from ranking in any significant way. Link churning can happen innocently to the assiduous link builder. Let's say you acquire a bunch of links and then you don't see a jump in rankings after a couple of weeks, or even after two to three months. You might conclude that the sites hosting the links are crippled or that the TrustRank being passed is just not enough to justify the compensation you are giving to the hosting sites. So it is reasonable to ask the webmasters who own those sites to take your links down, and furthermore to build a bunch of new links to make up for the empty space in your link-building program that you now perceive. And yet, this is the very definition of link churning. Done on a small scale (a few links at a time), this is passable behavior, but done on a larger scale (for example, more than 10 links at a time), this could trigger a penalty.

The best idea is to make yourself knowledgeable about which links pass the most TrustRank—a point you should already be at if you've read this book straight through—and actively solicit those links, knowing that you are placing a bet on them and should not be requesting their removal anytime soon.

As Google will be happy to note, most webmasters have no choice but to have an aged website with aged links pointing to it if they want to achieve a top ranking for a competitive keyword on Google. However, a super-focused individual who spends hours each day attracting and managing links could attain a top spot on Google in one year. A consistent but natural pattern of building high TrustRank links within a 12-month period could outdo a decade-old site with years-old links. So there is no excuse for readers of this book to slow down their efforts just to wait for a site or group of links to age. As long as all links appear to be the result of human effort rather than bulk, machine-added linking (stay away from link brokerages!), your work should be handsomely rewarded.

How to Find an Old Website Worth Buying

Unlike death and taxes, there *is* one way to avoid the sandbox, and that is by buying another website that has already gone through its probationary period. If you have never bought a website before, please do not be intimidated by the process. It's easy. You do not need to purchase an actual web business to get an old website; you just need to buy the website itself. Therefore, you don't have to worry about doing extensive due diligence. But let's hold off on that for a moment. First of all, what is the real goal of purchasing a website for SEO purposes?

People with SEO knowledge buy websites not just to avoid a few months of sandboxing but rather to avoid years of link building. The only websites you want to consider are ones that are many years old and have lots of links and are therefore enjoying their golden years of trust. It's kind of like marrying into a rich family—instant power! If you know precisely what you are looking for and engage in a systematic process of inquiring about the availability of websites, you will eventually find one that fits your criteria nearly perfectly. Although it does require time and effort to find a suitable website, that time and effort is a fraction of what you would have to undergo to build up a similar quality site from scratch.

So, how do you start? First, go to Google and type, in quotes, *"this website is for sale"*. That search query should bring up a few hundred sites whose owners have listed them for sale. You will quickly eliminate most of them because they fall into one of four "Don't Buy" categories:

1. **Parked websites**—A parked website has no functioning website on it and exists solely to make money through low-quality ads (see Figure 4.1). Usually it will have stock pictures on it, text ads plastered over the middle of the page, and an invitation to purchase the website on the side or bottom. These domains are essentially spam and cannot be obtained for any reasonable price. Skip them.

2. **Irrelevant websites**—If you find a website for sale that has nothing to do with your business whatsoever, it cannot be used as your main business website. It probably can't even be used as a sister website to get visitors interested in your main site because Google will already have it classified as being about a particular subject matter and will not allow it to rank for keywords of another subject matter. For example, if you own a pet store and you find a website called customtissueboxes.net that has been selling monogrammed silver tissue boxes for the past four years, you do not want to buy the site. Although it would be excellent for someone who has a tissue business, home accessories business, or silver knick-knacks business, it is too different from a pet store to have any use to you. The same principle applies to sites that contain your keywords but in a different context. For example, a site about salsa dancing is not a good home for your freshly made salsa business.

3. **Relatively new websites**—People put sites up for sale shortly after buying them, often because they think they have a good domain name. Of course, a website that is less than a year old is precisely what you are *not* looking for because it will not have especially high TrustRank. To find out a site's age, use the public whois lookup at http://www.internic.net/whois.html. (Just search for the words *Creation Date on* on the Internic domain page, and you will see the date the website was registered.)

4. **Linkless websites**—Even if a site is 10 years old, if it has not accumulated links in that time, it's as dead to Google as a completely new website. Before purchasing any website, look up its links using the Yahoo! Site Explorer. Just go to Yahoo.com and type in *linkdomain:http://www.example.com*.

If a site is relevant to your business, has had a functioning website running continuously for at least two years, and has at least a couple of links, it is probably worth purchasing.

A second, and typically better, approach to purchasing websites is to sort through websites that already rank for your keywords. Let's say you sell t-shirts. Type *t-shirts* into Google and look through the top 100 results. This method eliminates any chance of the site being classified in the wrong category and thus being unable to rank for your keywords—it already *does* rank for your main keyword. It also makes looking up the site's links fairly irrelevant because whatever number of links it has was clearly enough to earn it a decent ranking for your main keyword. In short, these 100 sites are all worth buying if you can get them for reasonable prices.

From this pool of prospects—like the "this website is for sales" pool mentioned earlier—a few traits should turn you away immediately:

- **Domain name doesn't make sense for your business or you don't like it**—If a site has a domain name you just can't live with, it's a no-go. As badly as you want to get a site that already has ranking power for your main keyword (and, if you don't already have a high ranking website, you should *really* want one of these sites), you can't ignore branding. For example, if you sell car parts and you stumble across a site for sale that is on the first page of Google for *car parts* but its name happens to be kidstoycarparts.com, you'll have to throw it back. Everyone will be confused by your name.

- **Ranking web page is part of a larger website**—You will undoubtedly find many web pages on a website that does something more general. For example, I wouldn't be surprised if a page on eBay was one of the results for a search of *car parts*. Obviously, you can't buy eBay. (Bill Gates, if you are reading this book, that doesn't apply to you.)

- **The website is clearly an active business**—Let's not forget that. In this scenario, you are looking to buy a website for SEO purposes. Many website owners will be confused by this, saying, "Why do you want to buy the website I spent the last eight years building?" You don't need to waste your time by trying to buy the website of a clearly active business. If you click the site and find that it is well maintained and the copyright at the bottom is up to date, skip it. The real opportunity is in looking for sites that say "copyright 2005" at the bottom or something similar, indicating that they are being ignored. A website that hasn't been updated in years is a gem because it means there is a chance you'll find a tired, busy webmaster at the other end of your email who is willing to part with his now-ignored web property (see Figure 4.2).

Ultimately, most of the 100 sites you look through will not be for sale for a reasonable price. However, buying websites is a game that is won with ingenuity and the power of the nudge. After you have a short list of websites that would be valuable vehicles for your business, think about each site and try to get a sense of the personality of the human being who owns it.

Old Copyright

Figure 4.2 *A website that ranks in the top 100 for the keyword sculpture. This is a good prospect to buy because it looks like it hasn't been updated in a while, judging from the years-old copyright at the bottom.*

Let's suppose you sell watches. Say that you're doing a search for *buy watches* and you notice an old site which hasn't been updated in a while that is dedicated to the joy of collecting antique watches. Before reaching out, you should be having this kind of thought process:

1. Okay, the guy who owns this site is probably passionate about watches.

2. He might have a collection of his own passed down from his relatives.

3. Maybe he discovered some old watches in his grandfather's attic when he was a kid, and the fascination began.

4. Either way, this guy created a site about watches without actually putting anything up for sale, so he's got to be a devoted hobbyist.

5. If I tell him I want to buy his personal project so that I can get a higher search engine ranking and sell my wares, he'll probably be turned off.

6. Instead, I should think about whatever interest I have in antique watches and communicate that interest to him, telling him I'd like to buy the site partly to continue what he started.

7. If he asks whether I will be selling watches, I'll tell him that I will, but that I'll keep a special section of the site in honor of his work that contains everything he's created and some of my own contributions. Everyone is happy.

As you can see, quite a bit of projecting and creative thinking was involved in determining the best way to obtain the website. If you are not prepared to think in this way, you'll have to think with your wallet. Of course, for some people, money is the only factor, and in cases like those, you should pay only what you can reasonably afford. Overpaying for a website is rarely a good idea because starting a site from scratch is still a viable option. In fact, it can be a valuable exercise in creating great content and building links, which you will need regardless of whether you buy an already-trusted site.

In the end, if you can get an old website for a livable price, go for it; but if you can't, it'll probably force you to adopt some better habits anyway.

How the Buying Process Works

When you and the webmaster have agreed on a price, it is time to get the purchase process underway. I've purchased many websites, and have seen the process completed in as little as two days; however, the average length of time from initial email to domain transfer is probably two to three weeks. Here is how the process generally works:

1. **Informal agreement**—Whether by email, telephone, or in-person meeting, you need to establish a "meeting of the minds," which is a casual agreement where both parties understand each other's responsibilities. Most likely, your main responsibility is paying money. The seller's main responsibility is transferring the domain, website, and rights to the content. This agreement generally occurs after both parties have had a conversation or two and gotten comfortable not just with each other, but with the idea that the other party will follow through on his or her promises.

2. **Letter of intent**—Sometimes a letter of intent (LOI) follows an informal agreement. An LOI is an agreement to agree; it's a statement of the major terms of the final agreement that seems to say this: "Here is what we're agreeing on, generally speaking. Once we determine that we're on the same page, we'll draft up something fancy and official." People use LOIs so that they don't waste time and money drafting formal agreements only to find that the major terms of the agreement are in dispute. In place of an LOI, I prefer to just shoot over an email with the basic terms, but some people prefer to do things the old-fashioned way.

3. **Contract of sale**—When it's clear that you and the seller are both cool on the main points of the transaction, it's time to make it formal. You may want to search Google for a contract for sale of a website. I usually use a contract template that I originally found online and have since modified. If the contract contains any elements that you aren't familiar with, Google some of the language to learn more about it. Aside from the main points about transferring ownership of the domain and content, most of the agreement is boilerplate that is meant to protect both parties from unlikely (but possible) occurrences. If in doubt, it is never a bad idea to seek legal counsel to ensure that the sale is handled properly.

4. **Due diligence**—After the agreement has been signed by both parties, you're *almost* there. Now the buyer just has to make sure that the seller hasn't been hiding or neglecting to mention anything important about the website. This is what due diligence is for. Due diligence, in this context, is the process whereby the buyer (and sometimes the seller as well) looks into the website in a more detailed fashion, often accessing domain records, financial statements, and outstanding advertising, business development, and service contracts. If you were to find, for example, that there is an advertising contract in existence that contains a clause prohibiting the sale of the website to a new entity (that is, you), that would be a deal-breaker. Typically, the sale of a website for SEO purposes does not involve extensive due diligence, and the transaction proceeds without too many speed bumps.

5. **Escrow/money transfer**—Ah, the most important part. Either at the same moment as, or just before, the domain and the web content residing on that domain are transferred to you, you must pay the seller. Typically, a seller requests a wire to his or her bank account because that method of money transfer is nonreversible and occurs within hours. PayPal and credit cards, on the other hand, are disputable, and checks take a few days to clear. But if you can pay by check, that's slightly safer from your perspective because, in the unlikely scenario that you are sold snake oil instead of a website, you can stop your check.

6. **Domain transfer**—The final part of the website buying process is receiving the domain. You need to have an account at the registrar with which the website you're buying is currently registered. As soon as the seller executes a domain transfer, you should see the domain listed under your domains when you visit your account page with that registrar. That event signifies that the transaction is complete with only one caveat, which is that the pages on the website are exactly the way they were before the transfer, and the domain is not parked or empty at the

time of purchase. It is important that the seller acknowledge that, in addition to the domain, you are buying all the pages of content on the site in the exact structure in which you first saw them (that is, pages haven't been deleted or renamed). Part of what you are purchasing is Google's trust in the pages on the website as visitors have been viewing them for months or years. If all is in working order, your purchase is complete, and you can start using your "new" Google-trusted website.

Common Pitfalls

Purchasing an old website is not without its perils, of course. Before forking over the cash for what appears to be an instant ticket to the first page of Google, you should beware of a few situations.

Beware When Shopping the Online Marketplace

One of these pitfalls concerns buying sites on an online marketplace. A few big marketplaces are known for selling websites, and a number of forums have active site marketplaces. Type *buy website* into Google, and you'll find most of them. As you're flipping through the listings, tantalized by the high PageRanks, age, and cool domain names advertised, keep in mind that many people sell their websites for one specific reason: There's something wrong with them. This is not to say "be paranoid," but rather "be cautious." I've come across many burnt buyers who innocently purchased old websites with great content and domain names only to find out that the websites didn't show up in any Google searches. The sites had been de-indexed or blacklisted, which is why the sellers were so anxious to sell them.

Sites That Have Nothing to Do with Your Business

Another common error new website purchasers make is buying websites that have all the right characteristics but have nothing to do with the product or service they sell. Even if you get an old website with old links, if you try to take down the previously operating website and replace it with something completely different, Google is going to get the idea that the website was recently repurposed and thus will do the only sensible thing from their point of view: reset its TrustRank. To them, the site might have been trusted in the past, but that was another life. A complete change in content often signifies a rebirth. You can get away with changing your Christmas website to a Hanukkah website, for instance, but not with changing your Christmas website to a life insurance site.

Avoiding Expired Domains

My last warning is to avoid expired domains. These are exactly what they sound like: domains that go back into the great big ocean of available domain names because their owners have either decided to abandon them or forgot to renew them. Mostly, the companies that specialize in expired domains are trying to profit off people's forgetfulness. I won't get into the details of this shady business, but suffice it to say that it's not a good way to acquire an old website because the moment the domain expires, it becomes parked, and that means its TrustRank goes bye-bye.

5

The Nuclear Football

Within my company, a certain strategy has been bantered about for years, usually in secret. We regard it as the ultimate way to dominate the search results. Only recently, however, did we feel comfortable enough to discuss it with certain key clients; before that, it was considered a trade secret. This concept never had a name until one day when I was having a conversation with a colleague and he called it "our nuclear football." And right then and there, I knew I had to borrow that name, for it was only fitting for the greatest concept in Google optimization.

Before I go into the nuclear football, I should address a question that every good, skeptical marketer or CEO should have: Why am I sharing this? The reason, reader, is that it's time. No secret can live forever, and this one has treated me well. It has built numerous businesses for me, and continues to build them for me today. But in the past few years, others have discovered it, too. Not many, but some; and my feeling is, if some can know it, anyone smart enough to buy my book should know it, too.

The Nuclear Football Defined

In government, the nuclear football is the briefcase the president keeps near him at all times that contains the nuclear codes, allowing him to authorize the ultimate retaliation during a crisis.

Figure 5.1 *The seriousness of the nuclear football in government reflects the grave damage this SEO technique can inflict on the competition. It's downright unfair.*

Similarly, this tactic is the most impactful one that you can undertake in your SEO journey. Unlike a nuke, it is a long-term solution that unfolds over a matter of years, but it does have in common with its atomic namesake a combination of ingredients that brings together the best research and experimentation on the subject. The nuclear football is about links. It's about age. It's about page titles. It's about URL structure. It's about keywords. And it's very much about content.

How to Execute the Nuclear Football

The overall goal of the nuclear football is to attract as much Google traffic as possible from long tail keyword searches. To do that, you need a lot of content and a lot of links. I have a favorite analogy for explaining the role of content and links in optimizing for Google. Your site is like a magnet trying to attract traffic from search engines. When your site is new, it is more like an unmagnetic hunk of dull metal; nothing comes to it. As you add pages to the site, however, each page increases the size of that magnet, making it more likely to bring in new traffic.

But still, without magnetism, even the largest magnet out there can't attract anything. That is where links come into play. Links are the magnetism. The more TrustRank your site acquires through new links pointing to it, the more attractive your site becomes, and suddenly new traffic begins to arrive from Google. The best situation, of course, is to have a huge magnet with tons of magnetism. Lots of content and lots of links. This will ensure that your site pulls in traffic from every corner of the Internet.

All the popular websites I've built have been big, highly attractive magnets. And every site that gets a ton of traffic from Google is too. It's the only real way to do it; you need to get traffic from lots of keywords to build a big site organically. No single keyword is so enormous that it alone can fill a site with traffic. In the fast-moving world of the Web, keywords go in and out of vogue, websites shift positions in the rankings, and people type a wide variety of searches. So even being at the top of Google for a monster keyword such as *games* will not a behemoth make. I know because I've done it.

Getting my kids' website, cartoondollemporium.com, to #5 for *games* brought it plenty of traffic, yes, but nowhere near as much as all of the long tail keywords combined. Keyword traffic brought Cartoon Doll Emporium more than 6 million visitors in one year. In the same year, *games* brought us about one-twentieth as many visitors. What is even more remarkable is that the 6.7 million visitors that came from Google that year found the site via 400,000 different keywords. That's a nuclear football, baby!

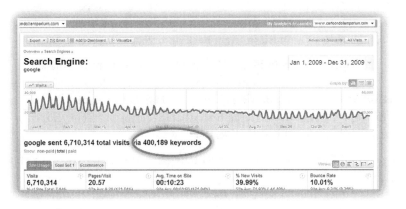

Figure 5.2   *The nuclear football in action: Cartoon Doll Emporium received 6.7 million visitors from 400,000 keywords in 2009.*

Although it is important to keep in mind that people keep coming back to a site because they like it—not because of a search engine tactic—the reason they know about the site in the first place is because of techniques like this one.

A broader question to address here is how important search engine traffic is to your overall customer-acquisition strategy. In other words, how much of your marketing budget should you devote to the nuclear football? I will say this: If search engine traffic delivers high-quality leads to your business, it is very important. But it should be considered alongside other types of traffic, such as word-of-mouth leads and website referrals. I know a law practice, for instance, that spends a third of its budget on SEO and the other two-thirds on a local legal site that regularly sends it relevant potential clients. It is important to look at your approach to marketing objectively: What brings in the most money for your company? And if you find that your business, like many others, derives valuable leads from search engine traffic, you want to start working on your own nuclear football.

The best way to begin crafting a nuclear football strategy is by slicing your business into all of its niches and making a separate page about each. Do you sell custom-made chairs? If so, you want to have a page all about *recliner chairs*. And another about *accent chairs*. Yet another about *dining chairs*. And don't forget *cheap chairs*. You get the picture. There are probably 500 different adjectives you can put next to chairs that people search for. And you can find them using the Google Adwords Keyword Suggestion Tool.

Because this strategy is known to a small but influential group of people nowadays, a number of companies have cropped up that sell custom-written articles for the same price as lunch for one at a local diner. These companies help you to effectuate a nuclear football by providing you with articles on niche subjects of your choice. You should feel free to avail yourself of services like these, but proceed with caution. If all your articles are written by their uninspired work-from-home armies, they will reflect that lack of enthusiasm right back onto your brand.

Consider the two articles shown in Figures 5.3 and 5.4. The first, from a site about theme parks, was produced by a mass-production article writer; the second, from a site about celebrities, was produced by a caring individual. Both websites are concerned with fun topics, but notice how the first article is closer to an encyclopedia entry, and the second article conveys real personality.

I acknowledge how difficult it is to create consistent great content for years at a time, but I also believe that everyone reading this book is capable of building a site that has charisma rather than content just for content's sake. So exhibit some balance: Commission a bunch of inexpensive articles just to get started (make sure they're original; Google sometimes penalizes sites for republishing content) and also write some witty, interesting articles. Put the better ones in the most visible areas of your site and minimize the exposure of the mass-written ones.

When writing all these articles, make sure each one is on its own page, and that each of those pages has a page title and URL structure that reflects the subject of the article. For instance, if the article is about folding chairs, the page title should probably be something like this:

Folding Chairs at Example.com | Metal, Wooden, Comfortable, and Cheap

And the URL should be something like http://www.example.com/folding-chairs.html.

Figure 5.3 *An article prepared by a company that mass produces articles in order to fill websites with content. It is a well-written article but does not have the character that the next article does, making it less effective as part of a nuclear football.*

Tip

By the way, notice how I threw in some extra keywords in the meta page title just to pull in long tail searches like *cheap metal folding chairs*.

After you have a plan in place for creating lots of pages of good content, it is time to focus on links. Your plans for getting links in the context of the nuclear football do not need to be any different from your normal link-building plan. Get lots of links in a natural way—some text links, some images links—and make sure they're pointed at various pages of your site so that Google learns to trust your whole site rather than just your home page. The latter point is particularly important when you're creating lots of content because Google does not include all pages in its index. It includes only pages that have enough TrustRank surrounding them to seem worthy of their acknowledgment.

Figure 5.4 *An article written with the intent of people reading and enjoying it, in contrast to the less-interesting, mass-produced article. This article would make a great addition to a site, contributing to a nuclear football effect.*

When you've got at least 1,500 articles and 20 high-TrustRank links to your website, you have created a nuclear football. It will probably take you between a few months and a year to attain that situation, by which point Google should consider your site properly aged. You know your nuclear football is working if you begin to see a substantial amount of traffic coming from Google organic search and that traffic is being sent by at least a few hundred keywords.

Ultimately, you should be creating content so voluminously that within two to three years your site has 5,000+ quality pages. The idea might sound far-fetched to you now, but when you see how many potential customers arrive at your site because of these niche subject pages, you'll want to keep the content coming. In my experience, the return on investment for a nuclear football is much greater than any form of advertising.

6

Google AdWords as a Complement to SEO

We have already established that SEO is the holy grail of Internet marketing. There is simply no substitute for gaining Google's trust and earning your way to the top of the organic results. So why devote an entire chapter to Google AdWords?

AdWords can be an effective companion to your SEO efforts. It offers a powerful way to analyze what is working and what isn't and to focus your efforts on more promising marketing strategies. Instead of throwing time and money at an SEO effort that might contain ineffective keywords, AdWords lets you just pay your way into Google's search results (right near them, at least) and see what happens. The results can give you a taste of what it would be like to be number one—instantly— and might guide you toward greater focus in your site and even in your business.

AdWords Defined

AdWords is the name of Google's pay-per-click, or PPC, marketing system. It has several different parts, but the upshot is simple: AdWords lets you buy advertising space on the world's biggest search engine. The main form in which this advertising appears is little text ads surrounding the organic search results. These are labeled

Ads, and they're four lines long. The thinking behind Google's creation of AdWords is pretty simple: People are already typing things that they are specifically looking for into the search engine, so what more perfect form of advertising could there be than showing them ads that respond to those searches? You want patio furniture? Here are some stores that sell it near you. You want a lemon chicken recipe? Here are some cookbooks from Amazon or Barnes and Noble.

Now let's not forget that when people search for something they want unbiased opinions—facts even—and not advertisements. That's why more people click the natural results than the sponsored results and why organic SEO, the subject of this book, is so valuable.

But Google has put real thought into these tiny blue commercials, which are the building blocks of its multi-billion-dollar empire. Two factors of equal importance have made this form of advertising so successful:

1. The relevance of the ads to people's searches

2. How closely the ads resemble natural results and thereby fool people into clicking them

Figure 6.1 shows how AdWords ads appear in relation to the organic search results.

Figure 6.1 *A typical page of Google search results. Note that AdWords ads appear both above and to the right of the organic results.*

Google's motto may famously read "Don't Be Evil," but the subtitle might say, "But Don't Be Poor, Either." For this reason, it is important to understand how AdWords campaigns are designed, priced, and placed. Google wants your campaign to work, but it also wants to maximize its profits along the way.

When you sign up for AdWords, you are asked to create three lines of text—a bold underlined heading and two lines beneath it, totaling 95 characters. Below that, you display your URL. You are also asked to choose the geographic locations where you want your ads to show up (worldwide, national, by state, city, or some combination thereof). Next, you must choose the keywords that, when typed into the search bar, will cause your ad to appear. Finally, you set a budget for each day and for each click. For instance, you might want to spend $50 each day getting the word out about your new company, and the most you're willing to pay every time someone clicks your ad is 50 cents.

If it sounds arbitrary and a bit costly, that's because it is. Google decides which of the many eager advertisers they will place at the very top of the results and highest up on the right side based partially on how much they spend. If you don't spend enough, your ad can end up on the second or third page of a search, getting it much less exposure. But not to worry: Whatever your daily budget is, Google finds a way to fill it.

A lot of people think that AdWords is a simple numbers game, like an auction: The more you pay, the higher your ad shows up on the first page of the sponsored results. Not quite. In reality, there is no escaping Google's love for complex systems, especially ones that make them a lot of money. True to form, AdWords campaigns run on an algorithm that is very much in line with those principles. In addition to giving higher sponsored placement to advertisers who pay more, Google determines who gets the highest spots based on how often ads are clicked. In other words, if you pay a lot per click, and lots of people click your ad, you get star treatment. And, by coincidence, this is the scenario that results in the most profit for Google. The situation is like a high-end retail store that rewards not just the customers who buy the most expensive clothes, but the ones who buy at the store most frequently; all in all, a better situation for the store.

Who Is AdWords For?

So do you need AdWords? Just who is this program aimed at, and what kind of results can you expect?

The answer in a nutshell: AdWords is a great solution for sites that are unable to earn their way to the top of search results organically for at least some of their keywords. This situation applies to most sites. New sites, for instance, are not able to rank organically because of the sandbox effect (discussed in Chapter 4, "Using Time to Gain Trust"). And no site can rank well for every keyword. This is where AdWords can be useful: You can see what it's like for your site to show up on the first page without having to wait months to achieve high page rankings through SEO. The most profitable keywords via AdWords are going to be the same keywords that perform well for you organically.

In short, AdWords is a good place to do keyword research when you start a new site and an excellent testing ground for sites that have many potential keywords. But if you think that your business has just a few clearly defined keywords and you know what those keywords are, you might not need to bother. Instead, you can just focus on SEO.

In the next sections, I cover some specific cases in which AdWords are a good investment.

Case 1: My First Site

New sites are the most obvious candidates for an AdWords campaign. Google might be able to serve you web results in a fraction of a second, but it does not include new websites in its search results right away. This is intentional and part of its probationary period, or "sandboxing," which I discussed in Chapter 4. Most webmasters won't see their sites appear in organic search results for at least three months, and even then it can take several more months to accumulate enough authority to achieve good rankings.

But new sites can jump right into the game with AdWords, testing keywords and creating campaigns that will be seen by potential customers across the Web. The visitors your site receives from AdWords might differ a bit in demographic characteristics and web-savviness, but the same potential for customers is there. And that AdWords campaign can go a long way toward helping you improve your new site, especially if you apply some of the tools I discuss later in this chapter.

Case 2: Diminutive Me

Every business has to start somewhere, and the Web offers a great way for upstarts to challenge the big players in their sector. Small companies do not have the deep pockets of their corporate counterparts, so it isn't always feasible to design and deploy an expansive SEO campaign and win the search war through marketing muscle alone. AdWords lets you ante up and take a shot. Instead of earning your way to the front page with size, authority, and mindshare, you can rent a spot and see what happens. Campaigns such as these are much less expensive than the cost of growing your business by a factor of 10, and sometimes a cleverly designed campaign can even help you rise above the fray and steal some traffic from the heavy hitters. Good and effective SEO takes time and money; if your small business doesn't have a ton of either, you can compensate with a PPC marketing campaign.

Case 3: The Long Tail

Most people in marketing have heard the phrase *long tail* by now. It was popularized by Chris Anderson back in 2004. The term expresses a simple truth: More sales come from the sum total of all the *less*-popular items than from all the popular items combined. The reason for this is because there are many more less-popular items than there are popular items. This applies to Internet searches even more than it does products. Popular websites get most of their search traffic from all the keywords that people have only typed in once or twice, rather than from the most popular keywords. This principle goes against most people's intuition. In fact, most of the time, webmasters focus on optimizing for the most popular keywords, not the aggregate of all the less-popular keywords. But they should always have an eye toward building a website that attracts long-tail searches. Although this might seem counterintuitive, webmasters who focus on optimizing for only the most popular keywords lose out on the business that a website which attracts long-tail searches enjoys.

So how does AdWords help your site target those lucrative long-tail searches? Well, let's say you own a board game website and want to analyze how people search for board games. You would probably expect that big names such Monopoly and Risk would get the most searches—and they do—maybe 5% or 10% of the total pie each. But when you add up the total number of searches for these popular games, they still comprise only about 25% of the total searches. The other 75% of the searches—the vast *majority* of them—are searches for more obscure games. Sure, only 1 person out of 500 might be searching for Happy Days: The Board Game, but the number of people searching for these less popular games will completely outnumber big blockbusters. That trailing line of less-popular events on the graph shown in Figure 6.2 is a fine example of the long tail.

AdWords lets you target literally thousands of keywords in your campaign. This means that, in the case of board games, if someone types in "happy days board game," your board game site shows up, most likely on the right side of the Google results, and has an opportunity to be clicked. Probably only one or two people would see the ad, and it's unlikely that anyone would click it. But if somebody did click it (and if you added the name of every board game ever made to your AdWords campaign, you would get some clicks on the rare ones), you would have successfully caused a customer to see your site who normally would not have. The only alternative to AdWords in this case would be to spend a year adding content pages to your site on every board game that ever existed—the nuclear football. Using AdWords for the long tail is quicker and easier for sites that aren't ready to make a large investment in content.

The best use of resources for most sites is to create a targeted SEO campaign for your most-desired keywords and use AdWords for the rest. You can throw hundreds of obscure keywords into an AdWords campaign at minimal expense because they almost never get searched. But if they do, and your ad appears, you have just acquired an extremely specific impression, one that could add up to significant results when purchased in bulk.

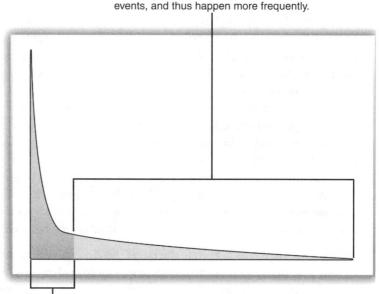

Less popular events outnumber popular events, and thus happen more frequently.

There are fewer popular events, and they happen less often.

Figure 6.2   *The long tail. The section at the left represents the most popular events: fewer choices that occur more often. The section to the right represents the long tail: less popular events in greater number.*

Getting Started and Understanding Match Types

Allow me to walk you through some of the basics of the AdWords universe—its rules, its lexicon, and what people are talking about when they start using acronyms such as CPC or CTR.

Anyone can start an AdWords campaign. You need a login, which your existing Gmail account provides, or you can create a brand new one. The system walks you through the rest—choosing your keywords, assigning a budget, and creating ads. You can see your ads appear almost immediately, and Google's account management tools make it easy to stay current on your campaigns and understand how successful they've been.

Keywords and Match Types

Choosing keywords is one of the most important ingredients in a successful AdWords campaign because it determines the amount of advertising you do. The more keywords you target and the more popular those keywords are, the more you will spend. It is important to keep in mind that spending more does not necessarily mean you will be earning more.

When choosing keywords, you will undoubtedly get the feeling that AdWords was designed by engineers, not communications majors. Engineers love to pick rules and then apply exceptions to them. In short, they are logic nerds. AdWords is based on this kind of thinking. So one of the first things you must become familiar with when you are choosing your keywords is a feature called *match types*.

Match types are basically a way of searching for the best keywords. The options involved are similar to the options you have in an organic search. When you are looking for something and you do not know exactly how to phrase it, you can use a search term without quotes: *shoe repair*. If you know how you want it phrased, however, you can put the phrase in quotes: *"shoe repair"*. You will achieve more specific results by putting the words in quotes.

The same principles hold true for search operators such as the minus (-) sign. If you are looking for shoe repair but want to filter out anyone who works on leather, you can make your search query *"shoe repair" -leather*. This trick offers an easy way to refine your efforts without scrolling through hundreds of pages.

Match types allow business owners to target desired search terms and filter out the terms that are not as applicable. Choosing the right match types is especially important in AdWords because useless clicks cost money, reduce your Quality Score (more on this soon), and drive traffic to your site with no appreciable benefit. It pays to be specific.

AdWords campaigns use four match types:

- **Broad match**—Broad match keywords involve no qualifiers at all; there is nothing to limit the range of terms you are interested in. A keyword such as *shoe repair*, with no quotes, would count as a broad match campaign. Anyone searching for those two words, in any order, is a candidate to see your ad—including people who use those two words along with several others. It's a way of casting the widest net possible. *You should avoid these keywords; they tend to be extremely expensive, competitive, and poor performing.* When the universe of potential customers is made up of anyone who types those two words into his or her search engine, you could find yourself paying to appear when someone types in, "How can I repair this glass I just shattered with my shoe?"

- **Phrase match**—Phrase match keywords are much more useful. Phrase match campaigns let you target specific phrases, typed in a specific order, much like using quotes in organic search. No more paying for useless clicks; phrase match lets you zero in on the people who are specifically searching for *shoe repair*, in that order. Phrase match campaigns are cheaper than broad match campaigns, and the traffic they drive toward your site is more valuable. When you get specific, your ad campaign's all-important Quality Score rises to reflect how well you have matched the ad to the customer.

- **Exact match**—Exact match is like phrase match, except more specific. Instead of targeting anyone who types your phrase into a search engine, exact match limits your pool of potential customers to the people who type only that phrase and nothing more. The main issue exact match avoids is people searching for your keyword in a different context than you expected (for example, "Can this shoe repair a broken heart?").

- **Negative match**—Negative match can be used with any of the other match types. You can make a phrase match campaign and then *add* negative match phrases to make it more specific. This works the same way as the - operator in an organic search: It filters out terms you do not want to appear. If your AdWords campaign is continually attracting people who search for *shoe repair free*, for instance, you might want to add the word *free* as a negative match. (This is assuming you enjoy your income and do not want to attract people seeking shoe charity.) Negative match is probably the most powerful tool in the bunch. Most money-losing AdWords campaigns fail because of inappropriate impressions. Study your site's traffic and you might discover search trends among the visitors who never buy anything. Identifying these terms is a great way to save your budget—and raise your Quality Score in the process.

Figure 6.3 shows the match type selection.

Cost Per Click

So now that you have set up your campaign and chosen your keywords and their match types, it is time to pull out your wallet. One of the unique aspects of AdWords is its pricing structure. AdWords is governed by a complex equation that takes into account everything from your past performance to whether your ad belongs on a given page. It is meant to show potential customers what they are most likely to click. You could compare this to a dating site that only presents you with people you find attractive. Come to think of it, Google really ought to go into dating.

You begin by entering the amount you would like to "bid" (auction style) against competitors to get a visible spot on Google search pages. This bid is expressed as a cost per click (CPC). For example, if you bid $.10, you are saying you are willing to spend up to a dime every time someone clicks one of your ads. But the amount you specify when you set your bid is not necessarily what you will be charged every time. AdWords is set up to automatically discount your cost per click rate if the ad is popular. This is a win-win situation; good ads get more visibility, and they cost less.

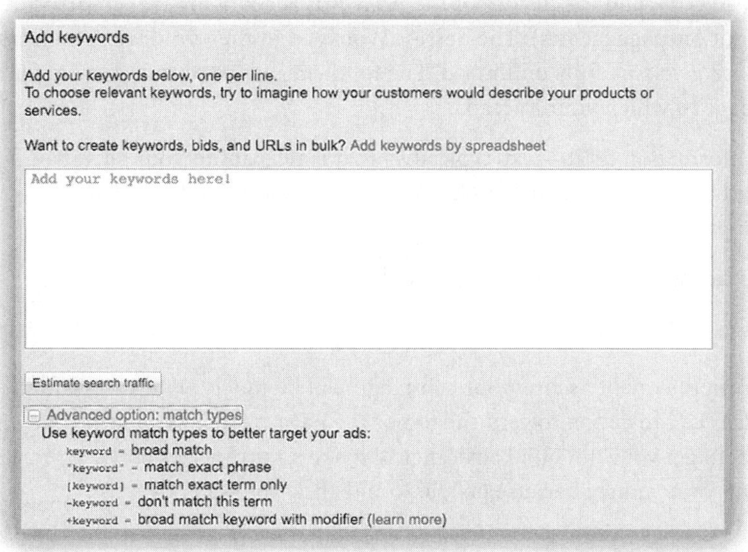

Figure 6.3 *Match types. Google distinguishes these with differing punctuation: no punctuation for broad match, quotes for phrase match, brackets for exact match, minus sign for negative match.*

Google provides AdWords users with something called a *first page bid estimate*, which is Google's best guess as to how much it will cost for your ad to have a chance of appearing on the first page when someone searches your keywords. It is also a useful overview of what Google thinks about your campaign and whether it has faith in your ad's relevance, quality, and ultimate popularity.

The more often visitors select your ads, the lower your first page bid estimate will be. When you start an AdWords campaign, Google has an estimate in mind of how much money it would like to make from you in exchange for giving your ad first page placement for a given time period. Let's say Google wants to make $10 per day from your campaign. If it shows your ad all day and only one person clicks it, it needs to charge $10 for that click to keep you on the first page. If it shows your ad all day and 10 people click it, it can charge only $1 per click. If 100 people click your ads in that day, you will only pay $.10 per click.

Of course, nothing is simple about Google math. The true first page bid estimate involves a number of factors, including your past performance and the perceived value of your landing page.

The Google AdWords quality score depends to some degree on a site's landing page—this is the only "on-page factor" that matters in Google AdWords (the click-through rate, ad copy, and the history of the AdWords account are bigger factors, but they are not on-page factors). The best AdWords ad in the world won't convert if the page it leads to isn't fully optimized. The following are important factors for the landing page to which your ad leads:

- It has information on it—text, typically—that is relevant to your ad. (So if you advertise Charles Dickens books, the page should not be about antique paper.)
- Google can spider the page easily, as well as your entire site.
- The page loads quickly.

Now, apart from the quality score, your campaign will be much more successful if you have a clear call to action toward the top of the page, as well as an attractive user interface, to get your potential customer to make a purchase; otherwise, you'd just be wasting your money because people would click but not convert.

Quality Score

The biggest factor affecting your CPC bid price is something called a Quality Score (see Figure 6.4). This is a general evaluation of your ad campaign by Google and plays a big part in determining where your ad is displayed and how much you pay for each click on that ad. Higher Quality Scores mean you can get away with bidding less and still appear at the top of the sponsored results. The Quality Score of your campaigns is the heart and soul of your success in the AdWords world.

Google tells us a large number of factors go into calculating an ad's Quality Score, including its historical click-through rate, your account's history, and the quality of your landing page. Google's Quality Score also offers a look into the way the company determines organic search results. If you can figure out how to raise your Quality Score in AdWords, you will have learned some important lessons about organic SEO.

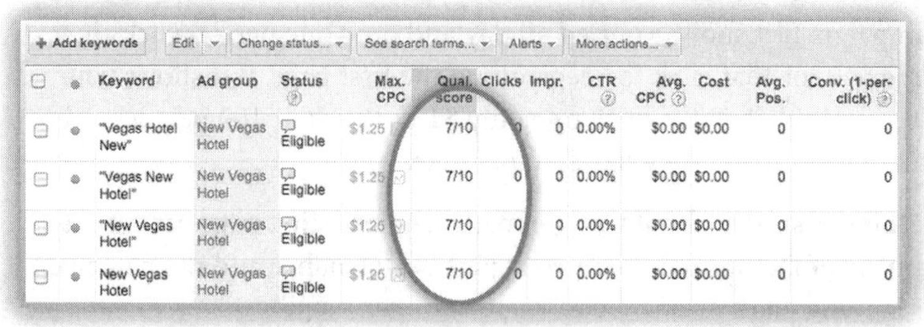
+ Add keywords | Edit | Change status... | See search terms... | Alerts | More actions...

Keyword	Ad group	Status	Max. CPC	Qual. Score	Clicks	Impr.	CTR	Avg. CPC	Cost	Avg. Pos.	Conv. (1-per-click)
"Vegas Hotel New"	New Vegas Hotel	Eligible	$1.25	7/10	0	0	0.00%	$0.00	$0.00	0	0
"Vegas New Hotel"	New Vegas Hotel	Eligible	$1.25	7/10	0	0	0.00%	$0.00	$0.00	0	0
"New Vegas Hotel"	New Vegas Hotel	Eligible	$1.25	7/10	0	0	0.00%	$0.00	$0.00	0	0
New Vegas Hotel	New Vegas Hotel	Eligible	$1.25	7/10	0	0	0.00%	$0.00	$0.00	0	0

Figure 6.4 *A look at Google's ranking system for Quality Scores. Note that these are limited to just three terms: Great, OK, and Poor. On Google's scale, 1–4 correspond with Poor, 5–7 with OK, and 8–10 receive Great markings.*

Click-Through Rate

The most important part of your Quality Score is your click-through rate, or CTR. Some estimates suggest that an ad's CTR is responsible for up to 60% of its overall Quality Score. Google gets paid by the click in its advertising programs, so it makes sense that Google reward ads that generate a lot of clicks. Even if your ad appears to be beautifully written and links to the world's most compelling landing page, Google sends it to the bottom of the pile if it fails to attract clicks on a regular basis.

CTR can be affected by many things, but the marketing copy itself is key; think about those four lines you are given to make your pitch. If your ads are written with an eye toward the customer's needs, you have a much better chance of motivating web surfers to check you out by clicking your ad. This is why it is important to try a number of strategies and continue refining the language in all your campaigns. Sometimes a little tweak or a new idea is all it takes to vastly improve your CTR.

For example, consider this typical ad for sleeping bags:

> Quality Sleeping Bags
> 10% off retail price
> Top brands, great values
> www.example.com

The ad would perform much better if it were more specific and geared toward a particular demographic. The tone should also be brighter and suit the potential buyer (in this case, moms). How about this:

> Kids' Sleeping Bags
> Perfect for summer camp!
> Price is right, kids will love them.
> www.example.com

It's all about thinking of a unique but down-to-earth way to communicate with the people who are searching for the product or service you're selling.

Your CTR is influenced heavily by *where* it appears. Your ad might be perfect in every respect, but if it keeps showing up for people who are looking for something else, Google will soon label it a dud. You could have a brilliant ad for sleeping bags, but if it keeps appearing every time somebody searches for ways to erase the bags under their eyes because they aren't sleeping well, your CTR rate will take a dive. This is where match types are important. Filter out traffic you don't want, reduce the impressions on the campaign, and you will discover how many more clicks you get from your target customer. It might feel a little counterintuitive to actively reduce your impressions in this way, but in AdWords, quality is essential.

A popular way to improve your CTR is to whittle down your campaigns until you are running only the most effective ads. I recommend beginning your process with a broad range of terms until it becomes clear which ads are working and which are not. If all ads are left running without closely examining the numbers, your CTR and overall account success will be dramatically reduced. Trim the fat, and work on optimizing the content and landing pages of your best-performing campaigns.

Account History

Quality Score is also affected by your overall account history. The number is based on the historical success of your AdWords efforts across the board. If you have traditionally run badly written, poorly performing, and irrelevant AdWords campaigns, Google notes it in your permanent record like a bad kid at school. As a result, even your new campaigns get slapped with a penalty that affects their Quality Score.

Of course, the opposite is true, as well: If you are an AdWords ninja who consistently pulls in a crazy number of clicks, Google is much more likely to give your newer campaigns a bump based on reputation alone. This is especially important if you are new to the AdWords universe and want to make your mark. Start with very specific and targeted campaigns, keep a close watch on them, refine the language as necessary, and you will soon build good trust with Google, which will be reflected in your account history. This is a much speedier process than you are likely to get from organic SEO, so it is worth using resources for maintaining an excellent account history from the outset.

You might have noticed that account history is reminiscent of TrustRank in organic SEO. The reasoning is essentially the same in both worlds: Either the people have voted on your site, or they have not. In AdWords, that vote is cast with a click. In organic search results, it is determined largely through your site's inbound links. Either way, Google is staying true to its DNA and honoring the system that keeps its results famously relevant: relying on humans to determine what is worth looking at and what is not.

Landing Pages

Yet another component of the Quality Score is the landing page where users arrive after they click an AdWords ad. Google employs search spiders and actual human beings to evaluate these pages. Landing pages are important to Google because they maintain the quality of AdWords as a whole. If many searchers were to find the sites they visit through AdWords to be of low quality, they would start to lose faith in the entire enterprise. Google knows all too well from years of fighting spam that there are plenty of people who make a living from leading users to harmful web pages through attractive ads and other convincing ruses.

Apart from eliminating spammers from its program, Google generally wants AdWords to be relevant and valuable to the searchers who click its ads. That is another reason why it looks at landing pages to hedge against the danger of well-designed, but ultimately misleading, ads. If your ad is getting a lot of clicks but its corresponding landing page is off-topic or misleading, Google will swiftly lower your Quality Score. Landing page quality is another area where AdWords meets organic SEO—quality counts everywhere.

The Other Components of the Quality Score

As you know by now, the keys to success on AdWords are having a good CTR, account history, and landing page, but there are a few extra elements that go into your Quality Score that are worth noting.

Display URLs

There are four lines of text in an AdWords ad: the headline, two lines of copy, and the display URL. Many business owners work on a great headline, add a couple lines of well-written text, and call it a day. But, the truth is that *all four* lines matter tremendously. They matter for your customers, who will scrutinize every inch of the ad for anything that feels like gimmickry, and they matter to Google, which evaluates your ad to help determine its Quality Score.

One of the most overlooked features of AdWords is that it lets you engage in a tiny bit of deception. The display URL at the bottom of your ad can be completely made up. If you run a site called www.greatfeatherdusters.com, and you want to place an ad for the keyword *pink feather dusters*, you can create a display URL called www.greatfeatherdusters.com/pinkdusters. An easy way to improve your performance is to make the display URL more relevant to the search. Look closely at the top ads for any common Internet search, and you will notice many repeat their keywords in this address (see Figure 6.5). More keywords mean greater relevancy, and often Google bumps up an ad's position as a result. Good display URLs are a smart strategy for your customers, who will typically find greater appeal and legitimacy in a URL that captures what they are searching for. If a site has gone to the trouble of dedicating a page to this precise product or service, surely that site must be useful.

Figure 6.5 *A selection of AdWords ads. Note that the Display URLs also include keywords.*

Geographic Settings

We already know the match type settings on your AdWords campaigns can affect the position, performance, and price of your ads. The same is true for your geographic settings. It is not uncommon for AdWords newcomers to target a wide geographic region, such as the entire United States. Even if you run a mail-order company that ships to every one of these places, you will undoubtedly take a hit in Quality Score because of your campaign's lack of focus. Businesses that zoom in on regions with the greatest CTRs can improve their Quality Scores. Look through your own site traffic and find where your customers congregate. Even if you do not operate a brick-and-mortar storefront, some areas will generate greater sources of customers than others. If you sell hunting gear, for instance, you will probably see a higher CTR from Texas than you will from Rhode Island. As with everything else in AdWords, Google loves specificity and rewards the most optimal geographic settings possible.

Quality Score is a *dynamic* calculation, meaning it is calculated every time your ad appears. You may have a high Quality Score when someone in Newark types in your favorite keyword but a low Quality Score when the same keyword is searched in a slightly different way from Barbados. You must maximize your campaign's overall value to the population you most want to attract.

Smart Strategizing

The thing that makes AdWords such a great complement to SEO is that it offers something SEO cannot: instant gratification. Whereas SEO operates in a time frame that is typically measured in weeks or months, AdWords lets you begin collecting clicks within a matter of hours. This time frame can yield valuable insights into your SEO strategy.

AdWords' primary benefit to SEO is that it offers a great way to zero in on the best keywords for your site. Whether you are optimizing a site for the first time or just looking to refine what you have, AdWords gives you instant access to millions of actual web surfers—and all their messy, mystifying, and occasionally inscrutable habits. You can throw out those proprietary keyword tools and instead get hands-on with your target Web customers.

Finding your SEO keywords using AdWords is purely Darwinian: Try a lot of stuff and see what works. Even if you think you have a strong understanding of what your best keywords are, surrender to the math. It is always right!

For example, if you have a store that sells handmade lockets in Des Moines, it might seem that your best keywords are *handmade lockets Des Moines*, *lockets Des Moines*, or *Des Moines lockets*. But after trying 100 other words that AdWords suggests to you, you might come across a keyword such as *cute jewelry Iowa* that has a higher CTR and converts to more sales. Who knew?

I recommend trying many, many keywords with the AdWords program. Try everything you can think of, throw hundreds of possibilities into the mix, and see what's most successful. This real-life research might point you in new and unexpected directions for your SEO efforts.

Another great way to find great SEO keywords using AdWords involves your competitors. Look at the ads that are currently being displayed when you perform a search for your most lucrative keywords. Generally, you will see the ads with the highest Quality Scores alongside the organic results. These are the ads that perform better than all the others. Study them closely because they may contain clues about the best way to design and deploy your own AdWords campaigns.

Your competitors' ads will probably also show you which other keywords in your industry are profitable. Simply look at the text of the ads to find other keywords hidden in them. Consider the "gift baskets" example from Chapter 2, "The Five Ingredients of Successful SEO." You might be focusing on *gift baskets* but subsequently learn that they are always including the words *gourmet*, *birthday*, and *food* next to that main term. If they're spending money on it, it might mean that they've *made* money from it.

Not everybody can reach the top of organic results through SEO alone, but AdWords lets you see the keywords that people *want to win*. And because the system is designed to reward well-performing ads, the ones you see on the first page are usually the ones earning the most clicks. Granted, you cannot tell how many conversions they are getting from their campaigns, but most businesses do not run ads long term unless the ads are working for them.

While we're talking about competitors, a word about trade names: AdWords lets you take advantage of any reputation your competitors have built by bidding on their name as keywords. Unsavory? A bit; and if you are not careful, you could be violating copyright law. But you *can* do it, and many people do.

The safest way to capitalize on a competitor's name is to focus exclusively on the difference between you and them. Think of it as a way to encourage comparison shopping. Suppose, for instance, that you make computer chips in your garage. You could bid on the keyword *Intel chips* and write an ad that emphasizes all the home-made loving care you put into each chip (as opposed to the impersonal Intel). AdWords campaigns based on competitive trade names offer an opportunity to change the minds of web surfers who think they know what they want—and to piggyback on the marketing muscle of your competition.

The AdWords system can also be an interesting testing ground for the language you use in your marketing messages, both on and off Google. AdWords campaigns are more than links; they are four lines long, with each line of text containing 35 characters and a great deal of careful consideration. Different strategies work for different campaigns, even within the customers of a single business or industry. A whimsical tone might work for one AdWords campaign, a touch of snark for another, marketing bombast for a third, and a warm and inviting tone for the last.

To demonstrate the importance of language choice in AdWords ads, let's use the example of a rabbit food seller. You might believe all rabbit owners to be open-hearted types who will respond to a sincere campaign, something like the following:

> Health food for your beloved rabbit
> Give the gift of better digestion

That is all well and good, and that precise phraseology may be an abiding source of impressions, but do not forget you have not tested the waters for other promising strategies. You might miss an entirely different group—twentysomethings who possess a greater sense of mischief and irony. And you will not know they are out there or willing to click a link unless you try something with a completely different tone:

> Hare today, hare tomorrow!
> Top chow to keep your bunny running

These experiments provide a peek into the minds of your customers. AdWords enables you to dig deeply into the metrics and see what each subset of people does when they arrive at a site. One campaign might draw tons of clicks for its outrageousness but very few conversions, whereas a more conservative tack could prove more profitable in the long term. You don't know until you try. After you identify these different customer profiles, you can refine your site with an eye toward optimizing for each group.

Ad Groups

Now that you know the value of testing different ads, one question lingers: How do you launch 100 AdWords campaigns and still take the time to write great copy for every one of them? The answer is called *ad groups*. It is Google's way of cutting through the clutter and dividing your AdWords campaigns into discrete, manageable chunks. With ad groups, you can deploy a single ad for any number of keywords, including dozens or hundreds at a time. Separating your keywords into sets is the only reasonable way to make sense of your campaign's results as a whole while keeping an eye on how individual keywords are performing.

Anyone who has spent a bit of time with the Adwords Keyword Suggestion Tool has noticed that keywords tend to divide themselves into natural cliques, as it were. If you sell shaving supplies, a keyword list could include the terms *shaving supplies*, *find shaving supplies*, *buy shaving supplies*, and *where to get shaving supplies*. Further down the list you might see another set of keywords that share a different theme, such as *learn to shave*, *shaving tips*, and *how to shave*. These groups of keywords belong together and do not warrant separate marketing strategies within each group. That is where ad groups come into play.

Google lets you create ad groups easily in its interface, so you don't have to spend an eternity entering everything manually (see Figure 6.6).

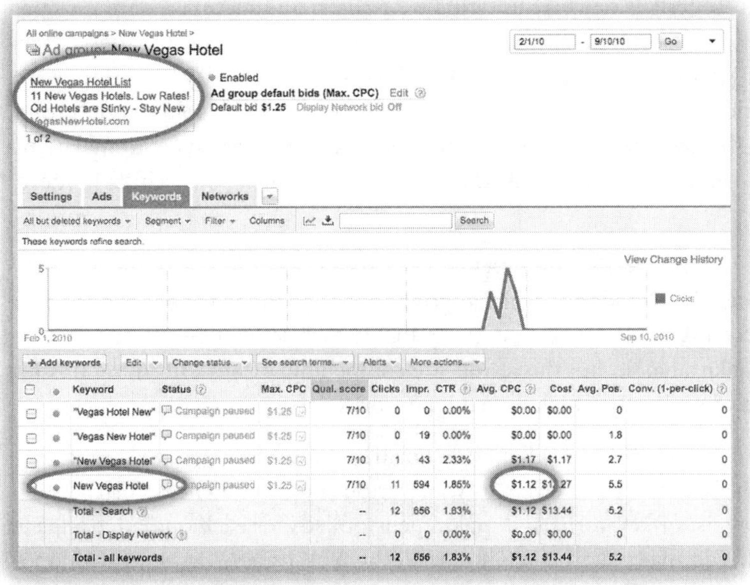

Figure 6.6 *An ad group page on the Google AdWords website, displaying all the individual keywords within the ad group.*

As you get better at using AdWords, you will begin to find that there is no such thing as a one-size-fits-all strategy. To that end, ad groups let you focus on the intent of users, or the reason they are typing in the search. Grouping keywords by the intent of the searcher allows you to focus on ads that make the most sense for each group.

Using the shaving keywords mentioned earlier as an example, you could create one ad group campaign for the people who are just looking for supplies by emphasizing your wide variety and sterling inventory. For the people who want to learn how to shave, you could make an entirely different ad group campaign that emphasizes your shaving manuals and vast array of handsome starter kits. Ad groups let you create a customized ad for every common intention for your product or service and to create landing pages that cater specifically to those needs.

Although ad groups are among the most useful tools in AdWords, they are ultimately a blunt instrument. When you throw a lot of keywords into a single group, it might not be immediately clear which ones are really driving the traffic and which ones are dead weight. More importantly, if you have too many keywords in one group, Google lowers your Quality Score, penalizing you for the extremely high-impression volume of your campaigns. Google loves specificity, and the same holds true in the design and deployment of ad groups. This is why most people recommend capping each group at a couple dozen keywords. Too many terms, and your group will lose its focus, and with it, its Quality Score.

Conducting split tests is one way to refine your ad groups and make sure they perform well. A split test is basically an experiment in which you isolate different factors in an ad group—such as keywords, match types, landing pages, or ad language—and see what performs best. For instance, you could split one ad group into two smaller ad groups and see which performs better, or you could make separate landing pages for two identical ad groups and see which page results in more conversions.

Some people use different match types on the same keyword groups to see which performs better. You could make one ad group that uses phrase match parameters, and then make a second identical ad group that uses exact match instead. This might sound like a hassle, but the results are compelling. After performing this test, you will know definitively which match type works best.

Ad groups are ultimately an excellent organizational tool, carving up all your keywords into useful chunks that relate to your various target audiences. Instead of having one big list of keywords and making custom ads for each one, ad groups let you take all the similar search terms and treat them as a single keyword with one unifying landing page. You can then test your ad groups to find the approach that suits each target audience best. These tests might even inspire you to create different sections of your site that cater exclusively to each audience.

Click Fraud

AdWords is touted as an excellent advertising solution, and in many ways it is. However, it has a dark side: click fraud. This aspect of AdWords is so menacing that, if not controlled, it could put Google out of business.

Click fraud is a simple concept, and it begins with the fact that AdWords is a pay-per-click product. Every time a searcher clicks an ad, the advertiser who created that ad pays. And every time the advertiser pays, Google—and any site that might be hosting that ad—makes money. A click takes no time at all, uses no resources, and can be repeated without much effort. You see where I'm going with this.

There are, in my opinion, two main types of click fraud:

- The kind that is done to make money for the publisher of a website that hosts Google ads

- The kind that is done to drain the bank accounts of competitors

Let's start with the latter. It is easy for competitors to steal money from you—all they have to do is click your ads. If you have used Google AdWords for at least a year, you have probably lost thousands of dollars to click fraud. Some experts estimate that up to a third of all clicks are fraudulent.

Google, of course, takes measures against click fraud. If someone were to click your ad 20 times in a row, you would not be charged for more than 2 or 3 of them. The rest would be labeled invalid clicks by Google and discounted. But if this person were to get more clever about it, clicking at different times of day from different locations, you could be charged for a significant percentage of his clicks.

Google is always looking for ways to rein in competitor click fraud, and, to date, has had reasonable success. There is only so much information it can collect from a single click (IP address, browser, time of day, rate of repetition, and keyword are the main ones), and Google has attempted to install safeguards for every one of those factors. The most obvious indicator of click fraud is repetitive clicks from the same IP address. If clicks from one IP address keep occurring over and over on a single ad, they lose validity because there is almost no chance that these clicks are well intentioned. Consistent click rates or patterns based on time of day are also scrutinized and generally flag a campaign for review. But Google does not discount clicks as easily as one might think. After all, it is considered reasonable behavior for someone to perform a Google search, click an ad, view the landing page for a few seconds, return to the search page, and then click again on the same ad a short while later. People comparing companies can behave this way, and because of that, multiple clicks on the same ad are often considered valid.

There are some defenses against click fraud. The most common defense is software that makes note of repeated clicks from the same IP addresses and lets you write a note that appears on the clicking person's computer screen warning them that they are breaking the law. Unfortunately, there is not much you can do to back up your threat. This solution is similar to putting a security company's sticker on your front door even if you don't actually have a security system; it is mostly a scare tactic. However, this kind of tracking software does log the offending IP addresses, which you can then pass on to Google for consideration in a refund request.

As bad as competitor click fraud is, in my opinion it doesn't hold a candle to click fraud performed by the publishers who host Google ads. With Google's Adsense program, the AdWords ads that normally appear alongside search results are hosted on any of millions of websites, which Google collectively calls the *display network*. This lets advertisers reach more people and target the audiences of specific websites. The trouble is that each of the sites in the Display Network is owned by a person who gets paid a portion of the amount Google receives every time someone clicks an ad. And many of these webmasters live in places where the money they receive from these clicks goes a long way. So pressing that mouse button a few times is darn tempting.

Because the Display Network is so prone to click fraud, I recommend that you always opt out of it when you run an AdWords campaign (see Figure 6.7).

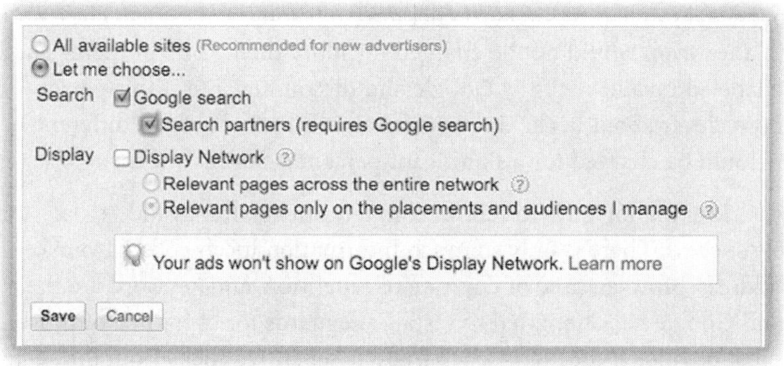

Figure 6.7   *The section of the AdWords website that lets you opt out of the Display Network—a wise move.*

If you need yet another reason to opt out of the Display Network, it also suffers from competitor click fraud. The algorithm that determines which website on the Display Network to place a given ad on looks for keywords common to the ad text and the website. So if someone wants to find his competitor's ad, all he has to do is look through a couple of sites in his own industry.

Because Display Network click fraud is much more profitable than competitor click fraud, a number of criminals have sunk considerable resources into mastering its deceptions. If you have ever seen banner ads online that promise great money to work from home—just by clicking the mouse!—there's a chance that Content Network click fraud is involved. Google has pretty effective safeguards in place to prevent webmasters from clicking their own ads all day, but they cannot put the same brakes on a far-flung network of confederates. It is not inconceivable for click fraud pros to employ hundreds of people whose sole job is to click ads all day.

Before I scare you away from AdWords too much though, I will note that if click fraud made up the majority of most advertisers' clicks, the Display Network—and Google AdWords—would not exist today.

The good news about the Display Network is that it is kept separate from the more reputable Search Network. All you need to do to avoid it is to opt out from the start, which you can do with one click of the mouse. When you begin an AdWords campaign, just look for the radio button during setup.

Common AdWords Mistakes

Up until this point, we have gone over many ways to properly use AdWords and covered only one part of AdWords that you should avoid. But it cannot be overstated how complex a system AdWords is. Without proper planning and care, you could drop a lot of money on a campaign that nets you little revenue. Following are the four most common AdWords mistakes. Take heed!

- **Bad match types**—One of the quickest ways to sink your AdWords campaign is to make every ad a broad match. You will pay a lot for each click and get fairly low-quality traffic for your troubles. Get specific with phrase match and exact match campaigns; you can make a lot more money and learn more about your customers.

- **Forgetting to keep up with negative match**—Make sure you refine your campaigns and trim the wrong search terms. Look for words with double meanings, words that do not relate to what you do, or words that simply indicate another intention altogether. The more specific you get with your campaigns, the better they perform.

- **Bad landing pages**—Keep your site sleek, clean, inviting, and primed for conversion. AdWords campaigns that land on home pages with overly broad themes, unattractive layouts, or ineffective URLs quickly lose points off their Quality Scores.

- **Failure to track**—AdWords is a treasure trove of research, but you can benefit from this data only if you have some way to collect, collate, and understand it. There are plenty of software solutions to supplement the standard Google Analytics, so be sure you are prepared to dig into your AdWords data and discover what it has to teach you.

Recap On AdWords

Even though AdWords is not the core strategy this book deals with, I've included a chapter on it because it can aid your SEO efforts in many ways and be a relatively inexpensive source of research. To this end, I want to close the chapter by summarizing the main ways that AdWords can be used to make your SEO more effective. Most of this material should be familiar, but here it is viewed purely from the standpoint of SEO utility.

The Page-One Party

With a little planning, AdWords can get you onto the first page immediately. Besides offering a quick and dirty way to pull in clicks, this practice lets you test your marketing strategies against the sites that have spent untold time and money achieving top organic results. The data you collect—who is clicking through, why, and what they do when they get to your site—is an invaluable wellspring of information for your business. Buying space via AdWords is a way to get on the map while you dedicate your time and energy to the five ingredients of organic SEO.

Wag the Site

AdWords lets you earn impressions from the thousands of searches that are not phrased exactly the way you expect. These endless iterations are called the long tail, and collectively they represent the majority of searches on any given subject. You do not want to write an article or design a landing page for every one of these searches, but you do want to have an ad on the results page when someone searches for one of these unusual keywords. Most of them are rare and easy to win, so you don't need to spend much money to grab a valuable impression.

Keywords, Keywords, Keywords

As you know, choosing the right keywords is one of the most important ingredients in effective SEO. No matter how great your intuition or research is, there is no better way to test a keyword's effectiveness than to get your site on the first page and observe the results. AdWords lets you try out your keywords in the real world right away, causing the most effective keywords to become apparent.

Eye on the Competition

Almost everybody who is serious about online marketing uses AdWords. Besides teaching you who your competitors are, AdWords lets you look into their own marketing strategies for tips and clues. Their ads might contain keywords you hadn't considered, their communication style might be worth noting, and their landing pages might be instructive. Or not. But AdWords lets you see every company that Google deems similar to your own and decide for yourself. A little comparison can go a long way toward refining your marketing strategy, both for SEO and traditional marketing methods.

Strike a Tone

In the SEO world, your company is often reduced to what is displayed in the search results—namely, a heading (your meta page title) and a line or two of description (your meta description). And although it is important to make these elements appealing to human beings, they are essentially website tags made for search engines. Therefore, a balance must be struck between keyword inclusion and human friendliness. Even though this balance exists in AdWords, there is much more emphasis on the marketing message itself. The four lines of an AdWords ad are a true Petri dish for themes, sentiments, and branding concepts. AdWords lets you try any number of marketing tactics in a hurry and parse the traffic that comes from each. Besides helping you focus your site's look and tone, this can help you understand the various populations that make up your customer base. Split tests, ad groups, and other techniques for slicing and dicing your campaigns make it easier to successfully optimize, telling you what your clients respond to best.

Put Quality First

If there is one dimension of AdWords that is most analogous to TrustRank, it is Quality Score. Your Quality Score is Google's best guess of the relevance and authority of your ad. If an ad earns lots of clicks, proves relevant to the search at hand, and points toward a landing page with a nice, clean design, you get a bump in Quality Score. That same list of criteria applies to organic search results. Instead of waiting months and months as Google learns to trust your links and content, however, AdWords can serve as an instant testing ground for different strategies in design and content, which will also have positive repercussions for your site's SEO.

7

Tracking Your Progress with Search Operators

By now, you should understand how to adapt your website to Google's standards, opening the arms of the Google traffic juggernaut. That means selecting the right keywords, optimizing your meta page title and URL structure, attracting links, and even using PPC advertising as an adjunct to those efforts. But one thing I haven't talked much about is how to check whether you're on the right track. Google is many things, but one thing it isn't is a mom and pop establishment that provides you with good, old-fashioned customer service. You are on your own, with only your experience and this book as your guide.

There are a few obvious ways to check your progress on attracting new business. The pathway that all search engine optimizers work with looks like this:

Keyword Rankings —> Traffic —> Sales —> Money

Let's start at the beginning:

- **Manually checking weekly keyword rankings**—You should be checking to see how your keywords are ranking on a weekly or daily basis. If your site was on page six for a competitive keyword a month ago and it's on page one today, you've done a good job. Usually, I make the process of manually checking keywords easier by clicking Advanced

Options next to the Google search box and selecting 100 results per page. Then I can just do a quick search for my domain name to see whether it's in the top 100 (see Figure 7.1).

Figure 7.1 *Showing 100 results per page on Google and then doing a search for your domain is a quick way to see whether your site is ranking in the top 100 results.*

🔍 *Tip*

Another option is to use one of the many keyword position checkers online. You can find one on the home page of my website, www.firstpagesage.com. It is useful to note your rankings each week so that you can understand the movement of your website within the results, especially if you correlate your rankings with your latest achievements in link building.

- **Checking traffic statistics**—The next way to check your SEO progress is to look at your traffic statistics. The industry standard is Google Analytics. I recommend using it to measure your traffic so that if someone requests a figure from you—be it a business development partner or an advertiser—you can give that person an easily understandable number. But whatever traffic analysis program you use, if you're pulling in more visitors this month than you did last month, chances are you're doing something right. The key, of course, is to attract the right kind of traffic. For the same reason a company that sells cleaning products wouldn't advertise on an anime fan website, you should be focusing on getting the right kind of people to your site. Creating lots of pages around niche subject areas à la the nuclear football is a great way to do that. But the most important way to make sure the right people land on your website is by choosing your keywords wisely. (Go back to Chapter 2, "The Five Ingredients of Google Optimization," if you need a refresher.)

* **Conversions to sales**—The final, and in many ways the most important, element of understanding your SEO progress is to see how your new traffic is converting into sales. This is such an important topic that I have devoted a whole chapter to it (Chapter 11, "Converting Your SEO Results into Paying Customers." Feel free to skip right to that chapter after reading this one if that is a core area of interest for your company.

Now that you understand how to navigate the pathway from keyword rankings to sales, let's explore how to track your progress toward achieving those rankings. Why are you kicking butt with one keyword and lagging behind the competition on another? Why did you get a huge traffic jump last Monday that mysteriously stopped?

If you had infinite time, you could use trial and error: Isolate one thing at a time, wait a safe amount of time, and then painstakingly write down everything that works and doesn't work. But that process should be undertaken only by those who have no help; and fortunately, I've already made the mistakes, so you don't have to.

Search Operators 101

Most people already know that the little box on Google's home page is more than just a place to string keywords together. Some of the most common methods for refining a search have by now become automatic: If you want an exact phrase, put it in quotes. If you want to exclude certain words, put a minus sign (-) before them. Advanced users may know some other tricks, including how to use AND, OR, and asterisks. There are actually countless things you can do besides your typical keyword search in Google. You can do math problems, get definitions, see tomorrow's weather, and check flight statuses. But another class of search tools gives you valuable insight into how your site is regarded by Google. These tools are called *search operators*.

Before revealing which search operators exist, I believe it's significant to note that Google's choice of operators offer us a great window into what Google itself believes are the factors that make a site most appealing to a search engine. Google has long been a pioneer in database analysis; they could create any operator they like. If they wanted, they could create a search operator that lets you search only for sites that have more than 10 pictures and one mention of baby birds. But the fact that they have chosen these operators in particular speaks volumes about the company's belief that these are the metrics that matter most.

Although there are more than 20 search operators, the most important are the site:, link:, and allinanchor: operators. Figure 7.2 shows a list of the operators Google provides.

Search Service	Search Operators
Web Search	allinanchor:, allintext:, allintitle:, allinurl:, cache:, define:, filetype:, define:, filetype:, id:, inanchor:, info:, intext:, intitle:, inurl:, link:, phonebook:, related:, site:
Image Search	allintitle:, allinurl:, filetype:, inurl:, intitle:, site:
Groups	allintext:, allintitle:, author:, group:, insubject:, intext:, intitle:
Directory	allintext:, allintitle:, allinurl:, ext:, filetype:, intext:, intitle:, inurl:
News	allintext:, allintitle:, allinurl:, intext:, intitle:, inurl:, location:, source:
Product Search	allintext:, allintitle:

Figure 7.2 *A comprehensive list of Google's known search operators.*

> ✉ *Note*
>
> Advanced search operators are a good way to parse out the SEO factors that affect your ranking; however, don't get addicted to them. An hour spent link-building is much more valuable than an hour spent with search operators on Google. And yet, it only takes one epiphany—gleaned perhaps from a competitive analysis using the Yahoo! linkdomain: operator—to gain a first-page ranking.

The Site: Operator

Let's begin with the most basic search operator out there: the site: operator. Like all of Google's search operators, it is executed by typing the operator word, with a colon after it, into Google's search box, and then following it up with a search term, *without any spaces in between.* For example, here is a site: search of my website, evanbailyn.com:

site:www.evanbailyn.com

What you will see when you press Enter after a site: search is a list of every single page that Google has indexed within that domain. It looks exactly like a conventional list of search results, but in this case all the results are pages from the same website. Look closely at the URLs associated with each, for instance, and you will notice that they differ only in the endings (see Figure 7.3).

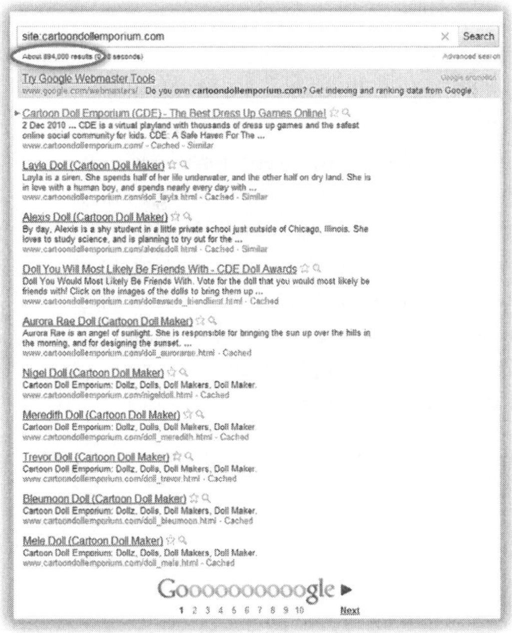

Figure 7.3   *The site: operator in action. Look up top and you will notice that my kids website has 895,000 pages according to Google.*

Why is this useful? On the most basic level, a site: search is a good way to confirm that your website has been completely acknowledged by Google—that it exists, in full, in their database. It is not uncommon for sites with poor page flow to show up in this search with several pages missing. Google's spider (the script that looks through every website for pages to serve in its index) can only follow methodically from one link to the next, so it is essential that your site's structure guide Google—and your users—from the home page to every single internal page. Creating a site map is the best way to ensure all your pages have their own links. You'll know that your site is being "crawled" by Google's spider if a site: search returns every page on your site.

But you can learn more from the site: operator than just whether your pages have made it into Google's index. Each individual result displays in exactly the same way it would in a regular Google search, so you can preview the way all the pages on your site will look when they appear in the search results. You might be surprised to discover that your page titles are displaying improperly or that they have become fragmented when truncated in the actual results. Or you might find that the two lines of text below the page title, which are taken from your site's meta description tag, are not utilizing their real estate in the most valuable manner.

The two lines of description under the title in a Google result is your opportunity to write about your page in more detail than the blue underlined title allows. Unfortunately, I often see random keywords taking up this space, put in place by the site's programmer when the website was first built. Even more frequently, a result has a random snippet of text in the description area that Google automatically took from the page. This is done when there is no information in the "meta description tag" area of the code. It is much better to put a short but complete description of your site in your meta description tag because this could be the difference between a visitor to your site or one of your competitors' results. These results are much like classified ads: You get just a couple of lines to make your pitch. And would you waste 66% of the lines in your classified ad? I think not!

Figure 7.4 shows three different ways search results might appear depending on how you have coded your website.

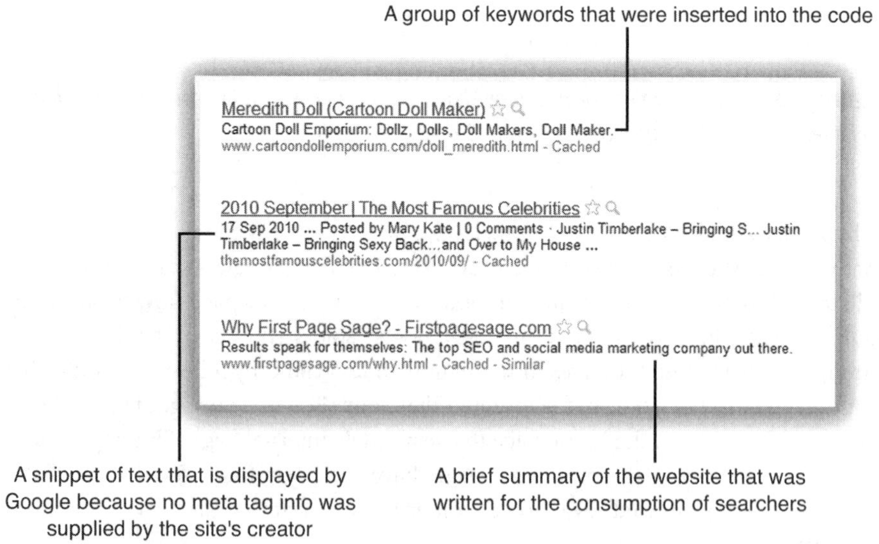

A group of keywords that were inserted into the code

Meredith Doll (Cartoon Doll Maker) ☆ ◌
Cartoon Doll Emporium: Dollz, Dolls, Doll Makers, Doll Maker.
www.cartoondollemporium.com/doll_meredith.html - Cached

2010 September | The Most Famous Celebrities ☆ ◌
17 Sep 2010 ... Posted by Mary Kate | 0 Comments · Justin Timberlake – Bringing S... Justin Timberlake – Bringing Sexy Back...and Over to My House ...
themostfamouscelebrities.com/2010/09/ - Cached

Why First Page Sage? - Firstpagesage.com ☆ ◌
Results speak for themselves: The top SEO and social media marketing company out there.
www.firstpagesage.com/why.html - Cached - Similar

A snippet of text that is displayed by Google because no meta tag info was supplied by the site's creator

A brief summary of the website that was written for the consumption of searchers

Figure 7.4 *Three examples of how the description can be formatted in a Google result.*

Following is more detail about what made each of the search results shown in Figure 7.4 appear as they're shown:

- In the top example, the description is just a group of keywords that were inserted into the code by a programmer. This is not the way you want a page on your site to be represented.

- In the middle example, the description is a snippet of text that was displayed by Google because no information was ever inputted into the meta description tag of the website's coding. This is not the way you want a page on your site to be represented either.

- In the bottom example, the description is a brief summary of the website that was intentionally written for the consumption of searchers. This is a great way for a site's pages to be represented in Google's search results.

The site: operator is also a nice way to monitor the speed at which new content is added to Google's database. Over the years, Google has gotten much better at updating its index as new content appears, but there is still a certain lag time before you begin to see your new pages in the search results. Depending on the number of links that are pointed at your site, your new content can get indexed by Google as infrequently as every two weeks or as frequently as every five minutes. Checking your domain regularly with the site: operator gives you a window into which pages Google currently knows about. If your SEO strategy depends on frequent revision and addition, this information can help guide your timeline and manage expectations as your changes are rolled out.

One final note about the site: operator: If for some reason you are afraid that Google may have de-indexed or blacklisted your site, you can use this command to make sure that Google still acknowledges your site. If results appear, your site is probably in fine standing with Google. If no results appear, you're in hot water. Of course, that won't happen to anyone following the advice in this book.

The Link: Operator

Whereas site: is the way to find all the pages on your site, there is another operator whose purpose is to show all the links pointing to your website. This is the link: operator. Link: is used in exactly the same way as the site: operator. For example:

link:www.evanbailyn.com

Despite the fact that link: is believed by many to show *all* the links that point to a given website, it does not do so at all. Instead, it returns a partial list of links to your website, a list that is old and polluted with multiple results from the same domain (see Figure 7.5).

Figure 7.5   *The link: operator in action, returning a random group of sites that link to the query site. Note that multiple results from the same domain are repeated as if they all have equal value. In fact, little information about the value of each link can be discerned from this result set.*

Why doesn't Google show us all of a site's inbound links? Because this is extremely valuable information, and it goes straight to the heart of Google's TrustRank system. If you could see every single page that links to a site, you might be able to determine exactly how pages are weighted and ranked. So Google deliberately obscures this data, much like the U.S. government allows GPS to be accurate to only a certain degree: It is protecting a powerful technology from prying eyes. In reality, the link: operator returns only about one-third of the sites that actually link to your own. It's still a pretty good thumbnail, but exhaustive it is not.

So just what is link: good for? A few things.:

- **Randomness**—First, even though it is not a complete list, the link: operator does offer something that at first glance might not appear useful: randomness. Before 2004, the link: operator used to return the most trusted sites that link to your own. Today, it is essentially a hodge-podge of pages—some big, some small, in no particular order. In fact, the links that Google shows might not have any TrustRank whatsoever. However, think about it this way: If you are focused only on the big players who link to you, you aren't actively researching other people you could reach. What the link: operator shows you is a diverse cross section of people who have linked to your site. You might discover an obscure blog post that opens the door to an entirely new community. Or you might find a mention in some local newspaper that represents thousands of untapped potential customers. Throwing a little attention and marketing muscle at these lesser-known contacts is a great way to grow your business and expand your presence on the Web.

• **Eavesdropping**—When you visit sites that link to your own, you will occasionally find conversations in which people are discussing your business. This is a phenomenon that is unique to the Web. Fifty years ago, the CEO of Burger King couldn't exactly listen in to what people were saying as they drove past his restaurants. Today, not only can he hear what people are saying, he can hear those opinions in candid, unguarded language. He could even find a discussion of how Burger King stacks up to McDonald's as easily as Googling *burger king vs. mcdonalds*. Conversations like these are a gold mine of market research.

Of course, you can do more than just listen in: You can participate. If you read something especially heart-warming or egregious on a message board, it is reasonable to post a response. Direct communication with would-be customers in this way can often go a long way toward repairing hard feelings and generating goodwill across the Web. One word of warning, however: The Web is a wild, woolly place, and message boards are famously prone to "flame wars" and nasty disputes. One warm and professional post can be an effective way to reach out, but beware of writing anything that makes you appear defensive or hostile. The "trolls" will respond vehemently. There is little patience on the Web for a CEO with thin skin. Figure 7.6 shows a discussion happening on the forum of a tween website.

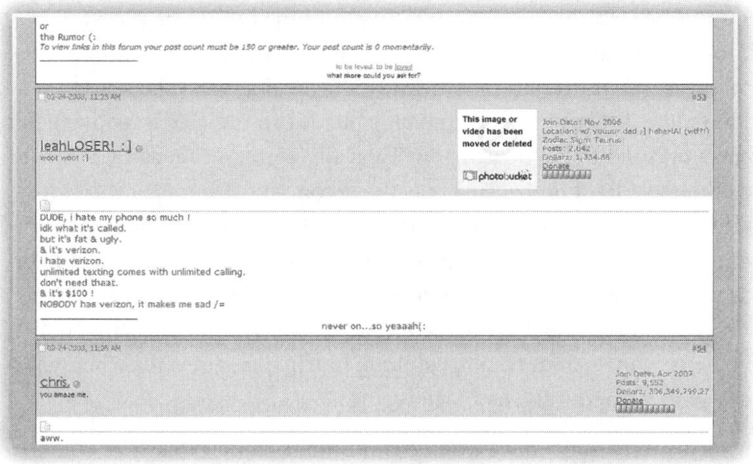

Figure 7.6   *A discussion on a tween website about Verizon, found using the link: operator. The CEO could potentially gain insight from reading one of his customers' complaints. It would not be a good idea for him to respond on this forum, though, unless his words were very sincere.*

- **Competitive intelligence**—A final use of the link: operator does not concern your own site, but rather the competition's. There is no rule that says you have to own the website you type in after link:, so why not use this tool to see what kind of links the other guys are getting? Sure, it won't be an exhaustive list (use Yahoo's linkdomain: search for that), and you might not even find the heaviest hitters in the lineup. But for a cross section of your competition's linking strategy, checking their incoming links is an easy place to start. You might even discover a major news portal that would be interested in running a follow-up about your business. Or you might find a bunch of bloggers you weren't aware of who focus on your industry. You never know unless you peek.

The Allinanchor: Operator

The allinanchor: operator is one of those special operators that I have used for years to give me insight about my link-building efforts. In essence, if you type in allinanchor: with a search phrase next to it, Google lists the search results as they would look if ordered solely by the number of text links you have pointing to your site about that search phrase. For example:

allinanchor:snow shoes

So if one of the keywords you care about is *cell phone accessories* and you have a lot of links like the preceding one pointing to your website, it is likely that your website will show up in the search *allinanchor:cell phone accessories.*

This operator is particularly interesting because it helps optimizers differentiate between the impact of text links on their rankings and the impact of everything else. As you know, text links are the most effective way to boost your rankings for a specific search phrase—but they are not the only way. Seeing what the search results would look like if text links were the *only* factor can indicate to you which of the other factors you need to be focusing on. Typically, aging is the factor that this operator sheds the most light on because it is the second most important factor in Google's ranking algorithm. If your site shows up much higher in an allinanchor: search than a regular search, you can almost always draw the conclusion that it, or its links, needs to age. In essence, the allinanchor: operator says this to you: "Here is what the results would look like if aging weren't a consideration. Using this tool, you can predict what your search results will look like in a few months when your site and its links have earned full trust" (see Figure 7.7).

In case you needed more proof that Google loves links, consider this: The allinanchor: searches are often almost identical to organic searches. This tells us something important about how Google's search algorithm works: The text inside a link—also known as anchor text—factors heavily into each site's ranking. For webmasters interested in improving their SEO, running an allinanchor: search is a great way to see whether your links are conferring as much benefit as they should. If you have optimized your site specifically for a certain keyword but you aren't ranking well for it, an allinanchor: search can help you analyze whether that keyword is showing up in the anchor text of your inbound links. Just don't forget what I taught you earlier—too many anchor text links will get your site penalized.

Figure 7.7 *An allinanchor: search, which shows how the results would be ordered if text links were the only factor in Google optimization. Usually, the results of an allinanchor: search are pretty similar to the normal results, which shows how important links are to Google.*

Probably the most common use of the allinanchor: operator among optimizers is a crystal ball into the future for sandboxed sites. If your site is brand new, allinanchor: will give you a rough idea of where your site would rank today if it had full trust. This is tremendously useful for new sites because waiting several months for your site to show up in the results can wear on your patience.

✉ *Note*

Probably the most common misconception about the allinanchor: operator is that it will tell you where your site will rank in the future. Just to be clear, that is impossible to predict because no algorithm could know what kind of links your site will acquire. It just tells you, all things being equal, where your site would land today if the age of your site weren't a factor to Google.

Yahoo's Linkdomain: Operator

Earlier I mentioned the invaluable Yahoo! linkdomain: search. Google is not the only search engine that gives webmasters useful tools. Yahoo! might have a different ranking philosophy, but it crawls the exact same Web that Google does. And Yahoo! has a few neat offerings in its Site Explorer area.

In theory, linkdomain: is similar to Google's link: operator; it returns a list of sites that link to a given domain. (Actually, linkdomain: shows all links that are pointed to *any page* on a domain, but hey.) But in practice, linkdomain: is a much more powerful tool than anything Google offers (see Figure 7.8).

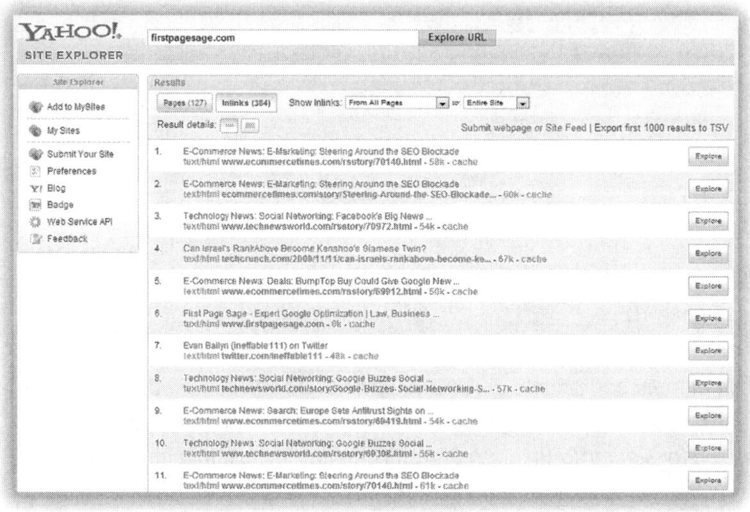

Figure 7.8 *A linkdomain: search on Yahoo!—the best way to discover which sites are linking to any page on your domain.*

First and most important, linkdomain: returns many more links than Google does—a complete set, actually. This is not a reflection of a better spider or a bigger database; it is simply a difference in philosophy. Google guards its link data to prevent anyone from reverse-engineering its algorithm. Yahoo! is less concerned with this possibility, and so it provides more exhaustive information on what it knows about your site.

Webmasters love this feature because it allows them to see a more complete picture of what is fueling their rankings—not as much on Yahoo! as on Google. It is also an amazing tool for researching your competitors. It's like having the rival team's playbook; keep in mind though, you only know what makes them rank, not how they achieved those links. I highly recommend studying your competitors' links, especially if they rank above you, because you might learn about an inexpensive online link campaign they're running or about a high-TrustRank directory you never would have considered.

The other big advantage to Yahoo's approach is its customizability. When you use a Google operator such as allinanchor:, for instance, you aren't allowed to add a second operator. That is, you can't combine two link: searches to find the sites that link to both you and your competitor. That's not the case on Yahoo!, where users can refine, parse, and narrow down the search results in many ways.

Let's consider how this might be useful in practice. Say you want to find all the sites that link to your domain. However, you've done a great deal of internal linking, and you've thrown in some links from other sites you own across the Web. You're not interested in seeing your internal linking; all you want to know is who has voted on your site from elsewhere. If you were using Google, you'd be up a creek without a paddle. With Yahoo!, you can run a search of all the sites that link to your domain, *minus* any links from within your own domain, *minus* links from the other sites you manage. Your search query would then look like this:

```
linkdomain:www.mysite.com -site:http://www.mysite.com
   -site:www.othersiteyouown.com
```

That might look complicated, but it's really just combining three simple search queries into one. By subtracting the site: operator from a linkdomain: search, you are eliminating all the results from inside a certain domain (in this case, your own). Combining operators in this way is extremely powerful because it enables you to zero in on any kind of data you're interested in. It also lets you get a fuller picture of where your links are coming from and what your SEO efforts would look like with any of these sources removed.

Other Operators: A Roundup

In this chapter, we have explored site:, link:, allinanchor:, and linkdomain: (the favorite operators of the SEO community). With just these four, you can learn a lot about your site and SEO efforts. However, I also want to highlight a few more search operators that can help you track your progress in specific ways. These are functions that tend to get overlooked because they are more limited, but each of them adds an interesting perspective to your outlook.

The Allintitle: Operator

One of the most basic operators out there is the allintitle: operator. Just like the other Google operators in this chapter, it is used by typing the search operator and then a website. No spaces, no *http://.* For example:

```
allintitle:toy planes
```

Remember how allinanchor: only searches anchor text? Well, this is another specific one. Allintitle: searches only the meta page titles of websites. You should remember these from earlier. The Meta page title, or title tag, is the brief phrase that appears on the top of your browser window when you visit any web page, which Google uses as the blue underlined heading for its search results (see Figure 7.9).

Figure 7.9   *A meta page title for my company website. A great deal of thought goes into these short summaries.*

As I said in Chapter 2, these titles are extremely important. Besides appearing in the results of every Google search, they tell search engines what your website is about through keywords. And when you run an allintitle: search for a keyword, you can see all the websites that are using that keyword in their title tags.

This is a great way to find out which sites are optimizing for the same keywords that you are. An allintitle: search can reveal competitors you weren't aware of, who you can then examine with a fine-toothed comb for any good ideas. You can also compare how your title tags stack up next to theirs. The allintitle: operator gives you a set of blinders to examine this one specific aspect of SEO by itself.

Tip

You already know the format I favor for these tags, but there are plenty of other good formats as well. It is certainly worth inspecting the title tags of your competitors because someone may have figured out a novel way to throw several keywords into a tag without making it sound forced. Somebody else might have refined a tag with different keywords designed to draw more targeted traffic.

The Allintext: Operator

A great debate in the SEO community has long gone on about the importance of on-page factors (things on the page) versus outside factors (links). The smarties—like you—know by now that links bestow more TrustRank than anything you could possibly write on a website. But Google doesn't *only* look at links when determining a page's relevance to a search. Google prefers that the content on the page meet a certain standard of relevance to the keyword being searched. And how does one measure a page's relevance to a particular keyword?

Lo and behold, there's an operator for that: the allintext: operator. The allintext:" operator determines how well optimized each page's content is for a specific keyword. It analyzes the written content alone, ignoring everything else. Think of this as the anti-allinanchor: operator. If allinanchor: is concerned only with inbound links, allintext: is concerned only with content.

The allintext: search results diverge widely from organic search. This confirms something we already know: Links matter much, much more than content. However, it is still interesting to look at which sites rank the highest in an allintext: search because it can indicate how heavily Google is weighing different content-related factors on the page. Every little bit of information counts!

Even though I am very much convinced that Google cares little about the content on a page (as far as on-page factors go, the meta page title is the main focus), it would be remiss not to share best practices for content:

- Address your keywords in an organic, unforced way. Avoid *keyword stuffing*, or using your main keyword in every other sentence.

- Put keywords near the top of the page, especially in *header tags*. Your web designer or programmer can help you with that, and most blogging software will help you identify your header tags. The H1 tag is most important.

- Include no more than two to three keywords per page, although focusing on one keyword per page and doing a bang-up job is always the best idea.

The allintext: search operator can help you check your progress with these strategies.

8

Google Optimization Myths

The purpose of this book is to teach you how to dominate the Google search results and gain lots of new business. However, it is often hard to transmit information if other, conflicting information is present. It would be ideal if everyone reading this book were starting with a blank slate, knowing nothing about SEO. But because most of you have read a bit on the subject, I have a little battle to wage with commonly held beliefs. There are tons of theories out there, most of them propagated in webmaster forums by so-called experts who actually know little about the subject. Here in this chapter, I plan to depose some of the most insidious, widely spread myths about Google optimization.

I can think of two reasons why there is so much conflicting information about SEO out there:

- The first is money. Lots of "gurus" have a financial stake in selling you their own optimization products and services, which means that they need to convince you that whatever they are capable of doing is the right thing to do. A person whose specialty is creating content will probably tell you that SEO is all about having lots of pages. A link broker will insist that you need to buy links on certain websites to win the first page. A web design firm will be convinced that the way your website is coded determines your rankings.

- The other reason is that this stuff actually *is* confusing. There are so many factors that might plausibly play a role in SEO, and sorting them all out can make your head spin. Between the onsite factors of website code, structure, layout, and content, and the offsite factors of linking style, speed of link building, and age of links—not to mention the constantly changing nature of Google's search algorithm—it's hard to know what's real. Not helping matters is the fact that Google is constantly spreading misinformation and tries to confuse the community of optimizers with false claims, bogus tools, and useless data.

The truth is that there are only three ways to know for sure what works in SEO:

- Put on a ski mask and creep into Google's headquarters in Mountain View, California, while the engineers are sleeping.

- Isolate every possible factor and conduct experiments for months on end.

- Trust the information in this book.

I recommend a combination of careful research and experimentation with trusting what I'm telling you. And if you do try the cat burglar approach, that should be the subject of another book. But seriously, although it might sound obvious to try different strategies and observe what works, few people actually do so systematically. The average person I've seen trying his or her hand at SEO is fixed on one or two strategies. If those strategies don't perform, he or she will focus on some other aspect of marketing instead. And yet, if this person had only tried out 10 strategies, spending a small amount of money on each, he or she would probably have found one that worked.

I have conducted close to 100 trial-and-error experiments over seven years. And by this point, you already know what I believe to be true about SEO. But, just to set the record straight, here are the things I am certain *do not* work.

Myth 1: Your Google Ranking Is Based on Your Website

This is by far the biggest and most widespread myth. The reason for its staying power is the fact that SEO in the early days *was* all about your website. It was about the keywords in your website's code and the density of keywords on your pages. Early search engines such as Excite and AltaVista relied heavily on these factors when ranking your website. But then a few people caught on, realizing that if they wrote certain phrases many times at the bottom of their websites, lots more traffic would arrive (see Figure 8.1). And then lots more people caught on—to the point where the search engines were overtaken by these early search engine optimizers. The results were polluted, and instead of changing their systems entirely, most search engines kept putting bandages on the problem by banning the most egregious keyword repeaters and creating filters for keyword density on a page.

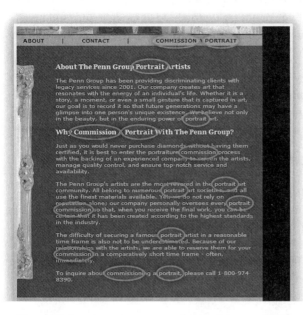

Figure 8.1   *This page was written with keyword density in mind. Clearly optimized for "commission a portrait," it contains the word commission 6 times and the word portrait 11 times. Although cleverly executed to sound natural, this type of optimization is no longer effective for ranking higher in Google.*

Google came along and changed the entire game with its concept of PageRank, which relied mostly on an external factor: links. Links were much more difficult to manipulate, which is why Google's results were famously relevant to your search and mostly spam-free.

Today, the only elements of your website that really matter to Google are your meta page title, domain name, and URL structure. Because your domain name never changes and your URL structure can be automated to be SEO-friendly, that pretty much just leaves your meta page title. And if you've written more than a dozen meta page titles, you can write a new one in less than two minutes. So you do not need to expend much time and effort on your site to get a high ranking on Google. It's all about links.

The caveat here, which makes this discussion tricky, is that nowadays Google's algorithm is much more about what you should *not* do than what you should do. And so, even if you have great meta page titles, a great domain name, a proper URL structure, and lots of links, you can still be prevented from ranking because of things you've done wrong. For instance, if you create lots of pages of content but you stuff your pages with keywords, or create lots of nearly blank pages, or link to every other website you own on every page, your site could be ignored. The key is to operate your website as if you're not trying too hard. If Google finds too much evidence of optimization on your site, it will prevent an otherwise-trustworthy site from ranking.

In summary: You should pay attention to your website, especially by not doing things that Google specifically doesn't like. But if you want to rank high on Google, spend your time building links.

Myth 2: Your Google Ranking Depends on Esoteric Web Coding

Here is another myth that can trace its roots back to the early days of the Web. The myth states that the code of your website—including a number of very specific techy things (XML sitemaps, meta keywords, robots.txt, and so on)—is the key to making Google raise your site in the rankings. Proponents of this myth argue that the Web was built by engineers, and Google is made up of engineers, so your code must make a huge difference in terms of how Google evaluates your website.

I think this belief continues to be propagated by the technical people who do all the coding and designing for websites. As soon as the Web became a place where the average person liked spending time (circa 1999), a large rift became evident—the one between the everyday people who use the Web and the software engineers who build it. Because we rely on these all-powerful folks to make our websites work, we also sometimes rely on them for advice about anything to do with the Internet. And that can be a mistake.

In reality, SEO is not a technical skill. Case in point: I majored in English in college and have never written a line of code in my life. And yet, I've attracted tens of millions of visitors to my websites through SEO, learning the art better than any techie I've met. But still, if my webmaster were to tell me tomorrow that Google has changed some technical standard that will affect my SEO and he needs to overhaul my website, I'd be tempted to listen. There is much power in being able to control something that people don't understand.

My point is that *some* tech folks overemphasize the importance of what they know and underemphasize the importance of what they don't know. And this leads to people paying for unnecessary things—and believing in those things—because they blindly trust their technicians.

With all that said, just like in the last myth, the exception to the rule that your code will not affect your Google rankings comes when you do something that Google specifically doesn't like. The most common code no-no's are as follows:

- Anything that slows down your site

- Site structures that are confusing and difficult for Google to spider

- Redundant or sloppy code that slows Google's spiders down

- Lots of broken links

- Black hat tactics (see Chapter 9, "White Hat Versus Black Hat SEO")

But then, any competent website coder should be able to avoid glaring mistakes that cause those issues. SEO is not about the kind of code you can't understand. It's about keyword choice, links, meta page titles, URLs, and aging.

Myth 3: Click-Through Rates Affect Google Rankings

This is a particularly tempting myth because it sounds completely plausible. The idea is that the more people who click your website in the organic search results, the higher it will rise. In other words, Google "learns" over time which websites are most useful to searchers by tracking their behavior. This system is in fact used by Google—not for ordering the search results but for trying out new features such as Google Instant.

The reason this methodology is not employed by Google for determining rankings is, first of all, that Google does not know anything about the way users behave once they have clicked a website. All Google knows is that they clicked it, and, perhaps, came back to Google later. But a click does not imply approval. The site could have drawn the searcher in with an inviting meta page title or description, only to disappoint him once he arrives. Nor could we conclude that a search result is irrelevant to a search because users clicked it and then returned to Google a moment later; this kind of behavior could easily be simulated by a script. Not to mention that if Google did allow searchers' behavior to determine the order of the search results, an entire industry would pop up around inducing people to click sites and stay awhile, both ethically and unethically. It would cause much more trouble than it's worth.

Google's actual strategy—relying heavily on inbound links to determine rankings—is much more reliable because links tend to be earned by people with real knowledge of what is on the other end of them. Most of us wouldn't post a link to another website without vetting it. And because links are built upon a deeper level of knowledge, they have proved over time to be a much more consistent gauge of value.

Myth 4: Pay-Per-Click Campaigns Affect Organic Rankings

Many people have asked me whether spending money with Google AdWords will improve their search results. Google is clear about the fact that no correlation exists between the paid results and the organic results, and for good reason: It would undermine consumers' trust of the search results, making its system more overtly capitalistic than it already is.

Some people refuse to believe that, though, insisting that Google uses its advertising program as a sort of backdoor bribe that gives you extra consideration in the rankings. It's like greasing the palm of a maître d'—a quick exchange, a nod toward the man in the back, and suddenly you hear "Right this way, sir."

Of course, any kind of "pay for play" system would be patently corrupt, especially for a public company. If Google sold its results, it would lose its reputation as a trusted search engine in a matter of weeks. After all, there is a reason *Consumer Reports* doesn't accept advertising of any kind: The first whiff of any kind of conflict of interest can destroy a reputation. And besides, Google already uses AdWords to get people to pay for first page placement and is making a few billion dollars a quarter from it. So Google doesn't really need to meddle with its most sensitive asset, the organic results.

Myth 5: Google Places Affects Organic Rankings

Google Places—the local listings of Google—plays a special part in Google's search results (see Figure 8.2). These listings often show up above the organic results, sometimes even among them, making them one of the most important sets of results on the page (see Figure 8.3). Google has given increasing appeal to these local results, rocking the SEO world shortly before this book was printed by making them almost indistinguishable from the organic results. If you're not sure exactly what Google Places results look like, they are two-line listings of local businesses with a little red balloon next to them, designated A through G, accompanied by a map.

> ### Tip
>
> Simply put, Google Places is an online version of your local Yellow Pages. If you're in New York City and search for Japanese restaurants, Google Places shows you listings for local Japanese restaurants. Click one of these links and you will see a map to the location and other information entered by the restaurant owner, such as photos, menus, and more. If the same user travels to Chicago and enters the same search, he will see Google Places listings for Japanese restaurants in Chicago.
>
> Google Places gathers information about businesses, culled from many resources on the Web, and meshes it with information entered by the owner

of the "place," and then displays results relevant to searchers based on where they are conducting a search. Places is especially useful for smartphone users (iPhone, BlackBerry, Android, Windows Phone, and so on) who allow Google to use their current locations to show relevant local listings in the search results. To learn more about Google Places, see *Sams Teach Yourself Google Places* by Bud E. Smith, published by Sams Publishing.

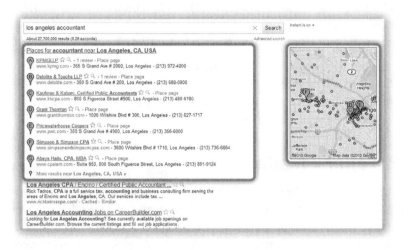

Figure 8.2   *The traditional format of Google Places listings: above the organic results in a "7 box" with a map on the right.*

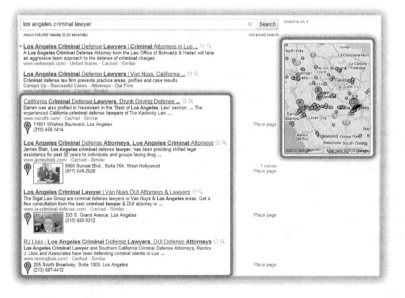

Figure 8.3   *Implemented in late 2010, this format of Google Places results sews them into the organic results. The "7 box" of local listings appears below the first two organic results.*

✉ *Note*

The term "7 box" refers to the number of Google Places results shown at the top of the organic search results page. Currently, a maximum of seven results are shown here.

Google Places is designed to make it easier to find local businesses that accommodate whatever you are searching for. Usually they show up only when you add a geographic phrase to your search, such as *New York*, *Austin*, or *Toronto*.

Just like organic results, Google Places listings are ranked according to their own algorithm. However, that algorithm has nothing to do with the algorithm that orders the organic results. What *does* the Google Places algorithm care about? It cares about keywords in business names, reviews, and links.

Myth 6: PageRank Matters

I started off this book with a discussion of the myth of PageRank. However, let me put it more succinctly here. Many people believe that PageRank is Google's rating of the importance of your website on a 0 to 10 scale. In reality, PageRank is a slippery, correlative measurement. It is a distraction from TrustRank, which is the real measure of a site's importance to Google. The fact that a PageRank bar is available for the Google toolbar is misleading—and somewhat mean—because it keeps people thinking about the wrong system.

One thing PageRank does indicate is the frequency with which your site is visited by Google to be indexed. But you can also learn that by monitoring when Google tends to *cache* (take a picture of) your site. You can find out your latest cache date by doing a Google search for your site. Next to each page, you will see a little link that says "cached." When you click it, the resulting page displays a date at the top (see Figure 8.4).

While PageRank does not tell you the importance of your site in Google's eyes, nor whether it ranks for any competitive keywords, it does tell you something. In truth, no matter how much I denounce PageRank, I still find myself looking at it from time to time, especially if I'm on a call with someone who tells me about his or her website and I want to get a quick picture of the site's credibility. If I see a PageRank of 4 or higher, it indicates to me that the site has been around a while and has links coming to it. In short, PageRank shows whether a site is established.

Click the Cached link to find out
when Google last indexed a site

Figure 8.4 *A search result on Google almost always has a small link to the right of the domain name that says "cached." Clicking it tells you the last time Google visited your site. Sites with a high PageRank tend to get cached more frequently.*

But in the same way that a person can have had a long career in a given industry but not be trusted by her peers, a site can have a high PageRank but a low TrustRank. Any site in this situation has only superficial value.

Myth 7: Commenting on Blogs and Forums Is an Effective Link-Building Strategy

In 2004, it was a fabulous idea to comment frequently on high-TrustRank blogs and forums, discretely leaving your link at the end of your comment. As long as you wrote something intelligent, people figured that the link was just your usual way of signing off, and the links passed TrustRank. All was good. But then the spammers came in. From 2005 to this very day, there has been such a plethora of linking being done in the comment section of blogs and forums that a new category has been invented to describe it: *comment spam* (see Figure 8.5).

I will end any speculation that putting links in your comments works. Not only do most blogs mark all comments with a nofollow tag, which, as you may recall, blocks the passing of TrustRank, but Google very likely de-emphasizes comment links anyway because the system has been so abused. After all, put yourself in Google's shoes: Links are supposed to be editorial votes of confidence from one site to another. But comments are not within the editorial domain of the owner of a website; they are written by the very people hoping to receive the benefit of those links. So there is no reason, in Google's eyes, to consider those links a vessel of trust. In fact, they are not.

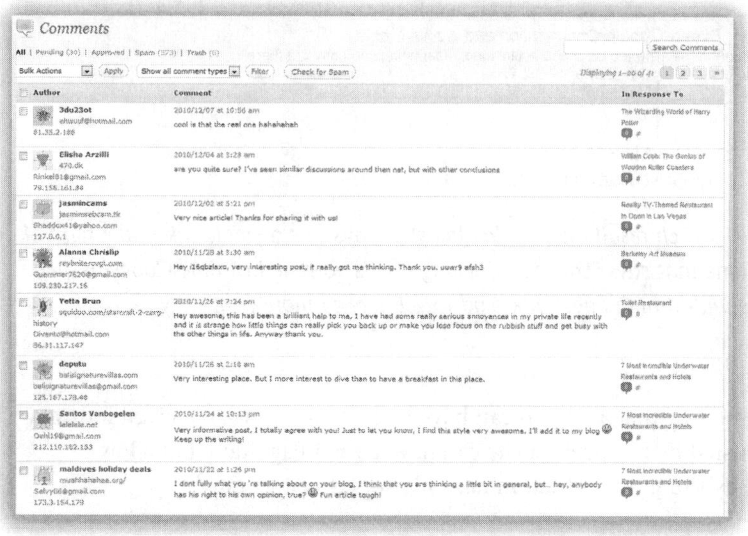

Figure 8.5 *A view of the moderation panel for one of my blogs. This page is 100% comment spam. All comments are meant to look real but are just a thinly veiled disguise for the spam they truly are.*

Myth 8: Submitting a New Site to Google Is an Essential Way to Get It Recognized

This myth, like many of the ones before it, has been around since the early days of search engines. It used to be that search engines asked webmasters to submit their websites so that there was a better chance the search engines would index those websites. Today, technology is much better than it used to be, and submission is no longer important. Getting a single link from another website typically gets your site indexed by Google in less than a week. The only time when submitting your site is a good idea is if you don't plan to get any links for your website, in which case Google might not know about your site until you make such a submission. But I have seen sites get indexed with no links countless times, so even in this situation, it's not a must to submit your site.

✉ *Note*

A related myth is that you must pay to get your site admitted to Google's index. This is hooey. I can't even imagine why people would think this myth is true unless they have been confused by the charlatans who charge for "submission to hundreds of search engines!" Putting aside the fact that there aren't hundreds of search engines that people actually *go* to, there certainly is no need to submit your site to them. Search engines follow links—that is how they discover the Web. And Google will find your site, whether you like it or not.

Separating Truth from Myth

So what is the larger lesson here? I think a lot of SEO myths rely on a rule-centric view of Google. If you hit a certain keyword density, you're golden. If you use precisely the right kind of markup code and XML site maps, your work is done. Engineers love rules such as these because rules govern the entire field of software design and because rules reduce the world to a set of comprehensible laws. Rules are comforting, easily explained, and easily achieved.

But rules are a pretty poor snapshot of reality. The real world simply doesn't abide by them, and the Web is a reflection of the real world. It isn't possible that all the most useful websites about sharks use the word *sharks* exactly 15% of the time, nor is it possible that the most useful websites about dental veneers are linked through images 20% of the time. In fact, very few things about great websites can be said to be universally true.

Google is well aware of the limitations of rules. That's why the company is always on the lookout for anything that appears suspiciously programmatic, homogenous, or precise. The actual Web is a messy and chaotic place, and sites that are truly valuable tend to have widely varying page factors and backlinks. There is no one "magic formula" for high rankings. Top-rated sites are all coded differently, written differently, and saddled with thousands of links beyond their control. Actual popularity doesn't look like a formula. In other words, it looks like randomness.

Your job as an optimizer is to simulate true organic behavior. This is why I say mix up your inbound links and the anchor text they contain. When a website magically acquires 100 links that are all phrased the same way, a bell goes off in Google headquarters that says "fake." When a keyword appears in precisely the same proportions on every page of your website, the bell rings again: "formula." Google's mission in life is to separate real value from artificial value, and one of the cornerstones of its strategy is to stamp out suspicious uniformity.

But now that we know that randomness is the only true reflection of reality, it's worth asking what randomness really looks like. Human beings are notoriously bad at identifying true randomness because of our tendency to find patterns in everything we see. If you flip a coin 1,000 times, the chances are that you will get a string of 15 heads in a row somewhere. Most people would view such a coincidence as exceedingly rare. But that string of heads is no more or less likely than any other combination of flips.

The same idea applies to the Web. Sometimes a good site *will* have a dozen links in a row that use the same exact words. Other times, they will have none. Sometimes a stellar article *will* use a keyword in every other sentence. Other times an author saves it for one big bang at the end. Statisticians describe such randomness using terms like *clumping* and *standard deviation*, but they are all just fancy ways of saying that anything is possible.

So what is the upshot for SEO? Go easy on the formulas. Do not aim for precise proportions, and do not try to control your entire link map. There is no one optimal set of proportions for achieving a top rank in Google. If there were, you can bet that optimizers would discover it and match it, and then the algorithm would have to change again. The only real commonality in all high-ranking sites is that they are older, have links from many different websites, and do not violate any of Google's rules. Everything I recommend in this book is meant to create that situation.

9

White Hat Versus Black Hat SEO

I want to pause for a moment now to orient you. By this point, you should know enough about Google optimization to be a force. And I hope that I have transmitted this information in an accessible way. But before going on to the more "advanced" chapters, which cover the corners and angles that go beyond the basic, I want you to know what school of thought all of this knowledge comes from.

I am what's known as a white hat SEO. Originating in the movies where the heroes wore white hats and the bad guys wore black, the terms *black hat* and *white hat* are used in the world of SEO to denote two separate optimization philosophies. White hat SEO is helping a website to rank at the top of the results using every advantage available *except* breaking the search engines' rules. It includes things like building keyword-optimized content, formatting your site's page titles in an SEO-friendly fashion, and building links organically by earning the attention of other webmasters. And it is the philosophy that underlies all of the advice in this book.

Although Google and the other engines do not like any form of SEO because it disturbs the objectivity of their indexes and competes with their advertising programs, they recognize white hat SEO and realize that it is a legitimate practice.

A black hat SEO, in contrast, uses hacker-like techniques to deceive search engines into perceiving that a site is more worthy of a high ranking than it actually is or to show human visitors different things than what is shown to the search engines.

These methods are in direct violation of the search engines' rules. Black hat SEO includes the creation of dummy sites and doorway pages, performing tricks such as cloaking and using hidden text—all described in this chapter. It is all about short-term gain; in fact, the expectation of getting banned from the results and needing to start over with a different identity is inherent in the black hat philosophy.

The Black Hat Way

So why do people become black hat SEOs? There are probably a few psychological reasons—a need to rebel, a desire to get attention by breaking rules, a thrill in out-witting The Man—but the most common reason is to make money quickly. Black hat SEOs are typically less successful in business than white hat SEOs because their vision is so shortsighted. Simply put, in business, playing just within the boundaries of the rules makes you more money. Play like a boy scout and you'll probably fail; break all the rules, and you'll also fail; but push the limits a bit while still staying within them, and you have a recipe for success.

Although it is getting increasingly difficult to pull off a really clever black hat trick, if you do succeed, you can get tons of traffic from Google for a few days or weeks of work. But the second Google's spam team notices what you're doing—and they will—your site will be permanently banned from Google. While black hat SEO tactics can deliver lots of traffic before they are stymied, they sacrifice long-term prof-itability, growth, respectability, and brand awareness.

In the following sections, I examine a few of the most common black hat tricks. I think it is important that you be aware of them so that if you do run into a com-pany that engages in any of these methods, you know to stay away.

Link Farms

Link farming is probably the most well-publicized black hat tactic, mostly because it has an intriguing name but also because it used to be very effective. Optimizers have been aware for years that links are the key to rankings, and it's easy enough to register a site, throw a design template up, and add links to it. So why not do that 100 times over, interlinking all 100 sites and creating a network of websites that all have 99 links pointing to them? Sure, the links on these brand new sites will not have much TrustRank, but surely they must have *some*, enough to send link juice to any other website you want to support. It's a logical thought, and one that many people have had. The only tiny problem with it is that Google specifically prohibits this behavior. It can get your websites crippled from passing TrustRank and most likely de-indexed.

Even the situation I just described is small scale for most link farms, though. Typically, there will be thousands of sites linking to each other, with 100+ links on each page. If you unknowingly pay an "SEO company" for links and receive this service, you will probably have to end up submitting your site for re-inclusion in Google's index—one of the most common reasons for doing so is that you unwittingly fell prey to a black hat SEO company (see Figure 9.1).

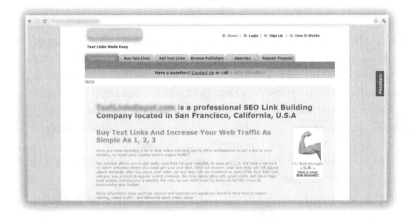

Figure 9.1 *A typical link-farm website. Notice how they call themselves "a professional SEO link building company" and mention their location so that visitors will believe they're a legitimate business.*

You can usually tell a black hat SEO company—the type that would employ link farms—from a white hat one by its website. If the website looks spammy, with a long page that keeps going on about "#1 rankings" and "thousands of links," it's probably best to steer clear. Also, if there is no phone number, take a pass. If there *is* a phone number, call and ask them to show you an example of a site that links to their clients. If what you see is a random-looking page with a separate area off to the side that has links to insurance sites, gaming sites, medical sites, and other shady categories, run far, far away.

Doorway Pages

Doorway pages are web pages that send visitors to websites they didn't click: "I won a free teddy bear? Cool! Wait, how did I end up on this page that's trying to sell me a credit report?" Doorway pages are often optimized for a high-traffic keyword phrase and, when clicked, show the relevant page for a second and then hastily redirect the visitor to a page that has nothing to do with that keyword. You may or may not have come across one recently, as Google has gotten very good with algorithmically blasting sites that contain doorway pages into Google purgatory. The practice of setting up doorways was so common years ago that Google specifically warns against them in its Webmaster Guidelines.

Cloaking

Cloaking is another black hat trick that involves using pages that nobody is ever intended to see. But unlike doorway pages, cloaked pages don't even appear for an instant. They are designed specifically to be visible to search engines and completely hidden from human beings. Thus the name: That cloak is of the invisible variety.

The advantage of showing one page to the search engines and another to human beings is that you can draw people in based on a particular subject and then show them a page they never would have clicked if they knew what the page was truly about. This sometimes leads to sales. An example of where cloaking turns insidious is where the technique lets black hat optimizers insert scam offers into innocent-looking pages on popular topics. One could be looking up some popular news topic, maybe the discovery of a comet or asteroid, and suddenly the site you were hoping to get information from tells you that your computer is infected with a virus and you need to buy a special antivirus program for $70 (see Figure 9.2). Most people realize this is a scam, but some of the less Internet-savvy among us might truly believe they have a virus and need the $70 program.

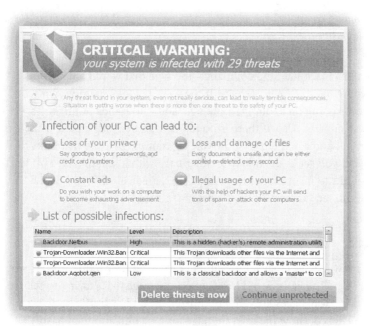

Figure 9.2 *A common scam of the late 2000s, the "fake virus" works by cloaking an innocent-looking page—the kind of page you might stumble upon while doing research—and then flashes a window like this one, warning you that your computer has been infected and offering to sell you a "solution."*

Google despises cloaking for the same reason it despises doorway pages: These tricks break its users' trust in the search results. Relevance and trustworthiness are the two greatest assets Google possesses. If you use any tricks that could undermine either one, your site is doomed to incur the wrath of the search behemoth—and, in many cases, the law.

Hidden Content

So now we have discussed pages that disappear in an instant and pages that never appear at all. Other black hatters employ a different trick: pulling a disappearing act with the content *on* their pages.

Hidden text in its simplest form is making text on the page the same color as the page's background (see Figure 9.3). To human beings, the text is completely camouflaged unless they know where to look for it. But to search engines, the content is readable and apparent. Some more advanced versions of this trick involve hiding text behind images and other media, or covering it with a foreground effect that renders it invisible without changing the background at all.

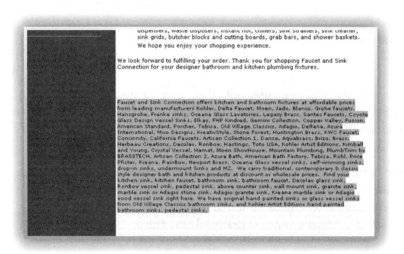

Figure 9.3 *Believe it or not, this page of spam is actually the "thank you" page of a sink website that customers see after placing an order. This site is attempting to attract search engine traffic by writing keywords all over the page. Below the gray paragraph are more keywords, but they are almost the same color as the background. This site was banned by Google for hidden text and keyword stuffing.*

Hidden text is an amateur's trick and sites that use this tactic never last long. All of the known ways to hide text are easy marks for Google's spam team.

Spam

The oldest and most common black hat practice is spam. Spam in the world of SEO refers to the creation of pages that have no value other than to attract search engine traffic and make money from scams or ads (see Figure 9.4). These pages are not hidden, or cloaked, or specifically designed to redirect the user somewhere else. Spam pages are, quite simply, useless pages littered with ads and links.

Figure 9.4 *A typical spam page. This type of spam is known as a "splog," or spam blog.*

Why does spam persist at all? Because, sadly, there is money to be made. Spam pages might attract only a sliver of traffic, but many are created in huge numbers by scripts without any human intervention, and they can throw off thousands of dollars or more for their unethical purveyors.

Google detests spam pages and can see them coming a mile away. The search giant treats them like the law treats criminals. So if you are thinking of creating lots of websites automatically and monetizing search engine traffic with ads, know that many minds have tried before you, and nearly all have failed.

Page Hijacks

The final black hat trick, page hijacking, is fairly sophisticated. A page hijack involves reproducing a popular website in an attempt to get Google to show some of the copycat site's pages in its search results rather than the original site's pages. When searchers click the links inside the copycat site, they are brought to a competitor's website or a spam page.

You won't find many page hijacks on Google nowadays, but as recently as 2006 a number of them were floating about. They are a clever trick, one that has cost certain popular websites a substantial amount of money in lost business because their customers were deceived. It can also cause reputational damage to the original website if the copycat website directs its visitors to a spam page.

As you might suspect, page hijacks are punished by instant banishment. Just like with every other black hat trick in this chapter, hijacking is the sort of gimmick that works for a short time and then quickly results in consequences far worse than low rankings: a bad trade-off for anyone looking to grow his or her business over the long term.

The True Difference Between White Hat SEO and Black Hat SEO

Some people like to say that white hat SEO and black hat SEO are actually pretty similar or that there is more of a sliding scale than a bright line between them. After all, both are ways to elevate a site's search ranking, possibly through artificial means. Aren't we just quibbling about how artificial we are willing to get?

I don't think so. White hat SEO is not about tricking Google, it is about *understanding* Google. Think of it as excelling at a sport: First you learn the rules, and then you figure out where you can acquire the maximum advantage. Football players don't spend all their time trying to hack into the scoreboard, for instance, or blind the ref. They don't subvert the game; they play it—by developing screen passes, gadget plays, and anything else they can think of. And if they do their jobs right and play by the rules, they can avoid the penalty flag.

We know what Google actually likes: links, page titles, aged domains, and keyword-rich URLs. White hat SEO is about capitalizing on these things successfully while never violating Google's Webmaster Guidelines. The results you can achieve through white hat SEO also help to reinforce Google's brand, ensuring that relevance and trust remain the only real arbiters of search rank.

Black hat SEO is designed to take the money and run, and its successes are accomplished through active deception. Google loathes these tricks because they attack the very core of what makes Google valuable—the trust it has amassed over many years of business.

Obviously, I don't recommend any black hat tactics. But now that you know what the most common ones look like, you can keep yourself safe from them. I also believe they can be instructive as a contrast to what actually creates successful companies. The thinking behind black hat SEO endeavors is defeatist. Short-term gain followed by needing to start from scratch is a cowardly approach to business. I say, jump in the game and do it right and build something that will keep growing in value in the future. Not to mention the fact that you only get one reputation in life and because of the preservative nature of the Internet, your sins can stick around a long time. Sure, you are probably so good at SEO by this point that you can just push the bad results back a few pages by optimizing dozens of good results. But that's a lot of work, and you're so busy as it is....

Just remember to play smart.

10

Optimizing for Yahoo! and Bing

Google commands a 65% share of the search market and doesn't seem to be slipping. That means that the rest of the pie is divided up by Yahoo!, Bing, and a smattering of smaller search engines. Although I don't know many people who use Yahoo! and Bing regularly, combined they apparently do make up about 28% of the search market, and so it is worth spending a bit of time understanding what makes them happy. My general rule has been "Optimize for Google first, and throw a few things in place for the other search engines."

Yahoo! Introduction

Say what you will about Yahoo!; it's a survivor. As of this printing, the brand represents one of the only remaining companies from the Internet's early portal days, when dialup access usually came with a customized "front door," or portal, to the Internet (see Figure 10.1). Yahoo! has evolved considerably over time, outlasting other creaky contemporaries such as Excite and Netscape that were slow to adapt. Yahoo! still tries to guide its users through the Web, giving people a home page to find news and content in which they are interested. But the company now also focuses on its search business because that is where they make much of their money, via advertising.

The history of search earned a new milestone in the summer of 2009 when Yahoo! announced that, after years of tweaking and refining its algorithm, it had decided to scrap it altogether and use Microsoft's Bing search engine to power its searches instead. The deal effectively combined the second- and third-place search engines into one, creating a potentially formidable foe to battle against Google. In reality, it has simply increased Bing's market share and not threatened Google in any significant way.

Figure 10.1   *The Yahoo! home page in 1998 during Yahoo!'s heyday.*

Yahoo! has been in decline for some time now and will probably be merged into another company soon. However, Yahoo! search will not go away for a while because so many users, especially older users, still associate the brand name with a place to start their Internet searches.

The Advent of Bing

Where did Bing come from, anyway? For most people, the rise of Bing occurred pretty quickly. First you saw an advertisement for it on one of your favorite websites. Then you read a news story about the $100 million advertising campaign that paid for the aforementioned advertisement campaign. Then you began to see it popping up in random places such as toolbars, maps, and travel sites. This was Microsoft's big attempt to grab a piece of the search pie. And Microsoft definitely got its share of publicity.

Bing grew out of Microsoft's long-held frustration with its stagnant share of online search. After more than 10 years of failing to compete with Google in products such as MSN Search and Windows Live search, Microsoft announced a massive code and interface overhaul, and a new name, in June 2009.

Bing was the result of that effort: a so-called decision engine that boasts interesting new tools, cutting-edge integration with travel information providers, and lots of other goodies. By most standards, Bing has been a success for Microsoft, capturing an additional 2% of search share in its first year, mostly at Yahoo!'s expense. It has also gotten plenty of attention in the media for its eye-catching photo-rich home page and innovative features. Even Google appears to have recognized that Bing has gotten a few things right, "borrowing" from its interface and design, and rather obviously adopting some of its features. Google fans remember the day in June 2010 when Google allowed users to upload their own Bing-like backgrounds to its famously simple home page.

Bing's taking over Yahoo! search is good news for the world of SEO because it means less confusion and fewer conflicting instructions. After all, it wasn't long ago that thorough webmasters had to optimize for three search engines in addition to, perhaps, Ask.com. Today, you're wasting your time if you optimize for any search engine besides Google and Bing.

How Optimizing for Bing Differs from Optimizing for Google

If Google's great innovation was organizing the Web around editorial votes, or links, Yahoo! went in the opposite direction for many years: analyzing the websites themselves and returning search results based around on-page factors. Today, Yahoo! is powered by Bing, and so it puts much more faith in links than it used to. However, Bing's technology holds onto this page-based legacy in some important ways. Most optimizers appreciate the fact that on-page factors matter to Bing because it makes optimization easier. Google's system of needing to essentially ask for other websites' votes is much more difficult than just following best practices when building your site. Exactly what those best practices are is a subject of ongoing debate, but a few basics are beyond controversy. Figure 10.2 shows a side-by-side comparison of Google and Bing.

Keywords in Your Content

The biggest difference between Bing and Google is their respective emphasis on keywords within the content of the site. I have already discussed the main ways that keywords matter to Google—namely when they appear in anchor text, the meta page title, and the URL. But Google does not care very much about keywords in the content of your site. That's why, when optimizing for Google, most people just write their keywords whenever they come up naturally in the site's content. Aiming for a particular "density" of keywords in your overall word count is a relic of the past and can actually have negative effects with Google.

Bing is much more receptive to keywords written within the text of your pages. Many webmasters report great strides in their Yahoo!/Bing rankings just by using keywords more often (see Figure 10.3). This isn't to say that you want to sacrifice syntax or intelligibility, of course; spam is spam, and every search engine knows it when it sees it. But you might see a bump in your ranking just by leaning a bit more heavily on the keywords you are optimizing for. Playing around with these keywords for maximum effect in this area is a must, especially because Bing is constantly refining its keyword detector. Someday, keywords inside content may matter less than they do. But for now, sprinkle liberally. First-page rankings may blossom.

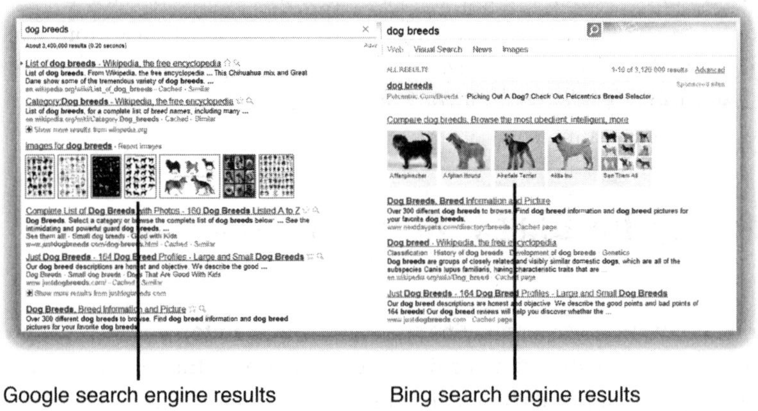

Google search engine results   Bing search engine results

Figure 10.2 *A side-by-side comparison of Google and Bing. The two search engines have different algorithms, and hence the search experience is fairly dissimilar.*

Meta Page Titles

Another area that Bing seems to care a lot about is the meta page title. You already understand the importance of this bit of code to Google, and it matters at least as much to Bing. Run a search for any popular term on Yahoo! or Bing, and you will notice that most of the first page results will use that exact term in their meta page titles. Google, in contrast, tries to return results whose meta page titles have the same words that the user searched for but not necessarily in the same order. So if you search for *best brownie recipe*, Google doesn't differentiate too much between web pages whose meta page titles are "The Best Darn Brownie Recipe" and "Mom's Recipe for the Best Brownie Ever" even though neither of those titles contains the exact phrase *best brownie recipe*. Bing, on the other hand, is more likely to rank a web page at the top if it has that exact phrase in its meta page title (see Figure 10.4).

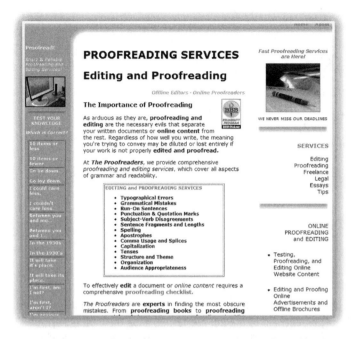

Figure 10.3 *A page that has keywords sprinkled throughout its content. This page ranks excellently on Bing for its main keywords.*

Meta Description Tags

Meta description tags are a factor about which Bing cares a lot more than Google. You learned about those back in Chapter 7, "Tracking Your Progress with Search Operators." Meta descriptions are—like meta page titles—text that is written into the code of every web page. They then become the two lines of text that show up underneath the blue underlined heading of every search result (see Figure 10.5). Unlike meta page titles, though, they usually don't show up anywhere on the web page or browser after you've clicked the search result. They exist merely to improve the experience of using the search engine.

Google cares about meta descriptions a small amount. Bing cares about them a good amount more, specifically looking for keywords in the meta description that also appear in the meta page title and on the page itself. That trio of keyword placements is a killer combo in Bing's eyes.

Figure 10.4 *Bing attempts to find sites whose meta page titles match what the user is searching for as closely as possible. All of the top five results have the inputted search designer jeans in their meta page titles. (The fourth result contains the phrase but the heading is truncated by Bing.)*

The meta description tag

Figure 10.5 *The meta description tag, a part of every web page's coding, appears in search engines as the line or two of text underneath the blue heading of each search result.*

So when you are optimizing for Bing, make sure your page's meta description includes your keyword at least once and that the same keyword appears in your meta page title. For instance, if your site sells scuba gear and your keyword is *caribbean scuba gear*, a good meta page title and meta description is this:

Top Caribbean Scuba Gear I Snorkels, Masks, Tanks & Cameras
Elite scuba gear for Caribbean divers at any level

Headings

Another important on-page factor to Bing is headings. Headings are the text at the top of a page, usually in larger letters, announcing the title or subject of the page. They're sort of like a meta page title except they're in the actual content of the page, front and center to visitors. Headings used to provide one of the bases of the early search engines' algorithms, but as soon as people started manipulating headings so that more traffic would come to their websites from search engines, headings became de-emphasized. Google, for instance, gives headings almost no weight in its algorithm. Bing must not have gotten that memo, though, because it still factors headings into its algorithm quite a bit.

Because most webmasters understand the importance of writing headings with real people in mind, optimizing your headings for Bing is a sensitive issue. You have to be one of those people who excelled at high school English assignments where you had to use vocabulary words in a sentence. *I walked to school surreptitiously today.* Remember that? Those are the types of skills needed for sewing keywords into headings naturally (well, better ones than that).

For example, if my keyword were *eco-friendly cleaning* and I were looking to write a page that is well optimized for Bing, I'd make a page with the following heading:

How Eco-Friendly Cleaning Can Tidy Up Your Home and Your Planet

My keyword sounds natural in that heading, making it good for both human beings *and* the Bing search engine. When Bing's spiders see that you have used the same term in both the heading of your page and the text of your page, it might conclude that your site specializes in whatever that keyword is. If this sounds simplistic, it is; so enjoy it. Bing will probably eliminate easy-to-manipulate on-page factors like this one in time.

Alt Tags

Alt tags are nothing more than little text descriptions of the images on your site. They are a required part of the code because as smart as the search engines are, they are not yet smart enough to look at a picture and identify precisely what it is. If you have ever seen a web page load slowly, you might have noticed a descriptive phrase sitting in the empty box that the picture soon occupies. That's an alt tag.

Bing shows images in its regular search results as well as, of course, its image search, and relies heavily on the alt tag in its algorithm. Google does the same and also puts a strong emphasis on alt tags. For that reason, I highly recommend that you properly describe all of your images. Searchers click pictures way more than most people realize, and having lots of properly labeled images can bring a ton of traffic to your site.

Although I encourage you to use keywords in your alt tags, do not go overboard or describe a picture totally inaccurately to attract more traffic. Indeed, it is tough for search engines to know whether your label is accurate—there is nothing to stop you from posting a picture of a scientific calculator and labeling it as "Jessica Alba"—but manipulating the system only annoys users and will be identifiable soon anyway, as image recognition software is already pretty advanced.

Outbound Links

Outbound links are the opposite of inbound links, or backlinks. Instead of pointing toward your own site, outbound links point *out* of your site toward other websites. The philosophy behind using outbound linking as a tool for SEO is simple: Acknowledging other authoritative sites is considered good Internet behavior and is the sign of a quality site. Whereas this philosophy is not held by Google in the least, Bing does abide by it.

The practice of liberally linking to other websites is not exactly a crowd favorite among webmasters, who generally want to hold on to visitors at all costs. But many of the same webmasters have found that a few well-targeted links to other sources can help demonstrate mastery of a subject. Also, the Web is very much an open place to explore, and so being too protective of visitors is not a winning strategy. Linking to authoritative sources will not cause a visitor to be lost for life if your site is providing something of genuine value.

Speaking of authoritative sites, outbound linking comports best with Bing's algorithm only if you direct your visitors to established and trusted sites such as news organizations and universities. And if you make the anchor text for that link one of your own keywords, Bing likes that, too; it further binds the keyword with your perceived area of expertise. In other words, this is another chance to use your keywords to improve your rank: Link out to well-known sites, and some of that reflected starlight should improve your site's rankings.

Site Structure

The final on-page factor that matters to Bing is site structure, or the layout of your pages and the way they are interlinked. This principle is common to all search engines including Google, and if you think about it, how could it not be? A site that is easily crawlable by search engines is usually easily navigated by people as well, and is therefore a good website to present to users in a search. Both Bing and Google favor clean, easy-to-navigate architecture, fast-loading pages, and easy-to-follow links.

What makes for clean site architecture? Think of it the same way you would when teaching a child how the natural world is organized. You start with the highest-level categories: the plant and animal kingdoms. Then you get more specific, going down to phylum, classes, and so on. (I'll stop the taxonomy lesson now because I don't really remember anything past that.) This kind of hierarchical structure is the same thing that web designers make when they create product pages. Bing likes sites that get increasingly specific as you link further into the website. Walking your visitors from category to subcategory to item is also a great way to ensure that all your product pages are focused on one thing at a time, which is a natural form of optimization that search engines love.

Links

If I were to summarize the entire chapter up until this point, I would simply say that Bing cares a lot more about what's on your site than Google does. But that doesn't mean it ignores what the rest of the Web thinks about your website. Bing actually uses an equation that works like Google's TrustRank system to determine which sites have earned the credibility of other webmasters. In fact, links are the most important factor in Bing's algorithm, too, although by not nearly as wide a margin as in Google's.

With that in mind, all the advice that you have read about linking throughout this book applies just as well to Bing. Whether your goal is to optimize for both search engines or just for Google, you have to focus on collecting highly trusted links from good sources—blogs, news outlets, social networking sites, and other popular websites. The many ways to acquire links are covered in Chapter 3, "How to Reel in Links."

Domain Age

A final element of SEO that is important to Bing is age. We know by now how important age is to Google, and Bing feels even more strongly about it. Of all the factors that affect a site's ranking, only links and age cannot be easily controlled by the webmaster, which is why they are so essential to the algorithm.

As with Google, there is no substitute for an old website, and the only way to acquire the credibility that comes with age is to buy an old website, preferably one with lots of inbound links.

A Word About Demographics

One of the biggest differences among Google, Yahoo!, and Bing has nothing to do with search at all. It is the crowd of people that frequents each search engine, which has a big impact on the type of visitors your site receives from appearing high in the search results. The people who use Bing are different from the people who use Google, and those people are different from Yahoo! users. Each group has unique habits and tendencies, and getting 100 visitors from Yahoo! is not identical to getting 100 visitors from Google.

Yahoo! is by far the oldest search engine of the big three, and as you might expect, its users tend to skew older as well. Many Yahoo! users have Yahoo.com set as their default home page, and have had for many years. These are not your typical Web-savvy surfers. They navigate the Web from their favorite portal and aren't the type to try and find the latest, coolest Web trends.

That is a demographic if I have ever seen one. Yahoo! users can be highly valuable to business owners. Because they are not as skeptical about online sales tactics, they are more likely to "bite" on a sales pitch or online ad. Also, Yahoo! users tend to spend more money on average than Google users—a byproduct of their more established place in life and the fact that younger searchers typically demand cut-throat comparison shopping and free services.

Bing is similar to Yahoo! in one respect and completely opposite in another. As with Yahoo!, the vast majority of Bing users run their searches from an old, established portal: MSN.com. MSN is typically the default home page on Microsoft's Internet Explorer, the most widely used browser. Most people who use Bing through their MSN home pages might not be aware of what is powering their searches or how to find other options. In this sense, they are similar to Yahoo! users in their online habits and are valuable visitors for the same reasons.

But Bing is unique in that it has attracted a completely different population, as well. The search engine was launched to great acclaim on tech blogs and media outlets, and as a result it has attracted a high number of *unusually savvy* surfers. Bing's innovations to the standard, colorless search interface appeals to Internet sophisticates and the general population alike, and its status as an upstart challenger attracts people who root for the (ironically, because it's Microsoft) underdog.

As a result, Bing is in the peculiar position of being represented among the very old and very young. And both of these populations are worth optimizing for: Older people tend to bring purchase power and trust, and younger people tend to bring advertising cachet and viral attention.

Bing even has the potential to challenge Google in the arena of brand name coolness, although it's certainly got a way to go. There is something satisfying about saying "Bing!" when getting something done. But it's not quite yet as much fun as saying "just Google it."

Pay per Click: Where Bing Shines

The demographic differences among Google, Yahoo!, and Bing are a big deal because they can lead to vastly different sales figures depending on which search engine your site's visitors are using. Google users tend to be more skeptical, whereas Yahoo! and Bing users tend to be more trusting. These are, no doubt, products of the different generations that the search engines represent.

These differences become especially interesting when we talk about pay-per-click (PPC) advertising. In Chapter 6, "Google AdWords as a Complement to SEO," I wrote about the many ways that Google AdWords can be an effective adjunct to your SEO efforts: It can help with choosing keywords and with collecting long tail searches, among other things. I only touched briefly on the demographic differences of the people who click AdWords ads.

Most people tend to ignore AdWords links unless they are so targeted as to be almost irresistible. So who is making Google their billions? Studies show that the people who click these ads tend to be disproportionately older and less current in the ways of the Web. Sound familiar? This is precisely the same population that is more likely to use whatever search portal came auto-loaded into their browsers: MSN and Yahoo! And so if you're going to take anything from this chapter, take this: Yahoo! and Bing boast a much higher click-through rate for search advertisements than Google. If you have a limited budget for a PPC campaign and your customers tend to be middle-aged or older, make your investment in these smaller, higher-producing search engines.

Yahoo! Distinctions

Up until now, I have been talking about Yahoo! and Bing as a collective. After all, for organic search, that is what they have become. However, both of these companies still retain their own individual features. In this final part of the chapter, I highlight a few of the things that make each search engine unique and how understanding those things can help your SEO efforts.

Yahoo! Site Explorer

The most popular Yahoo!-specific feature is undoubtedly its Site Explorer (see Figure 10.6). You've seen the linkdomain: feature of the Site Explorer throughout this book. Site Explorer encompasses other useful tools, as well, though. Most of them are accessible when you sign in to Site Explorer with a username and password and verify that a particular website belongs to you.

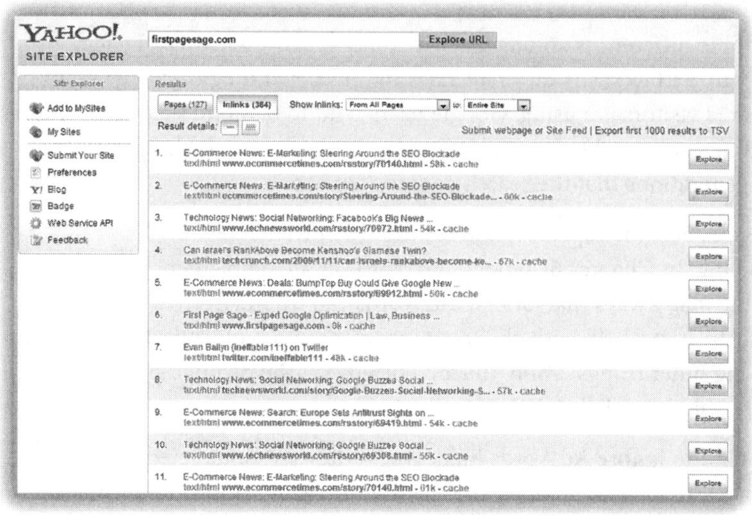

Figure 10.6 *Yahoo! Site Explorer, a useful dashboard of tools. This specific page came from going to Yahoo.com and typing in linkdomain: www.firstpagesage.com.*

After you have verified a site, you can do a number of things, some more important than others:

- **Include sitemaps**—One often overlooked feature is the ability to submit a sitemap (a basic piece of housekeeping that can save you the trouble of waiting for every page to get spidered on your site). Doing this can also help you identify problems with your site structure. If Yahoo! is not seeing a group of pages, this often means that they are not linked to in a direct, clean manner. Google lets webmasters do the same thing through its Webmaster Tools interface, but it is worth submitting your information to Yahoo! as well to make sure Yahoo! indexes your site properly.

- **Optimize slow-loading pages**—Yahoo! Site Explorer also points out areas in your site that are overly heavy code-wise or slow to load. Search engines favor clean code, especially when that code lets a visitor see the content of the site as quickly as possible. This often requires altering things that your web programmer or designer should be able to address relatively easily. Identifying site architecture issues is another area that Google's Webmaster Tools also covers.

- **Examine dynamic URLs**—Finally, Site Explorer examines something called dynamic URLs, helping webmasters clean up their code even further, removing certain content that slows down websites. This tool was included to make the Web easier to use and make Yahoo! indexing capabilities better. It is worth comparing the results of Yahoo! Site Explorer with Google's Webmaster Tools because both can make your site more search engine friendly.

The Yahoo! Directory

The Yahoo! directory has been around practically since the dawn of the Web (see Figure 10.7). It used to be the way people found information on the Internet before search engines were popular. When the Web became too big to curate in this way, search became the only option.

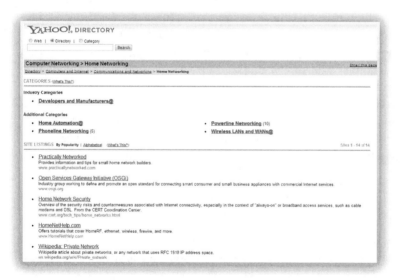

Figure 10.7   *The Yahoo! directory: one of the oldest and most Google-trusted directories on the Web and a great source of links.*

What does this have to do with SEO? Simply put, the Yahoo! directory is one of the oldest directories on the Web, and your site's inclusion in it amounts to one awesome link. At a cost of $299 a year, it is not worth it for everyone, but the price is actually reasonable compared to what most other high TrustRank links go for. The only thing that stops me from purchasing Yahoo! directory links for all my companies is the smidge of a suspicion that Google could have crippled listings on the Yahoo! directory, suspecting that these listings do not constitute genuinely earned links. After all, Yahoo! basically sells links for money in the same way as any link broker, and we know how Google feels about link brokers.

But because it definitely can't *hurt* your site to have a link in the Yahoo! directory, it might be an interesting way to try gaining a bunch more TrustRank.

Bing's Distinctions

Bing is, of course, the new kid on the block, but it has its share of interesting features. The most important is its unique list of search operators.

Search Operators

Bing's most talked-about search operator is probably linkfromdomain:, which generates a list of every site that a particular website links out to. It's basically an outbound link viewer. This is useful as a way of seeing the kind of sites that certain websites link to. For instance, I am always curious as to whether certain .edu sites—the sites of universities—link to regular sites that are not part of the academic world. If I can find a particular page on an .edu that gives out links for any reason at all, I want to jump on that opportunity. And Bing is the only search engine that lets me inspect all of a given website's outbound links. More generally, linkfromdomain: is a great way to analyze a website's linking philosophy. Remember how I told you at the beginning of this book to look for sites that usually do not sell links because they are more likely to be trusted by Google? Linkfromdomain: is a great way to analyze those potential candidates in your quest for links.

Bing also lets you search for sites that contain a certain type of file, such as a Word document or a PDF. This operator is called contains:, and you just pair it with the file suffix you're looking for (see Figure 10.8).

The contains: operator is handy for finding specific documents, of course, but it's also a good way to see what your competitors are doing media-wise. After all, SEO in its full bloom is about more than just gaining visitors. It's about improving your visitors' experience so that they eventually convert into paying customers. Using this search operator can help you see how many sites in your niche are posting videos, for example, or publishing e-books. The contains: operator also lets you find and download material quickly, which can be a good way to perform research quickly.

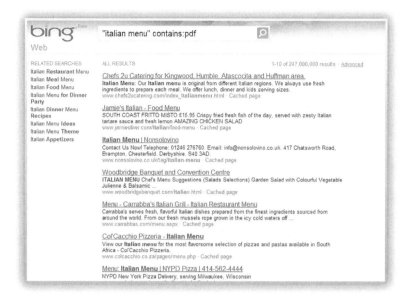

Figure 10.8 *Bing's contains: search operator is a great way to discover documents and media embedded inside websites.*

Bing Webmaster Tools

Last but not least, Bing also offers a set of webmaster tools that are similar to Google's. If you are serious about optimizing for Bing, it is essential that you sign up for these tools. Just like Google, Bing Webmaster Tools let you dig deeply into the metrics of your site, analyzing your traffic in several ways and monitoring the success of your optimization efforts. You can even customize how you want your site indexed and which pages, if any, you want Bing not to acknowledge.

For more advanced management tools, Bing encourages the use of a basic download for these tools called Microsoft Silverlight—its answer to Adobe's Flash plug-in. Through Bing's Silverlight interface, you can analyze data that stretches back six months, giving you access to a trove of research and data on everything from visitor behavior to backlinks. Although not more interesting than Google Analytics, Bing's way of organizing information is worth looking at, if only for comparison.

In the long run, Bing's and Google's algorithms will probably grow together. Both are interested in the quality of user experience and relevance. More important, both are watching each other closely to see the other's newest innovations and user reactions to it. Google is undoubtedly the king of search—that's why I recommend focusing the vast majority of your efforts on it. However, there *is* something to the mild threat that Google perceives in Bing. Ultimately, it is good for us, the consumers, that Bing and Google compete because we are the beneficiaries of their battle to help find information more easily on the Internet.

11

Converting Your SEO Results into Paying Customers

By this point, you know how SEO works. If you were to stop reading right now, you would see significant improvements in your rankings and website traffic. But there is still one itty-bitty thing missing. (Don't you hate that?)

That itty-bitty thing is getting your visitors to *buy* your product or service. Without this last step, optimizing your website is but a pretty distraction.

At first glance, the concept of customer conversion might seem as if it falls outside the purview of SEO. When you think about it, however, all the same factors we use in SEO—building trust, using good site structure, employing careful language to make a point—apply just as well to conversion. In fact, I like to think of conversion as another kind of optimization: human being optimization.

Optimizing for human beings is not nearly as mysterious as it sounds. In fact, I have found that four simple elements can get you to a healthy place. Conveniently, they all start with the letter *D*:

- Design
- Differentiation
- Data
- Deals

Design

Every day, it seems, a new study comes out analyzing people's behavior on the Web. Companies underwrite these studies because they are constantly trying to answer a simple question: What makes people trust one site and flee another? What exactly goes through our minds when we arrive at a site?

The first answer is, undoubtedly, design. Most people do not consciously notice web design, but there is no question that it plays an enormous role in gaining or losing a visitor's trust. Websites are like commercial buildings: If you walk into one and feel surrounded by symmetry, calm, and beauty, you feel comfortable transacting with the business. If you walk into a building and there's a sign for the business written on oak tag with magic markers scotch-taped to the wall, you feel a lot less comfortable spending money there. Websites that look spammy or amateurish simply turn visitors off. People turn away from them not just because they aren't pretty, but because poorly designed sites imply that the business behind them is inexperienced or unprofessional.

Design is less important than functionality for giants such as Amazon and Netflix, mostly because their reputations precede them. Most people know that they can safely use these sites. But smaller companies and new businesses do not enjoy this kind of built-in trust, and as a result, they often suffer from a high bounce rate, meaning many visitors leave their websites within a few seconds of arriving.

As far as we have come from the days of being afraid to make a purchase on the Internet, there is still a leap of faith involved in buying something without a human being present.

Put yourself in the shoes of a customer for a second. No matter how many adjectives a website uses to describe its credibility, when you send your 16-digit credit card number, you are placing your trust in the hands of a stranger. If that stranger is a celebrity like Apple.com, you probably have confidence enough. But if that stranger is a newcomer, you might want to seek a second opinion first. The great fear is not just that your money will vanish into the void; it's that you could lose your identity along with it.

Aesthetic

The aesthetic, or look, of a site is the first thing visitors notice. Their reaction to it is an important factor in whether they remain on the site or flee. It's sort of like going on a blind date. If that initial impression is positive, you might just stay for awhile. But if your date is a bomb, you're out of there as soon as the first opportunity arises.

Consider the two home pages shown in Figures 11.1 and 11.2. Both are from websites in the same industry, and both sell essentially the same service: restoration of your home after a flood or fire. Which site inspires greater confidence?

Figure 11.1 *The home page for Restoration SOS, a disaster restoration business.*

Figure 11.2 *The home page for RestorePro, another disaster restoration business.*

Now, I admit that there is an economic advantage acting here: RestorationSOS is a major corporation with offices nationwide, and RestorePro is a small, New Jersey company serving Princeton and Trenton. But what better way to underscore the power of design? You probably found the RestorationSOS page cleaner and easier to navigate, and the RestorePro site a bit confusing and homegrown looking. (In reality, RestorePro is a professional company, but its design doesn't communicate that.) I believe that the majority of visitors to both sites would choose RestorationSOS over RestorePro, regardless of name recognition, solely on the basis of design.

This chapter is not a primer on web design (I'll leave that to the experts), but it is worth noting a few things that stand out:

- The RestorationSOS site makes it easy to understand exactly what the company does and how to find it. The RestorePro site makes it more challenging to figure this out.

- The RestorationSOS site uses a confident picture of a professional seemingly preparing for the task at hand. The RestorePro site has no photographs other than the use of water drops as a background on its top banner.

- The RestorationSOS site has a cogent design aesthetic with clear edges and defined layout. The RestorePro site's color choices are all over the place, with blue, white, gray, fire engine red, and burgundy fonts.

Overall, RestorePro website's design elements are disconnected:

- The menu bar floats out beyond the edges of the header and the body of the page.

- The phone number gets lost in a sea of red.

- There is a misuse and overuse of formatting, including bolding and italics for the company name and paragraphs that are completely bolded.

- The website could use a good copywriter.

These little details, when looked at as a whole, undermine RestorePro's credibility. It's remarkable to think that if the company simply had a well-designed website, its client list might be twice as large. And an aesthetically pleasing website doesn't have to cost a lot more than a poorly designed website. But if it does, trust me when I say that the money is well spent. The simple fact is that when you look like a big player in an industry, people treat you like one. And that means sales.

Layout

Before we go any further with these examples, I want you to consider the design of fast food advertisements. Picture a billboard that features a giant juicy hamburger. Could you imagine what it's like to eat that hamburger? You could! The science of food photography has become so sophisticated that advertisements are specifically designed to invite this kind of unconscious action in our minds. Our brain says, "If I had that burger, I would lift it here and bite it there." Without fail, the place on the burger where you could best picture your mouth chomping down is the main focus of the advertisement.

Web design works the exact same way: You want to invite an immediate action with your layout. Let's look again at those same two disaster restoration sites. Beyond the different appearances, you might have noticed there is an organizational difference, as well:

- The RestorationSOS site has a neat little form at the top, just begging to be filled out. The RestorePro site seems confused about where you should click or why.

- RestorationSOS walks its customers through their choices with clear tabular categories. RestorePro leaves users wondering what to do next: Do you call for a free estimate, fill out the contact form, or learn more about water damage?

Put another way, you know what to do when you get to RestorationSOS. You don't with RestorePro.

Structure

That brings me to structure. Just like layout, structure is a way of organizing information. If layout is way of describing just one page, structure is a way of describing how your entire site works. Websites are a little bit like machines—you press a button, and something happens. Most websites by now use a familiar layout; there are big sections across the top and, if needed, smaller categories down one side. Some clever designers have strayed from this formula to great success, but most people do not want to tinker with a formula that already works fine.

A good site structure can make a big difference. Web users are fickle and impatient people, and the last thing they want is to navigate a dizzying set of links within links before they can locate what they're looking for. A simple hierarchy, moving from vague to specific, will speed your visitors along toward that all-important inquiry or purchase without any friction.

Differentiation

After you have achieved a clean and organized design, there still remains the question of what you should put inside that design. What do you need to say to convince people to take that leap of faith with *your* company instead of another one?

Differentiation refers to all the things that make your business special, unique, and worthwhile. The Web has completely eliminated the old adage "location, location, location." Today, your site is exactly the same distance away as all your competitors': one click. As a result, your visitors are probably checking out the competition in another window while they are browsing your site. That means your site needs to quickly answer the question "Why choose us?"

Us Versus Them

Differentiation comes in many forms, but the classic version is the Us versus Them comparison. You do a little research on your competitors, and then think about what you offer. Are your products or services unique? Do you approach your business in a different way from the other guys?

Suppose you run a cleaning company. Questions to ask include the following:

- Do you only use organic, nontoxic cleaners?
- Does your staff speak perfect English?
- Do they wear booties or take off their shoes?
- Will they use the customer's own special cleaning supplies if asked?
- Do you provide post-holiday party cleanup?
- Are you fully bonded and insured?

In an online age where barriers to entry are often low, your point of differentiation can't simply be "because we're the best." You need reasons. And making those reasons easy to find on your website is essential. Consider the proofreading company's website shown in Figure 11.3.

Although this site's design is a bit basic, the differentiation factor is there. On the top right, the site states

WE NEVER MISS OUR DEADLINES

The word *never* implies a comparison, and the copy further emphasizes that the company's proofreaders are professionally trained, work in the United States, and speak English as their first language. The owners of the site probably made that statement to highlight their own strengths and cause visitors to distrust the competition. They probably found themselves repeating certain points on sales calls and decided to emphasize them. Placing these points right on the home page is a smart way to capture visitors who may be comparing multiple websites.

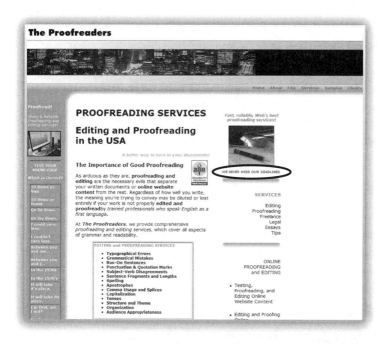

Figure 11.3 *A proofreading site that states its case confidently.*

Awards and Press

Of course, differentiation comes in many forms. One of the other big tricks in customer conversion is to mention awards you have won and press mentions you have received. The reasoning behind this method is the same as why people prefer organic SEO: We trust information when it comes from an outside and impartial source.

Awards come in many forms, and most can be beneficial to your business. Your company might have gotten recognized by some outlet or organization. Or it might have been cited as a favorite business or service provider in your local area. Better yet, it could have earned a spot on someone's "Best Of" list. Even if the most prestigious acknowledgment your company has received is becoming one of Bob and Jean-Anne's Favorite Websites (I made that up), you should consider putting it on your home page until something better comes along. Every little bit helps.

And what if you haven't received any awards yet? Well, then it's time to start lobbying. Look for bloggers in your industry, media outlets, critics, and columnists who compile award lists. Maybe they don't know about your business yet, or perhaps they will be flattered enough by the attention that they'll give your company a second look. Again, don't overlook the little guys. Any award is a good opportunity to show your customers that people prefer your company.

Press mentions are similarly useful but have the added advantage of binding your company to a well-known media outlet. Because of their value, a great deal of thought and strategy can go into earning them. You can try to get your own press using a site like HARO (helpareporter.com) and networking with bloggers and journalists on Twitter, or you can hire a publicist. If you don't have a publicist yet and can afford one, I highly recommend it.

After your company has found its way into newspapers, magazines, radio, blogs, or TV shows, you'll want to create a special section on your website to display your press. Of course, you should still display the best press on your home page. Customers who see the logos of local and national media outlets on a home page automatically assume that site has been vetted and approved by established arbiters of taste (see Figure 11.4).

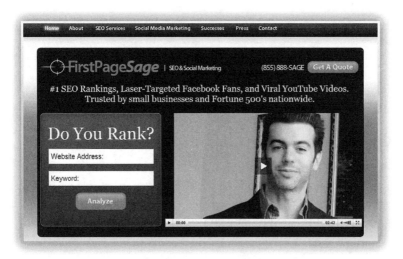

Figure 11.4 *My company is not shy about the press it has received, and yours shouldn't be either.*

Clients and Testimonials

Of course, not every endorsement comes with a famous name attached. You don't have to make the cover of *Time* to show that you are loved. Every message of support from someone outside your company is a vote of confidence in what you are selling, and quoting an ordinary customer can be more powerful than a press mention. The magic is in people being able to relate to the person who is quoted. If, for instance, I were thinking about hiring a web design firm, and I saw a testimonial on the firm's home page from the CEO of a technology company the same size as First Page Sage, it would make more of an impact on me than seeing the logo of a local newspaper.

Testimonials are especially important if your company is new. To go about getting them, start by contacting your most satisfied customers and asking their permission to quote them on your site. Some people might blush at the publicity, but others will appreciate it. A lot has to do with your delivery when asking. Saying "I would be honored to have you write a few words about your experience with our company" is a confident but humble way of proposing the idea. Remember to ask for testimonials from past or current customers who best represent the future customers you want to attract.

Social Media

A lot of these differentiating factors fall under the category of credibility. When you demonstrate that people like and respect your business, people view that as proof of legitimacy. Popularity is a self-fulfilling concept on the Web. Everybody loves an established member of the community.

Which brings me to the final way you can show that you are loved by others: social media. This is a topic big enough for its own book (*Outsmarting Facebook* anyone?), which is why I reserve most of the discussion for the next chapter. But I do want to point out a couple of simple ways you can use social networking sites to help differentiate your company:

- **Facebook**—Do I need to convince you of how massive it is? I won't even go into how, if it were its own country, it would have the third largest population in the world. Or the fact that some studies have suggested that Facebook is responsible for one-quarter of all the page views in the United States. No, I won't even go there. A good way to tap into that epic audience and prove that your company is recognized by others is to create a Facebook business page. By gaining at least a few hundred "likes," you will demonstrate that people are fond of your business and that you encourage an open dialogue with your customers. Once your community of "likers" is sizable, affix a link to your Facebook page to the home page of your website (see Figure 11.5). Doing so has become a standard good practice for businesses nowadays.

Link to Facebook, Twitter, LinkedIn
and more from your website

Figure 11.5   *A New Jersey doctor, Joel Fuhrman, M.D., links to his Facebook and Twitter pages from the home page of his website (top right).*

- **Twitter**—Twitter is a somewhat different animal, but we can simplify it by saying that it's a community of people who like to see what other people and businesses are doing. People express this interest by "following" your company's Twitter username, and you can send out short messages anytime telling people what your company is doing. This practice can lead to new business. And just like with Facebook, you should add a link to your Twitter account to your home page.

Data

We have now covered design and differentiation: building a clean, professional site that highlights your company's advantages. After you've accomplished these two goals, and visitors are regularly impressed by your company's aesthetic and credibility, they will now look for more information. This means providing your visitors with answers to the many questions streaming through their minds. What do you sell? How does it work? What does it cost? And who are the members of your team?

Simply put, give your customers everything they need to commit. Too many websites hide information behind unnecessary walls, such as making people request a quote. Unless your product is so customized that general information cannot reasonably be given, you should be up front with your potential customers.

Price

Price is by far the greatest area of sensitivity for business owners. So many websites are chock full of information but shy about listing prices. At some point in the past, it must have become common practice to withhold your prices so that you could collect more information or do the sale over the phone. That is the only way I can explain the trend of asking for a potential customer's contact info for them to ascertain your business's prices. In an age where competitors are just a click away, it just doesn't make sense to withhold the answer to a question everyone is asking. Rather than risk turning off a potential customer, give at least some idea of your company's prices.

When you announce your rates publicly, you send the message that your company stands by its products, believes in what it's worth, and is unafraid to compete in the open marketplace. You project confidence, transparency, and convenience, which are three things new customers love. In addition, you prevent yourself from having to take calls from people who can't afford your services.

Products

Clarity is also important when showcasing your products. Many sites boast enormous inventories but have no photographs or copy to support those claims. Others might include pictures, but they are grainy, small, and lacking explanation.

Consider this: When you walk into Sears to check out a new electric drill, you can weigh it in your hands, hold it up against other models, pantomime a home repair, and load multiple drill bits. The Web is a visual medium, so you must substitute for all that physical contact with pictures, diagrams, and words. Customers are much more comfortable buying something on the Web if they believe they have seen it from every angle. Good photography and videos can dramatically increase your conversion rate.

And don't forget the words. There is a reason the J. Peterman catalog was an American institution for so long despite the fact that it contained only watercolor illustrations of its products. Words can paint a picture, evoke the emotions you want, and answer countless technical questions about what you're selling. Words also demonstrate that you are paying attention to detail and that you care about the shopping experience on your site. Words can also help define your site for indexing and ranking. The moral: Don't think of your site as a computerized inventory machine. Think of it as a catalog, complete with glossy photos and plenty of professional copy. Your customers will reward you for it.

One final note about product information: There is one way the Web actually outshines physical stores, and that is *comparison*. Effective sites often have side-by-side tables that line up the features on electronics, spa packages, what have you. Customers who like comparison shopping—that is, most people—tend to return time and again to the one resource that puts everything in front them in a clear format. And from there it is a short trip to the Buy Now button.

Process

What if your business sells services instead of things? All the same rules apply, but they must be catered toward *process* rather than *products*. It is equally important to explain exactly what you do, how it works, why it works, and how long it takes. It doesn't matter if you are a dentist or a dry cleaner; people want to know what they're getting into.

One of the simplest ways to explain your process is to walk customers through everything step by step. Tell them a story. You could create pages for each step or simply show the process visually with a flowchart. If you do plastic surgery or web design, show before and after pictures. If you're a lawyer, describe every step of the process from initial consultation to conclusion. If you're a massage therapist, talk about what happens from the moment your customers walk through the door to the time they leave totally zonked out, water in hand.

Resources

Another good way to increase conversion rates on your site is by creating a Resources section. This section is devoted entirely to educating customers about topics related to your business. If you sell cars, consider writing some articles about how to buy a car. If you sell ant farms, write an article about the communal behavior of ants or how to extend the life of an ant community.

Sites that contain lots of useful information tend to be "stickier" than sites that do not, which means that people keep coming back. Adding expert-level information also enhances your site's prestige and respectability, showing your customers that you know this subject inside and out. Implicitly, you are saying, "I'm an expert, and I would never offer anything but the best products." Good resources are also an effective form of link bait, drawing attention from bloggers and other companies who want to share useful information with their audiences.

People

One final way to fill out your site's data is to create a page about your team. Let's go back to the Sears example for a second. In the physical world, you know exactly who is trying to sell you something. You can look that salesman in the eye, shake his hand, and decide whether you trust him. The Web is an anonymous place, however, and often it is not clear who is on the other end of that sale (if anyone).

Business owners are sometimes reluctant to add detailed bios to their sites if they are not eager to be in the spotlight. But everybody wants to attach a face to a purchase, especially online. My advice is to hire a photographer to take a professional headshot. Then, underneath that beautiful photo, tell your life story simply and talk about your passions a bit. Often when purchases are made, it is not just the product or service being sold; it is the people behind it.

Deals

And so we come to the final *D*: deals. By now, you should have a pretty good idea what goes through your visitors' heads when they arrive somewhere new. There is an initial snap judgment based on the look of the site (design), followed by a quick decision about whether to stay or go (differentiation), followed a bunch of questions that require answers (data). At this point, your visitors are actively looking for a reason to buy. Give them one.

Deals are a good way to make your products more competitive, attractive, and affordable. An intelligently crafted deal can also give your visitors a sense of urgency, encouraging them to buy now instead of later. Sales are some of the oldest tricks in all of marketing, but they have been around so long precisely because they work. There is something about the notion of a "special offer" that just taps into our natural instincts.

Sales and Promotions

The simplest kind of sale is a discount. If you charge $10 for a widget, you will sell more of them when you tell people it's marked down from $15. Everybody loves a bargain, and one of the surest ways to inspire immediate action is to create a special value, then put a ticking clock on that value. One-week deals, weekend deals, holiday deals—these "bargains" are everywhere online because they are so effective.

Bundling items is another time-tested way to get your customers to buy more than they otherwise might have. If you sell baby onesies, throw in a free one for every four they buy. If you run a book-of-the-month club, create an annual rate that is much cheaper than the month-to-month rate. Bundling products lets your customers buy more and save more simultaneously. Everybody wins.

Another promotion that works well on the Web is the "first time" offer, in which new customers have a limited-time opportunity to save substantially on their first purchase. Also in the "new customer deals" family is the concept of a referral program, in which you reward your customers for spreading the word to their friends. Because the Web works in such a viral way, you can greatly increase your reach and brand awareness just by giving customers an incentive to market your site for you.

Finally, you can invite guests to submit their email addresses for future correspondence with the company by *offering* something with that signup information. A lot of people offer guides or other types of resources that will give potential customers useful information within your area of expertise. You can also make a coupon or a discount code available with signup.

The goal of all promotions is to make your customers feel as if they are getting something, not giving something; so think carefully about what you would genuinely want if you were in their shoes.

An important point about sales and promotions is that different types are appropriate for different businesses. If you offer too many discounts on a medical website, for instance, you will seem desperate for business. But for a mobile phone site, all the discounts in the world will be appreciated. Professional services businesses and other companies selling more expensive products should feature free consultations, high-end handbooks, and other similarly fitting fare.

Point of Purchase

My final thought on conversion may be self-evident, but it's worth repeating: Nobody will buy anything if he or she can't figure out how to get it. For commerce sites, this means you want to create a big Buy Now or Add to Cart button on every product page. For services, it means offering an extremely simple way for people to book your services. If you take appointments, have your webmaster create a simple appointment form with a calendar that people can understand instantly (see Figure 11.6).

Figure 11.6 *The Midas front page appointment invite. Figuring out how to make an appointment couldn't be easier.*

A big part of moving customers closer to purchase is the so-called call to action, which is industry lingo for encouraging people to take an action (usually, completing a purchase) right now. Some of the most effective conversion tricks involve nothing more complicated than putting a call to action on every page. Nobody should ever have to click more than once to become a customer. So put a call to action on every page. It doesn't have to be big and gaudy, and you never know when your customers are ready to check out.

SEO is worth little without a website that is optimized for conversions. Put thought into your customers' psychology when they arrive on your website and make sure your site addresses their anxieties, questions, and expectations. Then, simply stand out of the way of them making a purchase.

Conversion optimization is work, but it's time and money well spent. Doubling your conversion rate is much more profitable than doubling your traffic because only conversion translates directly into revenue. Give your site the consideration it needs to thrive, and it will give you the economic reward you deserve.

12

The Intersection of Social Media and SEO

If marketing were a family, SEO would be the smart, hardworking daughter. Her parents would be very proud of her, and nobody would have any doubt of her growing up to be an independent, productive member of society. But she would have a hotter sister who always gets more attention than SEO for no reason other than her good looks. That sister's name would be social media.

As people interested in growing website traffic, it is important that we understand these two sisters for who they are. SEO is the one that, through time and understanding, will bring you the most traffic, most consistently. She is ultimately the better investment of time. But social media can do some surprising things for your business. SEO may work hard for you during the day, but social media can take you out at night, wink at the bouncer, and dance the night away with you. And happily, there is a way for SEO and social media to complement each other.

The main way that SEO and social media intersect is in the area of links. Social media sites have them, and SEO needs them. In this chapter, I reveal the ways that you can use social networks such as Facebook and Twitter to generate inbound links from popular, high-TrustRank websites—without even asking. These methods involve using carefully engineered social media campaigns (and a little bit of luck) to attract links from news sites, social bookmarking sites, and popular blogs.

Social media as an SEO tool basically works like this: Big websites like Nytimes.com, CNN.com, and Huffingtonpost.com are the ones that everyone seeks attention from but are largely controlled by an elite group of journalists. Social networks like Facebook, YouTube, and Twitter represent the masses. And while a single link or status update on one of these social networks has no significance, there is great power in numbers. If you post a link to a video you took of your dog doing a back flip, and it strikes a chord in the average person, she will share it with her friends, who will share it with their friends, and so on. The reach of a single output of content that is adopted by the social hoi polloi can be much greater than the reach of a mainstream media outlet. And if that content is popular enough with the common man, it will reach the elites as well. It's all about "going viral."

If you are the creator of a piece of content that goes viral, your website can get links rained upon it. This is why social media is a powerful complement in the world of SEO. In the future, SEO and social media will evolve together to incorporate our profiles, preferences, and relationships into search results. Imagine typing *gift shops* into Google and seeing a list of results based not just on your location, but also on your personal preferences and friends' recommendations. In short, imagine Google acting like someone who knows you, who can suggest things to you based on its knowledge of you as a human being. Sound far-fetched? Right now it does. But in a few years it won't be. In the next chapter, I give a lot more details on what the future of search will look like. In the meantime, however, let me show you how you can use social media sites right now to boost your website's ranking on Google.

Social Media Sites and the Flow of Information

As a business owner, you already know that exposure is the key to success. Traditionally, the most powerful ways of getting exposure have been advertisements, press, and word of mouth. Although these tools have always been the backbone of marketing, the rise of social media websites has opened up a whole new world of possibilities for online marketers. If we were to compare the types of exposure available to online businesses nowadays versus what used to be available to traditional brick-and-mortar stores, it might look something like what's shown in Figures 12.1 and 12.2.

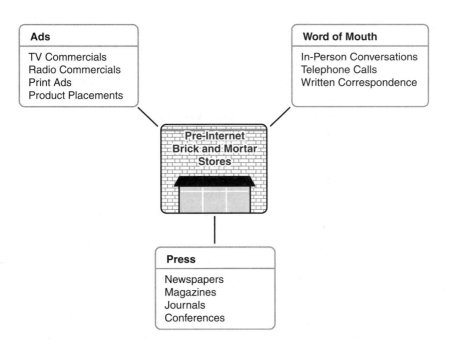

Figure 12.1 *Exposure available pre-Internet.*

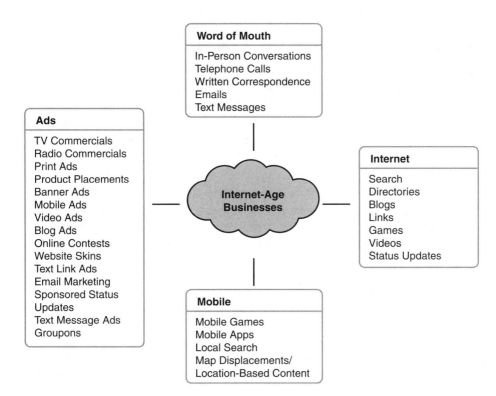

Figure 12.2 *Exposure available today.*

The main thing the Internet has changed—other than vastly expanding the number of outlets for communication—is the flow of communication in our world. While opening it up and speeding it up, it has also made communication occur more on our own terms. The Internet has added a new dimension to communication, largely because it involves interactions that we can control. Instead of having to experience the social pressures of an in-person encounter or even a phone call, we can now write an email or text message, which we respond to at our own will.

I remember experiencing the benefits of Internet-era communication back in 1998, when AOL chat was extremely popular. If a girl I liked was online, I could chat with her, saving myself the awkwardness of having to call her or ask her to meet up. Obviously, I wanted to do those other things, but I needed a bridge, an intermediary, before gaining the courage to do so. Chat was perfect. I would write something, she would write back 30 seconds later, and I would write back in another 30 seconds or minute. If I needed to think of something witty to say or consult a friend, there was always the built-in excuse that I was involved in other chats or had a phone call come in. I have AOL chat to thank for many an interaction I might never have had due to shyness.

The convenience I just described is a huge reason why the Internet—particularly social media—has had such a profound influence on our culture. And it extends into the world of marketing as well. Let's take ads as an example. In the past, I might see an ad in a magazine, stare at it for a few seconds, and then either remember it or forget about it. If the advertiser were persistent (and deep pocketed) I might hear ads for that company on radio or see them on TV.

Now the same company might place an ad on Facebook. Recognizing the company, I might click Like underneath the ad, indicating my acceptance of the brand. The next day, because of that "like," I might get a status update showing me a humorous YouTube video that company made as part of a campaign for a new product. Finding the video funny, I might then post it on my friend's profile page. His 1,000 friends might then see it, and 3 of them might post it on their friends' profile pages. An additional 2 of my friend's friends might tweet about it, exposing it to their 800 combined followers. One of those peoples' followers might then submit it to a social bookmarking site such as Digg, where the best content of the day gets posted on the home page. If enough people voted for this video, it would hit the front page of Digg, get 150,000 additional views and 550 comments, and even more sharing would occur. Because of the Digg exposure, 15 blogs might repost the video, including a major outlet that gets millions of visitors per month. And on goes the sharing. That entire journey started with just one click.

Forgive me if I have lost the thread of where SEO plays into this concept. The significant event, SEO-wise, in that story was the part where the blogs reposted the video to their sites. If 15 blogs repost a video, that's 15 links to a single web page. In this case, the web page hosting the content was on YouTube, but it could easily have been hosted on your website. As you know from earlier chapters, acquiring a link can be pretty tough in an age when most webmasters understand the value of linking. So 15 links in a single day is quite a payload. Social media regularly delivers that kind of link jackpot; you just have to make a piece of content that is creative enough to earn it.

In Chapter 3, "How to Reel In Links," I covered some of the best ways to create viral content to tempt webmasters to link to your site. Straight link baiting is important, but social media can be a great way for content to find its way to webmasters in a less pushy way. It's one thing to write to the owners of blogs and tell them you created this awesome nature diagram. It's another thing for them to come across it in their stream of status updates one morning and think it's really cool. The feeling of discovering something is much more powerful than having that something pushed on you.

Marketers understand that social networking sites such as Facebook and Twitter are the breeding grounds for virality. But most go about their social marketing strategy incorrectly, simply posting links to their latest blog articles every day. In fact, as I think about it, almost every company I know that has a Facebook page does exactly that, so let me be clear about how effective it is: not at all. If you want to attract links to your content via social media, you have to follow some rules:

- **Build a rapport with your audience**—If your social media page is nothing but an automaton of content with no humanity emanating from it, it is sure to be ignored. This idea confuses a lot of in-house marketers because they think it's a social media page's job to deliver content from the company. But in reality, it's the page's job to build a rapport with its audience. And that is done by acting like a real, thinking, breathing person. So let's say you're a sport shoe store in Newark, New Jersey. The content of your posts should not be purely about the specials and promotions your store is having (or just about the new inventory it gets in). If people liked to read about that, they would read circulars all day long. Instead, post about what a fine day it is today in Newark. Post about a local guy who built an airplane using spare parts from his garage. Post about how crazy the potholes are on the main avenue near the store. People can relate to those things. They can't relate to 15% off hiking boots from now until Friday.

- **Only promote the stuff that's genuinely good**—Imagine if a comedian got onstage and made 10 bad jokes in a row followed by 1 good joke, then repeated that pattern for 30 minutes. He wouldn't be working much longer. Now imagine if that same comedian used only his good jokes and stayed onstage for only 5 minutes. The guy would be a hit.

That's what you need to do with social media. The less-than-awesome content can still have a home; put it somewhere on your site, and the people who really want to see it will find it. But reserve social media announcements for really good content. Everyone misses more than they hit; but you have a choice not to publicize your misses.

🔍 *Tip*

There is a more technical reason to only post your best content, as well. Facebook, Twitter, and YouTube look at the percentage of people who interact with your posts. If everyone ignores your content, it might be algorithmically demoted and shown to smaller audiences in the future.

- **Respect that social networking sites are their own community**—As much as marketers would like all social networking sites to be a traffic funnel to outside websites, they simply aren't. Most people who are on Facebook, YouTube, Twitter, Tumblr, or any other big social network want to be there. To get people to see content that is on your website, you do need to direct them outside of the walled garden, but the key is to do so sparingly. For instance, suppose your viral content is a simple game. Allow visitors to your social media pages to play that game on the sites themselves for awhile but offer a better version of the game, or more games, if they come over to your site. The same would be the case with a great video. Keep users on YouTube for the video, but then tell them if they want to see other, exclusive videos, they must go to your website. Lure them over.

The overall thing to keep in mind if you want to respect the social networking environment is to remember that everyone is there to socialize and pass around fun content. There is no social networking site that is built to send traffic off the site. All of them allow it, but it is not the main activity. So just be conscious of that, and if your content is exciting enough, the masses will visit your website in droves. It is that kind of mass adoption that will lead to more links.

Creating Great Content

For all I talk about the importance of posting great content, I feel a refresher is in order about what that really means. Sure, different people find different things entertaining. But there *are* certain categories of content that are interesting to most of the population. Through studying the popular content on major social media sites, I have come up with a guide to the types of content that the masses love:

- **Amazing or dramatic stories**—True or half true, wacky or amazing things happen every day that most people don't know about. I remember a story about a guy who set out to trade a red paper clip for a new house. By trading the paper clip many times for increasingly more valuable items, he eventually got his house. This incredible chain of events occurred back in 2006, but I never forgot it. Believe it or not, there are plenty more out there like that one.

- **Scandal**—For better or worse, people love to share scandalous stories on the Internet. No matter how distasteful the situation may be, never underestimate the power of the "Can you *believe* she did that?" factor.

- **Exclusivity**—People love to read a story directly from its source. If you are the first to get the scoop, you will get linked by every other blog that finds your content interesting enough. And if you don't have an exclusive for a story, you can still take an exclusive angle on the story and use the *E*-word nonetheless. Just make sure you have made the story your own by filling in missing background info, adding new facts and opinions, and overall looking at the story differently than other outlets did.

- **Pictures**—Which would you be more likely to click: a link that says "Gorilla Saves Injured Boy" or that same headline above a picture of a massive primate swinging at a lion with a scared boy cowering beneath him? The picture, obviously! Words can be more vivid than images sometimes—as when a book is better than a movie—but for quick Internet consumption, a picture will win every time. And by the way, videos are even better than pictures.

Promoting Your Content Through Social Media

Let me back up a bit. To promote your content on the various social media sites to which you belong, you need to have friends, fans, followers, or subscribers. Whatever the "audience" is called on each site, you need a solid base of them to promote your article, image, or video.

Building your audience is a pretty straightforward process: You just start by adding all the people you already know, and then send friend requests (or the equivalent) to friends of theirs. For every friend you add, you gain the potential for members of that new friend's network to become future connections of yours. Not everyone will accept your invitations, but a lot of people will, and you don't need that many people to start anyway. New connections naturally sprout just from being active on a social network. Also as a general rule, do not send more than 10 requests in one day or you will run afoul of the rules.

After you establish your presence on the various social networks you've joined, the steps for sharing your content are pretty straightforward. Here is how to do so on a couple of the big sites:

- **Facebook**—After you've established a personal page, you can create a business page. Business pages want to attract likes the same way that personal pages want to attract friends. To gain likes, send a page suggestion to all your friends. Hopefully, at least one-third will like it. When people like a page on Facebook, the action will usually be announced on their "news feed," the page that lists all their friends' status updates. Here is an example of a typical announcement that you would see in a news feed:

  Mary Jo likes Donuts Galore.

  In this case, most of Mary Jo's friends will see the announcement about her liking Donuts Galore in their news feeds and, if they click the hyperlinked "Donuts Galore," it will take them to Donut Galore's fan page, where they can click Like, too, which will then show up in their friends' news feeds, and so on. Of course, Donuts Galore's Facebook fan page will want to have a link to the actual Donuts Galore website in order for the Facebook exposure to help sell donuts.

- **YouTube**—After creating an account, which will establish your own channel, start uploading videos. Until you have friends or subscribers on your channel, you will have nobody to share the video with. You can send friend requests to other YouTube users. Gaining subscribers, however, is usually a matter of people enjoying your videos. The best way to get a YouTube account some initial traction is by posting your videos on Facebook so that any of your social connections with YouTube pages can become friends or subscribers on YouTube. Twitter is another good channel on which to post your videos. Ultimately, if your video is so good that thousands of people watch it, it has a chance at gaining "honors," which means that it shows up in the list of YouTube's most viewed or most popular video pages across many categories. Once a video begins to get honors on YouTube, it is typically seen by thousands more people because it appears on YouTube's highly trafficked Browse pages.

- **Social bookmarking sites**—The main social bookmarking sites at the time of this printing are Digg, Reddit, StumbleUpon, and Yahoo! Buzz. Creating an account on each of these sites is simple. Then all you have to do is post a link to your content. The community will then see your link and determine whether it's worthy of promoting. If people like it, they can give it the equivalent of a thumbs up. With enough thumbs ups, the link will appear on the front page of the site and get a huge burst of traffic, as well as many new links.

- **Twitter**—Starting a Twitter account couldn't be easier: Just fill out your name and a line or two about you, and begin talking about the random things you think about or find on the Internet (beginning with your own content). The main way to gain followers on Twitter is to ask your friends to follow you and then "tweet" interesting status updates to them. Twitter also has an algorithm that encourages people who are similar to you to follow you, so you might see followers appearing like magic. If your status updates are scintillating enough, they will get "retweeted," meaning echoed by other people in their own status updates. If your updates include a link to your website, retweets can be especially valuable because they can lead to links.

As your website gains exposure and links from social media virality, you should look to sustain that success by adding cool content on a regular basis. Remember to always sprinkle in personal, down-to-earth status updates with your links to your own website. Ultimately, figuring out how best to create status updates comes down to asking yourself "What do *I* like to see on websites I visit?"

As search engines become more sophisticated, the intersection of SEO and social media will not just be about links. SEO and social media will be mixed together as social preferences, location, friends' interests, and other "social" factors influence what we encounter in our search results. As we look forward to the future, the rule of thumb for social media is always to contribute quality content to the community and engage in real conversations with people. Do so, and you might find yourself knee-deep in traffic and TrustRank.

13

The Future of SEO

Learning how to get your website to the first page of Google is a huge feat. I hope that by now you feel proud to be among the few who understand the workings of the Giant. This book has been a privilege for me to write; rarely does one get a chance to sum up seven years of discovery, invention, and hard work. But now we must address what will happen after the last page is turned.

You, the reader, have something that can never change: a record of Google's algorithm as it was at a certain moment in time. This part of Google's history can never change, and just as the works of the famous Italian Renaissance painters influenced art for hundreds of years after them, the way that Google's search algorithm is constructed today will always teach us about the way Google functions tomorrow.

In a broad sense, Google is an information-discovery tool, a way of sifting through the mountains of data that the Web possesses to find, hopefully, the most relevant response to your search. In an even broader sense, Google is a publicly owned advertising company. The first way of looking at Google is important, for the business will always have at its core the curiosity of its founders, who sought to revolutionize the way people retrieved information. But the second viewpoint is probably even more important to understand. As an advertising company with a duty to its shareholders, Google is motivated to do two things:

- Make money
- Beat out competition by being both innovative and popular

To make more money, Google will continue serving advertisements on all platforms—Web, mobile, radio, and TV—into the foreseeable future. It will focus especially on the mobile Web, making a larger share of its revenues by licensing its popular Android platform to handset manufacturers so that those companies can associate their new phones with the brand that makes everyone's lives easier. It will also make money through selling applications, extensions, and other add-ons for Internet users. But advertising is still the revenue model that Google cares about most, and the one the company is gearing up to focus on for the long haul. You can tell advertising is Google's top priority because it continues to acquire as much data about users' online habits as possible, creating incredible free products such as Gmail, Chrome Internet browser, Google Earth, and Google Maps. That free model means Google is getting its money by serving ads, all the while gaining a richer set of data about its users so that it can release better-targeted, more personalized ads.

Google is darn good at what it does. And like Newton's first law of motion states, Google will keep moving forward until it is acted on by another force. (I think Newton was a shareholder.) Currently, Google admits on its investor relations web page that it considers Microsoft and Yahoo! to be its main competitors. However, its biggest competitor is actually Facebook, the only site on the Internet that people spend more time on than Google.

There is no doubt that Facebook will continue to pose a threat to Google in the coming years, but Google also faces competition from smaller, niche sites that people turn to for answers about popular topics such as restaurants, hotels, and outdoor activities. When people aren't going through Google for everything they need to know, Google gets insecure. And let's face it, even Google is mortal. To stay relevant, the company will have to keep innovating.

Following are the search-related innovations that I predict Google will focus on in the future, as well as the competitive landscape around those innovations.

Social Search

Other than local search, no project is more important to Google than the integration of social preferences into the search experience. It wasn't too long ago that only a small number of people actively maintained a Facebook page. I even remember the days when talking to someone online was considered nerdy and weird, let alone physically meeting someone you had met online. Now, people share their lives—including very personal details—with their friends and acquaintances through social networks. The amount of personal sharing that has taken place has created a tremendous opportunity for search engines.

The crux of the social search opportunity is this: Do you care more what Google thinks about a subject or what your friends think? Most people would say the latter, that a recommendation from a friend is much more valuable than information from a random website that pops up in Google's results. This is not always the case, of course; I probably care more about what Wikipedia says about a subject I'm researching than what my loud-mouthed poker buddy has to say about it. However, in the areas of lifestyle, entertainment, and maybe even health and wellness, a friend's opinion is the most valuable referral of all.

At the time of this writing, Google has little insight into what your friends think about. It knows what the population in general thinks about (quite well, actually), but not your specific friends. Facebook, on the other hand, has a wealth of data about your social relationships. This is because it brilliantly popularized the concept of the "like": a simple statement, made my clicking the mouse, which says "Yeah, I like this." The Facebook Like button appears underneath almost every status update or mention of a page throughout Facebook. This is because Facebook knows that people enjoy talking about themselves. After all, the vast majority of us feel we're special and deserving of attention. We're interesting to ourselves, and so other people should find us interesting too, dammit! This principle allows Facebook to collect huge amounts of data about us.

Just to make sure you understand the cleverness of Facebook, I want to describe what happens when you start a Facebook profile nowadays. You are asked to provide your name, birthday, gender, relationship status, high school, college, and place of work. You are also encouraged to list all the media you enjoy, especially books, movies, and music. Finally, you are asked to give the password to your email so that Facebook can search through your contacts and ask whether you'd like to become Facebook friends with each of them. By the time you've finished filling out your profile (which is kind of fun because of Facebook's snappy interface), Facebook knows about 20 times as much about you as Google does.

Google, you see, only knows your location and what you search for. Granted, what you search for tells a lot about you. But the sheer amount of information that Facebook collects in that 20-minute-long profile creation is incredible. Google may know that I'm looking for an accountant in my area, that I always call the same Italian deli for lunch, and that I am concerned about a callous on my toe. But Facebook knows that I am engaged and the name of my fiancée; that I love Whitney Houston; both my brothers' names and locations; that I like the book *The Giver*; that my birthday is in March; the name of my gym; my religion; my personal website, business website, and blog; and hundreds of other things. Get the idea? Facebook knows almost everything about me!

Now just imagine the possibilities:

- My brother's birthday is coming up in a week and his favorite movie is *The Shawshank Redemption*. If that film's studio or distributor buys Facebook ads (which it probably does), Facebook could suggest that I buy the new anniversary edition of the DVD for him. And it would be a good suggestion.

- Winter's coming up and I live in New York, and Facebook knows that I'm a fan of Axe shampoos. The next time I log on, Facebook could suggest Axe's new moisturizing shampoo product, perfect for the damage that cold weather can do to hair. I might actually buy that product, seeing as how the ad was so customized to my needs and preferences.

- The newest season of *American Idol* is happening soon, and Facebook knows not only that I'm a fan of the show, but that I'm a fan of season one's winner, Kelly Clarkson. Facebook could inform me that all members of Kelly's fan club get 15% off *American Idol* products and a chance to win tickets to that season's finale. By combining two of my interests, Facebook targeted me way better than a generic ad on the side of the screen for the new television season.

And what does all this have to do with Google? Well, Facebook has the data set that Google is gunning for. As spoiled as we are by Google's search experience, which filters out spam and irrelevant results and shows us a useful list of websites in response to our queries, we will all soon find Google's results to be too static. I predict that, at some point in the near future, the majority of people will stop using Google for anything except research unless Google knows more about who we are and what we are truly interested in. The only reason for this shift in behavior is the presence of Facebook, which will no doubt start making more and more intelligent product and service recommendations to us, like the previously mentioned examples, while Google's "10 result" method will seem stale. Google knows the threat that Facebook poses to it, which is why social search is just around the corner. It would be safe to say, then, that the pressure of competition is going to force Google to become a better search engine.

Google has already dipped its toes in the water of social search via an experimental feature called Social Results. This feature returns search results from the personal websites of people in your Google contact list who have a Google Profile (see Figure 13.1). A relatively small number of users have this feature turned on, mainly because the social connections it knows about are limited to your email contacts (a weaker social link than your Facebook friends). Yet it still marks the beginning of a new era in Google search.

Going forward, here is how I predict Google will change its search result page to incorporate social data from your circle of friends:

- When you do a search—let's say for *flower shops los angeles*—just below the ads but above the organic results, there will be horizontal listings representing local flower shops. (In Figure 13.2, the arrow marks where I think these local results will appear.)

Figure 13.1 *Google's early foray into social search: a feature that shows results from the blogs of people in your Gmail contacts list who maintain a Google Profile.*

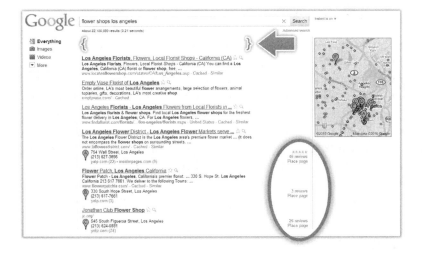

Figure 13.2 *A search for* flower shops los angeles *will probably incorporate friends' preferences in the future. Just above the first organic result, you might find a few listings of flower shops your friends like. Alternatively, your friends' opinions of each Google listing could appear to the right of the result, bundled with the ratings and review links that are currently there.*

- Underneath each listing in the local results will be a row of little thumbnails with pictures of friends who like each of the local flower shops, along with the phrase "4 friends like this."

- This format will show you a different kind of result set than the organic results below it; it will indicate, in a way, what your friends recommend.

Google's greatest concern in implementing social search is where it will get the data about what your friends like. Sure, it could partner with Facebook and get the jackpot of social data. But Facebook would probably require an onerous amount of compensation for it. In fact, there is a chance that Facebook might not even give Google access to its social information for any price, given the feeling of competition between the giants. (Facebook *did* give Bing access to its social data so that Bing could create a social search, but Facebook feels infinitely less competitive with Microsoft.)

Most likely, Google will end up building its own set of social information. There are three feasible ways of acquiring such a tremendous amount of data, and all three require participation from hundreds of millions of people. The challenge is formidable, but Google has no choice if it is to compete with Facebook in the next 5 to 10 years. Here they are.

A Google Social Network

The first way for Google to get access to the world's social data is to create a Facebook killer—a social network so popular and so addicting that everyone and their mother, aunt, grandpa, and dog wants to use it. (Hey, my dog's on Facebook.) The arguments against Google taking this route are many; the most common one is that people don't feel like re-inputting all their social preferences into another version of Facebook. Google also has PR considerations in such an endeavor: If it fails, people will begin to look at Google as the company that can't do social networking right. After all, it has already had two social-related failures that were rather notable in the tech community: Google Wave and Google Buzz. For these reasons, it is unlikely Google will try to create a social network to compete with Facebook.

A Portable Social Identity

The second way that Google could capture social information on a large scale is by backing the concept of a *portable social identity*. A portable social identity is a sort of "movable profile" that contains all your personal information, including your likes and interests, and which you can plug into any site you visit so that it can instantly customize your experience. The underlying intention is to democratize the social Internet and take some power away from Facebook, which currently has a kung fu grip on your personal information. Facebook proclaims (correctly, at least in the legal sense) that because you typed your social information into Facebook, it belongs to Facebook to use responsibly. In other words, it won't openly share your data with the world, but will use it to make itself—and nobody else—advertising revenue. There is a group called the Diaspora Project that is probably the best known in the effort to thwart Facebook's jealous guardianship over your information and create a portable social identity (see Figure 13.3).

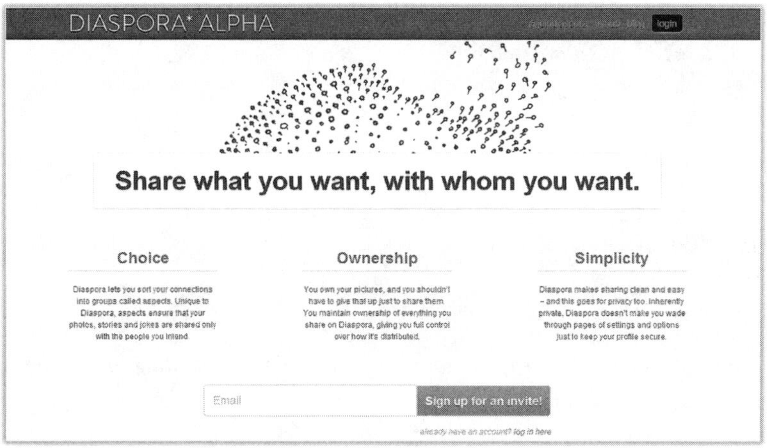

Figure 13.3   *The Diaspora Project is the best-known effort to create a portable social identity and free people from Facebook's monopoly on their personal information.*

If the concept of a portable identity caught on and everyone created one, many people would probably share that identity with Google while searching so that Google could return more customized search results. In reality, you'd be helping it make more money, but it would also be helping you to make better and quicker purchasing decisions.

Building Niche Websites that Collect Social Data

The third and most likely way that Google will acquire social data is by creating websites around different niche areas such as restaurants, movies, and nightlife and collecting user ratings and reviews in the process. This is a difficult strategy because it requires coming up with a user experience that is fun enough that people don't mind spending their time filling out surveys. So far, though, Google's strategy has shown some promise for the same psychological reasons that filling out a Facebook profile is sort of fun; it capitalizes on people's desire to dwell on themselves.

Google's first foray into niche rating and review sites was Hotpot, a site acquired in November 2010. Hotpot is a site that lets people rate and review restaurants, museums, and other venues, and those ratings and reviews become a part of your personalized search results (see Figure 13.4). Eventually, those ratings and reviews become a part of your friends' search results, and your friends' ratings and recommendations show up in your search results, as well.

Figure 13.4   *Part of Google's strategy for collecting social data is creating fun, addictive rating and review sites. This format shows the typical Google style: a picture, location, 5-star rating system, and an opportunity to write a quick review.*

How Does Google Get There from Here?

This strategy of collecting information is all well and good, but in order to compete with Facebook, Google needs a critical mass of user information. If enough people find the concept of Hotpot appealing, Google will have a neat little set of data about places. But to match Facebook, it needs to create a highly successful rate and review site in *every* business vertical, from products to professional services to online businesses to entertainment. How will Google do that?

As the Wave and Buzz failures show, Google cannot make a product successful based on brand recognition and access to users alone. Even the tens of millions of Gmail users aren't enough to make a Google website flourish. Those people are using Gmail because they like Google's email product, not because they necessarily like anything else Google does. And Google's reputation does not extend to being great at maintaining a trusted reviewing community, like, say, Yelp or TripAdvisor.

My feeling is that Google will need to get very good at game mechanics to make this strategy of data acquisition work. Having built a popular kids website, I understand how unforgivingly a community reacts to a new product; it usually either soars or fails. Google's success at gaining enough user data to make social search work will depend on a few factors:

- **Fun**—Is this site genuinely fun to play with? Is there a reason I am going to spend two minutes of my free time reviewing a fitness center when I could be playing Tetris or texting my friend? Fun comes in many forms: Graphics, sound, the concept of what you're doing (something about popping bubble wrap is just...fun!), motion, cuteness, and humor are just a few of them. Google Hotpot demonstrates some competence in the area of "funness": After you rate a venue, the box flips around like a revolving door and asks you for a quick review. I could get into more detail, but I'm sure Google can find my email address if it needs some advice.

- **Competition**—If you're competing against someone (friends would be best, followed by strangers, followed by a computer), something in your brain just wants to try harder. I could be competing against a 10-year-old from Reykjavik over who can count to 10 quickest, and I'd be distracted for a half hour. And, if I were to win, I would appreciate placement on a scoreboard so that I could feel a sense of achievement and scope out the rivals I need to beat next. If Hotpot pitted me against my Gmail contacts to see who could review the most, I'd be more interested.

- **Collection**—The reason why badges, medals, and ribbons are so popular both in real life and location-based sites such as Foursquare is because people like to be decorated when they win. It's a nice feeling. This aspect of game mechanics is related to competition; I'd like it if my friends saw my medals after I out-reviewed them.

- **Community**—Hotpot already has this highly important element at the top of its mind. By encouraging users to invite friends to review venues so that they can use each other's recommendations, Google is bringing the community into the experience, making it more informative and enjoyable.

- **Reward**—In addition to leaderboards and badges, I would love to earn some sort of virtual currency (call them GoogleBucks) for my time spent rating and reviewing. Google could come up with some cool prizes to trade GoogleBucks for—maybe getting your own personalized version of the Google Logo on your home page or a new Gmail theme or something.

Don't be surprised if you see some of the elements listed here incorporated in Google's review sites. They are the company's best shot at gaining the personal information that it needs to create a truly worthwhile social search experience.

Taking the idea of social search a bit further into the future, I can imagine a Google that not only delivers you results that include your friends' preferences, but also filters those results based on which of your friends is most trustworthy about a particular subject. After all, Google is famous for diving into a heap of data and coming up with the 10 results that are most relevant to your request; why couldn't it do the same with a huge pool of friends' opinions about a place or product?

I believe that identifying the tastemakers among your group of online friends—not to mention identifying your *actual friends* among your group of online friends—is part two of the process of making social search truly useful. If you think about it, isn't there a friend whose taste in movies is really similar to yours? And isn't there also a friend that likes prewar western indie horror flicks with subtitles, and you just can't understand how he or she sits through the darn things? A filter is definitely in order. In fact, as I browse through Facebook, I am often pleasantly surprised to notice things such as the fact that the girl I talked to twice in Shakespeare class likes the same kind of music I do. Funnily enough, if she starts listening to a new band, I would like to know about it. To me, she is a tastemaker.

So how do we prepare for this new world of social search? To begin with, the focus on SEO should remain constant. Most of you reading this book are running a business, and for the majority of businesses, the best return on investment will come from showing up at the top of Google's organic search results. Google's social recommendations have yet to be implemented, and after that they will have to be accepted by searchers before they become a real threat to SEO as we know it. That could take years. We will have to reach a point where everyone we know has given a thumbs up or thumbs down on almost every business they've interacted with before social data becomes meaningful enough to inform our every buying decision.

For now, a smart move is to begin investing in social relationships on both Facebook and Google. Meeting people and connecting with them online is a good idea for business in general; it's networking in the age of the Internet. But not everyone makes sure the second part of that networking, the connecting online, happens. Although business social networking is purported to be LinkedIn's domain, Facebook is increasingly becoming a place where business contacts "friend" each other. You can choose to do so on your personal account, knowing your pictures and status updates will be exposed, or you can make a separate account for business use. However, the most important decision you can make to prepare for the future of social search is to create a business page on Facebook.

There are two reasons for making a home for your business on Facebook. The first is that, as stated earlier, it is possible that Google will end up licensing Facebook's extensive user data to fuel its social search. This partnership might very well occur if Google fails to collect its own social data. (Having conquered search and made significant strides in the mobile and local arenas, this shouldn't seem like a failure, but for Google, it would be.) The second reason that creating a Facebook business page is important is that no matter what happens with Google, Facebook's user data will play an important role in millions upon millions of buying decisions in the not-so-distant future. It is easy to envision a Facebook search engine, for instance, that responds to users' queries with a rich array of products and services that your friends like.

I advise all my clients to start attracting likes to their Facebook business pages in the same way that I advise audiences at my speeches to attract links to their websites. Both are a currency that matters. Links may matter more than likes in 2011, but in 2012, it is possible to imagine the reverse being the case. Even if it's not, likes will matter a lot, and here's why: The payoff all businesses hope for with each new like they gain on Facebook is that a friend of that liker will do a search for something related to their business and will become a customer because of it. For example, if my friend likes a dentist named Constance Flosser, D.D.S., and I, in need of a dentist one day, search *dentists* on Facebook, I will likely see a picture of Dr. Flosser and a picture of my friend underneath, with the words "So-and-so likes Constance Flosser, D.D.S." Providing my friend so-and-so has nice teeth, I would click Dr. Flosser's page and make an appointment.

Once you understand that the goal is to get people's friends to like you, you begin to see the mathematical possibilities. Basically, the more people that like you, the greater your universe of potential customers becomes. If one person likes you, and he has 227 friends on Facebook, those 227 people will probably see your business page if they search for the general category of what your business sells on Facebook. Now, a pool of 227 potential customers might not be large enough to generate any sales, but imagine this: You have invested in attracting Facebook fans for years and, instead of your page having 1 like, your page has 1,000 likes. If we assume that on average, each of those 1,000 likers has 200 friends, that means that your pool of potential customers is 200,000 people! The net of what I'm saying here is: Get more likes!

As the owner of an SEO firm, it is not just my job to effectuate top Google rankings for my clients. It is also my job to anticipate what is important for the future of SEO and advise my clients to focus on it. That is why Facebook "like building" is almost as large a part of my business as SEO now: Everyone wants to be prepared when social search happens.

Social (Contextual) Discovery

The future of SEO does not only include search as we know it. Search is but one way to encounter new information that responds to our needs and interests. Another way is getting a recommendation. I like to think of search engines as omniscient personal concierges who can tell you almost anything you want to know and show you almost anything you want to see. (I'm not the only one to think this way; a butler was the gimmick behind the Ask Jeeves search engine.) In practice, though, an omniscient concierge would be better than a search engine because he could anticipate your needs before you even ask:

"You seem hungry. Would you like a sandwich?"

"You're going for a walk today? Make sure to wear a coat; it's chilly out there."

"I understand you're planning to travel to France in May. You should really check out Chartres Cathedral. It's absolutely stunning."

In essence, this kind of anticipatory recommendation is what social discovery is meant to be. Once again, Facebook, rather than Google, is best positioned to execute social discovery. And, once again, Facebook's advantage comes from its much-richer set of personal information deriving from hundreds of millions of users. But Google is plowing forward with a slightly different concept: contextual discovery, which forms opinions about what you might like based on your search history and location. Whereas Facebook's recommendations will come from its users' social connections, Google's recommendations will come solely from the context of the user's searches—at least until Google gets its hands on our social data.

In December 2010, a representative from Google announced the company's interest in contextual discovery for the first time, saying that recommendations will probably be made to users on a panel that resides on the side or bottom of your Internet browser. She also stated that mobile search will have a version of contextual discovery that delivers different information depending on where you are at the time. For instance, if you were inside an airport, all you'd have to do is open your browser, and Google might deliver a map of that airport. Figure 13.5 shows an example of how contextual discovery might work.

Figure 13.5 *An illustration of how contextual discovery might work. The panel on the right contains movie-related suggestions and deals. It is responding to the fact that the browser is on a movie website.*

Contextual discovery is a fun idea with wide-ranging possibilities for Google. While it is easy to picture that right panel becoming a repository for ads, if Google plays its cards right, it could become a fascinating tool that increases the number of new web pages that people visit—a net positive for Google.

When I imagine contextual discovery, I think about my first experience with the music-recommendation site Pandora.com. The way the site works is, it asks you to type in the name of a song you really like. Then it plays a few similar-sounding songs and asks you what you think of them. Based on what you say about each song, Pandora analyzes your musical tastes and starts playing songs by various artists you might not have heard but whose styles match the style of music you like. Astonishingly, the site works really well, and I have discovered hundreds of great songs I never would have heard without Pandora.

Google will have to try for the same effect as Pandora: truly useful suggestions that people enjoy receiving. This model works especially well for music—Apple has since developed a similar program for iTunes called Genius—but does it work for website recommendations? I really think it can. The reason why Yelp and TripAdvisor rose to Internet prominence is because they deliver truly honest view-points that help people make decisions about which places to visit in the real world. In some cases, the collective opinion of the masses can misfire, but more often than not, you can discover some really cool places with these sites. Users of Google's con-textual discovery will need to feel that same sense of trust for its recommendations.

The problem Google will have with contextual discovery is filtering out websites that aren't truly interesting and bringing forth only recommendations that make people say "Wow, this is cool!" Because Google search does not currently do this well—the results are relevant but not necessarily compelling—Google will have to create a special algorithm for contextual discovery. In my opinion, this algorithm needs to be based mostly on users' reactions to the recommendations they are served. Google will need to *learn* which sites are interesting to each person.

Google has always shied away from using user behavior as a criterion in its algo-rithm because the data seemed too easy to manipulate. In this case, however, the risk of manipulation is much less great because users will each have their own per-sonalized set of recommendations based on their specific search histories. A web-master who is trying to game the system might, for instance, pay people to click "like" or "5 stars" next to his or her website when it is suggested; however, that wouldn't work with contextual discovery because recommendations are so person-alized that you couldn't easily predict when this website might pop up.

Like Pandora, Google will have to ask users "Do you like this recommendation?" And when users respond, Google will have to go back to its databases and say "When users in the past responded that they liked this particular website, they also responded that they liked this *other* website." As the likes stream in and Google's data gets richer, it will soon have a good idea about which websites people truly enjoy discovering and spending time on. And, as likable websites gain additional traffic, webmasters will realize that creating a truly compelling environment is the new way to attract Google traffic. This scenario will bring Google ever closer to its goal of suggesting websites that provide searchers with real value rather than just search engine shininess.

When contextual search does come out, the response from the optimization community will be puzzlement at first. No longer can the same rules of pushing search results to the top of the page apply, because there *are* no search results in contextual discovery. If contextual discovery is a hit and it changes the way people find information, it will turn SEO on its head. Many people will panic. But you don't need to. After all, SEO is a continuously evolving field that, while requiring patience at times, is ultimately a survivor.

The way to begin thinking about optimizing for contextual discovery is to recognize that it is a paradigm shift. Whereas SEO is solely based on factors having to do with websites, contextual discovery is based on factors having to do with people as well. And so, links will not be the only factor used to determine whether sites show up with recommendations in someone's browser. Instead, those coveted recommendations will be based on the searcher's location and web history, too.

So what will optimizers set their sights on in the area of contextual discovery? Because at first glance it is difficult to imagine influencing someone's location, black hatters will look at the web history aspect first, trying to artificially fill a browser's history with sites that the owner of the computer never visited. Google will be prepared for this kind of behavior, though. Let's look instead at the real question of how webmasters can get users to engage in legitimate behaviors that will cause Google to recommend their websites. Consider the following example.

Google notices me going to a travel website and booking a ski vacation. My contextual discovery panel might then suggest some stores that sell warm clothing. Now, how will Google decide which clothing stores or specialty ski stores to suggest? If I am on my mobile phone, it might just be the closest store to me that also has high reviews. If I am on my desktop, it will probably look for winter clothing sites with a high TrustRank or ones that I have visited in the past. And with those educated guesses in mind, we have some real criteria to examine:

- **Location**—Can you really influence where someone is at a given point? Maybe not, but you *can* locate your business in a densely populated area. Or you could fake it. I predict that contextual discovery and local search will influence the rise of "ghost locations" (unoccupied addresses that are rented just so Google Places will perceive that a physical store is located in a certain area). This tactic wouldn't be helpful if you needed to actually *go* to the store in question, but if you were sitting at home looking to order some new ski hats and an online ski clothing site has a location less than a mile away, contextual discovery might suggest it.

- **Reviews**—Fake reviews have been around forever, and they are probably the biggest threat to group review sites like TripAdvisor. If contextual discovery catches on, the epidemic will become worse as the owners of every venue will be tempted to boost their reviews. Of course, a more ethical approach would be to simply ask satisfied customers to review your venue.

- **Sites people have visited in the past**—Getting someone who has never heard of your site to visit it is not an easy task. Some of the link-baiting tactics I reference in Chapter 3, "How to Reel In Links," are great approaches to getting noticed, as is the creation of viral content for social networks as described in Chapter 12, "The Intersection of Social Media and SEO."

- **TrustRank**—Google always seems to manage to sew TrustRank into its algorithms. That is one reason why I recommend following all the practices in this book to build TrustRank, despite the many changes that will occur with Google over the next few years.

Although I have a strong feeling my predictions will be helpful if and when contextual discovery becomes popular, we will have to wait until the product is launched before making any conclusions. Then we can begin reading about people's experiences with contextual discovery and drawing conclusions about the actual factors that engender a recommendation.

The Rise of Google Places

I learned that Google Places would be an important part of the future of SEO during the writing of this book. One day, I was doing a typical Google search for a professional services client located in Chicago when I noticed that all the local results had been integrated into the organic results with almost no differentiation. Suddenly, the #1 result in the organic listings that we had been trying so hard to achieve became #8 by default, as there were suddenly seven Google Places listings above it. So yeah, I'd say Google Places is important.

At this point, it would be reasonable for you to ask: Doesn't the dominance of Google Places make organic SEO almost irrelevant? The answer is no; Google Places makes organic SEO more challenging, but organic SEO is still extremely important.

There are three main reasons why organic SEO still matters a lot. The first is that not all searches generate Google Places results; only searches that contain a geographic location in them, such as *chiropractor new york city* or *cleaning service in philadelphia*, will generate these local listings (see Figure 13.6).

Figure 13.6 *The "classic view" of Google Places listings, as they were before Google integrated them into the organic results. Otherwise known as a "7 pack" or "7 box," these listings always appeared above the organic results in their own separate-looking area. This format still exists for certain search result pages.*

The second reason is that Google often keeps the top two organic results above the Google Places listings. Actually, there is no standardized number of organic results that appear above or below the Places listings. At the time of this writing, there are either 2 above and 5 below, 1 above and 4 below (see Figure 13.7), or none above and 10 below. Google appears to not be sure what the right allocation of search results should be either, so consider the numbers subject to change at any time.

The third reason that organic SEO remains significant is that Google Places operates on an algorithm similar to that used to generate its organic results. Although I suspect that the Places algorithm will continue to evolve as Google Places occupies a larger part of Google's result set, its main ingredients will always be links and titles, just like those generated by Google's organic search algorithm. (In this case, "title" means the name of the business as written on its Google Local profile page rather than the meta page title of the website.)

So where will Google Places go? It seems to be a part of almost all of Google's future plans, which I have discussed in the context of organic search, social search, contextual discovery, mobile search, and maps. But the amount of information Google has about every place on earth is, understandably, incomplete. For Google to be able to guide people in the granular sense they are expected to desire in the future—giving them information about every physical location they go to, suggesting restaurants, nightlife, and things to do—they will need to get a solid community of reviewers onboard. They can either earn those reviewers or buy them from Yelp, Citysearch, TripAdvisor, and other Places competitors. The parallel to Google's conundrum with social search, where it needs to either compile social data itself or buy it from Facebook, is striking. And it highlights a larger issue that the sleepy search giant woke up thinking about sometime in 2009 or 2010: In an age where being able to find what you're looking for is taken for granted, how will Google transition from search to *meaningful discovery*?

Figure 13.7 *One of several new formats for Google Places listings, which integrates them into the organic results, making them especially prominent. In this format, there is one organic listing above the Google Places results and four below.*

Put another way, people are no longer impressed with the idea that they can search Google for *best restaurants in san francisco* and get a bunch of editorial opinions. In 2004, that technology was amazing. Now, it's passé. Yelp, Citysearch, and TripAdvisor have come along and given the company a perspective into the desire for user-created guides. More than anything, these businesses have shown Google that being the conduit to all things on the Web is not enough; they also need to provide human-curated information relevant to each specific person.

In the coming years, Google is sure to make big moves in its quest to be your local concierge. Expect to see the following:

- Google Places continuing its domination of the first page of search results. Not only does it serve users about as well as the organic results, but it encourages users to visit the Place pages for businesses and leave reviews and ratings, thus adding to Google's data bank.

- The mobile search experience improving, with suggestions for nearby venues aplenty.

- Google Places working with Google Maps to create an online mirror of the real world, with users labeling and reviewing almost every element of that real world.

- Mobile ads looking more and more like Place pages so that people trust the ads more and can see all the positive reviews and five-star ratings advertising businesses have received (see Figure 13.8).

Figure 13.8 *A screenshot from Google's mobile web page touting voice command technology and the simple interface of Google Places listings on a mobile phone.*

- Improved voice command technology on Google-powered phones, so people can simply say *candy stores in Las Vegas* and instantly get suggestions.

Another aspect of Google Places that is sure to make a big showing in the near future is local deals. Google's attempted acquisition of Groupon for $6 billion in late 2010 spoke to Google's interest in the space very clearly. Groupon proved the simple concept that people love getting bulk discounts at local establishments, and nothing could play into Google's mobile strategy better. Not only will Google suggest nearby venues to you while you are out and about, but it will offer you deals at those same venues.

The idea of connecting people on a local level has been fascinating to Google for many years. I remember hearing that Google had purchased a site called Dodgeball.com back in 2005, way before the days of its high-profile acquisitions. (This was pre-YouTube.) Dodgeball.com's basic concept was that you could receive text messages on your phone when your friends were nearby so that you could meet up in person. Although Google never did anything with Dodgeball, it clearly had a premonition that people would want to use their mobile phones to facilitate real-world interaction. I believe this idea will be revived, riding on the coattails of Google Places and contextual search. I can picture notifications popping up on your mobile phone saying things like "Andrew Jones is in your area" or "Debbie Smith is at Ben's Brewery." And I think it will be incredibly appealing (see Figure 13.9). The question is whether Facebook can do it better than Google. After all, Facebook has a much better idea who your friends are.

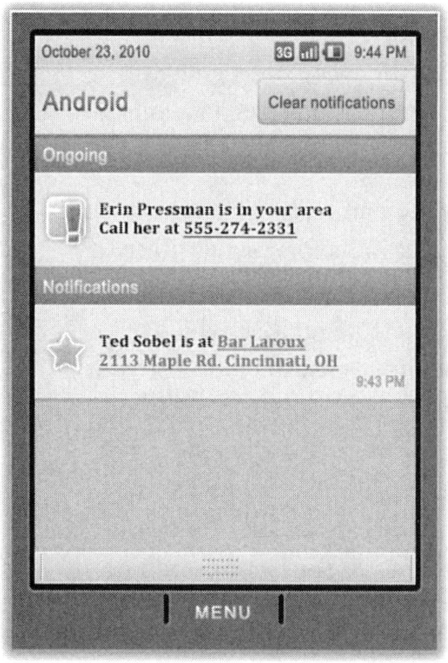

Figure 13.9   *A likely implementation of the way mobile phones will facilitate real-world interaction in the near future.*

Google already has a product that is aiming to connect people the way Dodgeball was meant to. It is called Latitude and is bundled into most Android phones. At the time of this printing, it had not gained traction but was being pushed by Google in a major way. I predict this product will gain traction in the coming years, as people grow more comfortable with people knowing where they are at all times. As unlikely as it might seem now that people will basically open themselves to being stalked, it is the next logical step up from status updates, which announce what you're doing at any given time.

Now that you have an idea of the ways that Google Places will evolve to become a more important part of Google's business, let's address how webmasters can optimize it to get the most new customers to their websites.

Optimizing for Google Places Now and in the Future

Of all the projects Google is currently working on, none is seen by more people than Google Places. Google plans to keep it that way, considering local search to be one of the most important parts of its future. The formula for showing up on the first page of the Google Places listings is partly based on traditional classified-ad factors such as location and business name and partly based on SEO factors such as other people's opinions of your website. Here are the elements that matter now and will continue to matter down the road:

- **Links**—The most important ingredient of SEO is a big deal in local listings, too (probably the biggest). Simply put, the more links going to your website, the more Google trusts that your local listing (the one associated with that website) is well reputed.

- **Place page information**—Google counts the name of a business much more heavily than most people would expect in its Places algorithm. If you've been reading carefully, this fact shouldn't surprise you because business names play a very similar role to meta page titles, which Google also prizes. For this reason, it is helpful to list the name of your business with a keyword in it. However, as I stated earlier in the book, do not stuff your business name with keywords, or Google Places will delete your listing. You basically have an opportunity for one natural-sounding, carefully placed keyword here. If you are an auto body and collision shop and your business name is Jones & Sons, you would be remiss not to call yourself Jones & Sons Auto Body and Collision Repair. Similarly, if you own a web design company called White Clouds, you would definitely want your business name to be listed in Google Places as White Clouds Web Design.

- **Reviews**—Reviews are probably the smallest factor in the Google Places algorithm because they are so open to human manipulation. Nonetheless, I rarely see listings in the Places section of the search results with fewer than three stars, and experience has taught me that four- and five-star businesses have a slight edge. More important than edging that four-star rating to four and a half is the number of ratings and reviews. Google will consider the rating more credible if at least 30 people have participated in it.

- **Location**—Much like the situation with contextual search, location is a crucial factor that is difficult to manipulate. The best hope for the enterprising few of you who want to beat this system is to set up addresses in many locations under slightly different business names. I can imagine striking a deal with local business where you pay a tiny amount of money to them to receive mail there. Of course, any family member's home or office would also do. The key is that Google will call or send a postcard to the location when you set up the Places listing, and someone has to be there to receive it. I do not recommend doing these things, though, because Google does look out for inauthentic listings, and your time is probably better spent optimizing the one listing you legitimately own.

The best frame of mind to have when optimizing for Google Places is one of customer participation. When customers are satisfied, you should ask them to write reviews. If they have websites, ask whether they wouldn't mind linking to yours. And more than anything, don't forget that real-world referrals are more valuable than virtual ones. So ask for those, too.

Real-Time Search

One of the projects that Google got really hot on in late 2009/early 2010 was real-time search. Since then, its interest appears to have waned, but the product could have interesting uses for your business as it evolves. Real-time search is a way to search through status updates from Twitter, YouTube, Tumblr, and other sites that encourage you to talk about what you're doing at any given time. Although it might seem pointless to wade through people's announcements about what they had for breakfast and comments on their cats' antics, there is some valuable customer information in there.

The best use of real-time search is probably finding status updates that indicate a need for your product or service. Imagine this scenario: You sell wedding invitations. You go to Google.com/realtime and type *"just got engaged"* into the search box. Out come hundreds of updates from people who got engaged that day. Being that these are all people who will be planning a wedding soon, it is an excellent opportunity to message them and ask if they would like to check out your invitations.

Optimizers have long attempted to gain traffic from real-time search by flooding search results with messaging about their products, but that is equivalent to spam. Truly the best use of real-time search for marketers is the method just described.

Other Innovations

In addition to the major innovations described earlier, other, smaller search products are likely to come from Google in the next few years:

- **Improved image search**—Google's image search is already a popular product. But during the writing of this book, it has placed a greater focus on it than ever, streamlining the search results into a huge, borderless collection of images and speeding up indexing of images to lightning levels. Meaningfully, it has also changed the display of a clicked-on image so that the site it comes from is more visible in the background than it used to be. This change to the user interface has brought webmasters who feature lots of images on their sites a greater click-through to the actual site. In the future, I suspect Google will make images a greater part of the search experience, following in Bing's footsteps by featuring lots of beautiful, visual content. As image-recognition technology improves, I also believe Google will have better filters so that you can search in a much more specific way. Google already has a little-known way of searching for images of faces only. (Simply add &imgtype=face to the URL after performing an image search.) I can see it extending this functionality to other categories such as living things (for example, plants only) and materials (for instance, wood only).

- **In-video search**—I liken the concept of in-video search to Google Books, an extremely ambitious project that lets you search the text of millions of offline books that Google has scanned. Like Google Books, video is an area that was hitherto unsearchable because there was no way to know what was inside a video without actually watching it. However, the technology to search videos has existed for a while now, and it is only a matter of time until Google releases an in-video search feature. Not only are the words of a video interesting to search through, but also the sound effects and music. Google currently employs song-recognition in YouTube to prevent copyright violators but hasn't given the public access to this tool.

- **Social comments on search results**—Although Google has attempted the concept of annotated search results in a product called SearchWiki, it never really did it right. What was missing was the ability for friends (or at least trusted connections) to comment on the search results. If I knew that my thoughts regarding a website would be seen by all my Facebook friends, for instance, I would have a ball with it, giving my honest opinion about websites in the same way that I'd guide a friend through a city I once lived in. It would bring about that "let me help you" feeling. I believe that Google's main search product will undergo

more and more personalization in the future, and this is one great way
to do it.

- **Natural language search**—Typing keywords into a search box is something we all had to get used to. But technology seems to be going in the direction of making our lives more intuitive, hence the rise of touch screens and video games that respond to the motions of your body. Most people would agree that it would be great if your search engine understood you better. This is the sentiment behind natural language search, which attempts to return meaningful results in response to queries such as "What is the second fastest animal in the world?" Google wouldn't do too well with that one because it would just register *what / second / fastest / animal / world* and return results about the cheetah, that mention how many *seconds* it takes for it to accelerate from 0 to 60 miles per hour. Technologists have been focused on natural language search for many years, and it is all but a certainty that it will make its debut on Google in the coming decade. After all, can't you just picture yourself 10 years from now, saying "Remember how primitive Google used to be? You would type keywords into a box, and it would try to guess what you meant!"

The Common Denominator

There are many things about Google's future I feel sure of: an emphasis on local search, the rise of social search, and at least a solid attempt at contextual discovery. But what all of these search products have in common is personalization. In the future, every person's search experience will depend on what they like, who they know, where they are, and anything else Google knows about them. Personalization will change SEO as we know it. Gone will be the golden days when most people could go to Google and see the same set of results, making an optimizer's work easy to evaluate. This will mean a new kind of work product from search engine optimizers. Instead of delivering pure rankings, they will have to deliver traffic, perhaps even leads. The burden to show real evidence of your optimization's effectiveness will increase, and that's a good thing; it keeps people accountable and weeds out the charlatans.

But what is a search engine optimizer to do when Google takes away his bread and butter? I am tempted to say "adapt," but you already know that. Instead, I will leave you with this: In an environment where Google is increasingly making SEO more difficult—probably to strengthen its golden goose, ads—the smart marketer will become an expert on optimizing ads. Someday, we can all talk around the fireplace about the wild days when you only had to write your keyword a hundred times on a page to make it show up at the top of the search results. But until then, we have but one absolute certainty: Google will always make sure that people see ads. So it is wise to try to understand how to make them work in your favor.

Reader, you have a world of opportunity in front of you. With every big change Google makes to its search experience, 99% of the population will remain mystified and need someone to help them with it. If you are a search engine optimizer or marketer, be that person. If you are a business owner, be a part of that 1% that understands what's going on so that you can apply it to your own business. The fun of SEO is in the thrill of beating the system. And with so many products coming from Google each year, there are lots of systems yet to be beat.

Index

Try Safari Books Online FREE

Get online access to 5,000+ Books and Videos

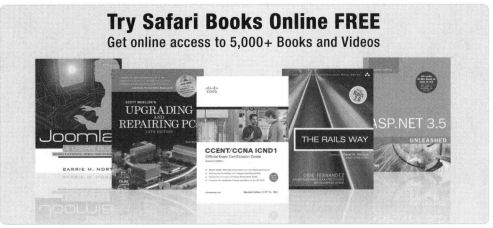

FREE TRIAL—GET STARTED TODAY!
www.informit.com/safaritrial

Find trusted answers, fast
Only Safari lets you search across thousands of best-selling books from the top technology publishers, including Addison-Wesley Professional, Cisco Press, O'Reilly, Prentice Hall, Que, and Sams.

Master the latest tools and techniques
In addition to gaining access to an incredible inventory of technical books, Safari's extensive collection of video tutorials lets you learn from the leading video training experts.

WAIT, THERE'S MORE!

Keep your competitive edge
With Rough Cuts, get access to the developing manuscript and be among the first to learn the newest technologies.

Stay current with emerging technologies
Short Cuts and Quick Reference Sheets are short, concise, focused content created to get you up-to-speed quickly on new and cutting-edge technologies.

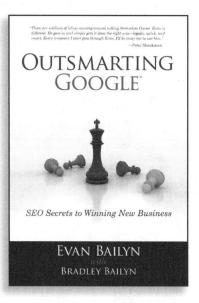

FREE Online Edition

Your purchase of **Outsmarting Google: SEO Secrets to Winning New Business** includes access to a free online edition for 45 days through the Safari Books Online subscription service. Nearly every Que book is available online through Safari Books Online, along with more than 5,000 other technical books and videos from publishers such as Addison-Wesley Professional, Cisco Press, Exam Cram, IBM Press, O'Reilly, Prentice Hall, and Sams.

SAFARI BOOKS ONLINE allows you to search for a specific answer, cut and paste code, download chapters, and stay current with emerging technologies.

Activate your FREE Online Edition at www.informit.com/safarifree

STEP 1: Enter the coupon code: UVODHBI.

STEP 2: New Safari users, complete the brief registration form. Safari subscribers, just log in.

If you have difficulty registering on Safari or accessing the online edition, please e-mail customer-service@safaribooksonline.com

Addison Wesley   AdobePress   ALPHA   Cisco Press   FT Press   IBM Press.   lynda.com   Microsoft Press   New Riders

O'REILLY   Peachpit Press   PRENTICE HALL   Que   Redbooks   SAMS   SAS Publishing   Sun   WILEY